Praise for *Income Disparity under Welfare and Poverty Dilemma in Emerging Countries*

"Emerging economies are highly impactful in the continuous growth of the global economy. Increasing the organizational footprint allows for diversification and expansion of the business. This position will only heighten in significance in the future and as a result, any thorough study of global inequality trends must include rising economies."

—**S Waleck Dalpour**, University of Maine Farmington

"This book outlines pathways that rising nations may follow to restore their power to act and improve people's living standards in the long run. Markets, according to the prevailing economic theory, are vital engines of prosperity and poverty eradication. Financial markets and capital flight may penalize policy efforts aimed at achieving a more equitable income distribution or increasing public investment . . . it is a must-read for policymakers and practitioners striving to combat global poverty, as well as economists and students interested in gaining a better knowledge of emerging economics, poverty, and financial economics."

—**Peter Rabb**, Budapest University of Technology and Economics (Hungary)

"Growing inequality is now a global megatrend. Unlike other megatrends, which benefit some stakeholders and harm others, in the long run inequality harms everyone. In the aftermath of the pandemic and against the backdrop of rising geopolitical tensions, inequality is becoming a harder challenge. Reducing it is a unique opportunity to improve the state of affairs for future generations. For this reason this volume is both very important and timely."

—**Alessandro Lanteri**, ESCP Business School

INCOME DISPARITY UNDER WELFARE AND POVERTY DILEMMA IN EMERGING COUNTRIES

INCOME DISPARITY UNDER WELFARE AND POVERTY DILEMMA IN EMERGING COUNTRIES

Edited by
Ufuk Bingöl
and
Meltem İnce Yenilmez

LEXINGTON BOOKS

Lanham • Boulder • New York • London

Published by Lexington Books
An imprint of The Rowman & Littlefield Publishing Group, Inc.
4501 Forbes Boulevard, Suite 200, Lanham, Maryland 20706
www.rowman.com

86-90 Paul Street, London EC2A 4NE

British Library Cataloguing in Publication Information Available

Library of Congress Cataloging-in-Publication Data

Names: Bingöl, Ufuk, 1984- editor. | Yenilmez, Meltem Ince, editor.
Title: Income disparity under welfare and poverty dilemma in emerging countries / edited by Ufuk Bingöl and Meltem İnce Yenilmez.
Description: Lanham : Lexington Books, [2023] | Includes bibliographical references and index.
Identifiers: LCCN 2022042899 (print) | LCCN 2022042900 (ebook) | ISBN 9781793646248 (cloth) | ISBN 9781793646255 (ebook)
Subjects: LCSH: Income distribution—Developing countries. | Equality—Developing countries. | Developing countries—Economic conditions. | Developing countries—Economic policy.
Classification: LCC HC59.72.I5 I4638 2023 (print) | LCC HC59.72.I5 (ebook) | DDC 339.2/091724—dc23/eng/20220914
LC record available at https://lccn.loc.gov/2022042899
LC ebook record available at https://lccn.loc.gov/2022042900

Contents

List of Illustrations

List of Tables

Acknowledgments

WE WOULD LIKE TO THANK all the authors and researchers who are experts in their fields, for their devotion and diligence, and we hope to help our readers. We are also grateful to their families and children who are the source of motivations for our authors with their support and patience during the creation of these valuable works.

Yours Truly,

Assoc. Prof. Ufuk BİNGÖL
Prof. Meltem İNCE YENİLMEZ

Introduction

Emerging economies are playing an increasingly important role in the global economy. It is a position that is projected to grow in the future. As a result, it is critical that any thorough evaluation of global inequality trends take the rising economies into account. We must all recognize that reducing inequality does not happen by fiat, nor does it happen automatically as a result of economic development or policies that equalize earnings downward through mindless taxation and expenditure. Inequality reduction necessitates a joint endeavor that must drive all parties involved, one that represents true political and social innovation, and one that frequently goes against dominant political and economic pressures. The case studies in this volume highlight the intricacy of the new systems necessary to meet each country's needs.

The case studies in this volume highlight the intricacy of the new systems that are necessary to meet each country's unique economic, political, and cultural conditions. These systems include technological, financial, legal, fiscal, and organizational aspects with a high level of applied competence, and they must be linked within a coherent, well-understood, growth- and job-creating development plan. Their long-term viability is dependent on their capacity to encourage collaboration among stakeholders who frequently have diametrically opposed interests, beliefs, and rationales.

This book has 13 chapters, eliminating the introductory overview chapter, on income disparity, poverty, and economic well-being. These chapters were authored by academics who publish articles on these issues on a regular basis. The literature on these issues is substantial, and research interest in these topics has a long history. Furthermore, it is fairly unusual for academics' viewpoints on these subjects to disagree. In light of this, the subjects of the chapters may best be regarded as representing the contributors' different viewpoints.

It was a delight to edit this book, which took a little more than two years to finish. The unreserved support of our colleagues, on the one hand, and the publisher and his team, on the other, has contributed significantly to the success of our project. Another aspect that contributed to the project's success was the collaboration and assistance of the contributing writers, who were meticulous in preparing the chapters and finishing their revisions to take into account the reviewers' and editors' remarks. The assistance of anonymous reviewers was vital since they thoroughly examined the articles and provided comprehensive evaluation and suggestions. It gives us great pleasure to express our gratitude for their outstanding assistance.

1

The Nexus between Income Inequality and Job Satisfaction

Cenk TUFAN

Abstract

Studies in the literature have shown that high income inequality negatively affects individuals and societies. Surprisingly, studies examining the relationship between income inequality and employee job satisfaction are scarce. In this chapter, I present a framework for examining the relationships between income inequality and job satisfaction. For this purpose, I am trying to contribute to the literature by drawing my work on literature review on the basis of income distribution and job satisfaction theories. Based on these theories, I argue that income inequality will negatively affect job satisfaction.

Keywords

Income inequality, job satisfaction, income distribution theories, job satisfaction theories.

Introduction

Today, one of the issues that states focus on is the problem of unequal distribution of income, which can cause social unrest and economic collapse. As countries grow and become richer economically, how to distribute the additional national income created comes to the fore as an important economic problem (Temin, 2017). When the goods and services produced in the country are not shared fairly among the citizens, economic growth occurs, but development does not occur. This situation, which is frequently seen in some Middle Eastern and African countries today, is a problem that increases social explosions and tendency to crime in countries. Realizing this situation, some countries, especially Saudi Arabia, have chosen to distribute money to their citizens in order to survive the Arab Spring events with the least damage (Çelik, 2015). However, these are temporary solutions and do not have the potential for a long-term solution.

As Karl Marx stated in his book *Capital* published in 1867, when the added value obtained from production is not shared fairly between employees and capital owners, this will bring social explosions in societies over time, which will pave the way for the workers to come to power (Uztopal, 2017). Countries that have a social state understanding are trying to take the necessary measures to prevent problems between employees and employers (the rich) and those who run the state, by providing social assistance to those in need, to prevent these people from being involved in crime. While doing this, states try to provide health, education, and other services in a way that all citizens can access and try to ensure income equality in their countries. At this point, academic studies to eliminate income inequality and policy proposals to be developed based on these studies are of great importance. In order to reveal the real aspects of the issue, it is necessary to examine the global socioeconomic outlook of the early twenty-first century. In this context, the Second Millennium Report of the United Nations (UN) secretary-general reflects the negative socioeconomic situation at the beginning of the century and the associated concerns. These concerns largely address the effects of globalization, emphasizing that the free market system on its own is far from solving these problems. According to the report, the creation of a common future is possible with human values that will embrace all groups in common. In its current form, globalization has conditions that make billions of people live in despair (UN, 2000: 19–20). Moreover, while inequality is presented as an increasing problem worldwide in recent years in the ILO's 2014/15 Global Wages Report, it is stated that growing inequality not only distorts social justice but also causes very negative economic problems. For these reasons, the struggle against increasing inequalities and social solidarity gain great importance (ILO; 2014/15)

Income inequality is a concept for explaining economic inequalities in society. Although conceptually different, income inequality can often be treated as part of broader analysis that includes satisfaction and well-being. Inequality is a broader concept than well-being because it covers the whole distribution, not just the distribution of individuals or households below a certain poverty line. Therefore, in any organization, the quantity and quality of existing personnel affect the productivity level of the organization. As a result, employees are one of the most valuable resources of an organization. They coordinate all other resources of the organization to achieve maximum results. Therefore, it can be said that an organization cannot exist without employees (Booth, 2012). In addition, the relationship between income inequality and job satisfaction is important for several reasons. First, the link between income inequality and job satisfaction is important to human resource managers. Mc Shane (1984) showed that job satisfaction is associated with absenteeism, Chahal and Mehta (2010) with turnover, and Loke (2001) with productivity. Second, it is important for the functioning of the labor market and public policy, as income inequality affects the labor supply and wage profiles, savings, and optimal tax policy. Considering all these, the employee in organizations plays an important role as a change factor. With this aspect, an employee not only manages change but also has the power to change every environment he is in. For this reason, in order to recruit and retain the right personnel, wage distribution should be made to satisfy the employees in the organizations. Remuneration is a function of human resource management, which includes rewarding employees for performing organizational tasks. With this aspect, wage management is one of the most complex functions of human resources managers (Dessler and Varrkey, 2005).

In this context, providing job satisfaction has received great attention from social scientists as it includes all monetary and nonmonetary goods and tools used to reward employees. Because the job that ensures the satisfaction of one's needs is a personal value system that is assumed to increase the dignity of the individual at the same time. It creates a desire to improve productivity and organizational functioning by increasing the quality of work experience in employees. In addition, the degree of job satisfaction is related to one's quality of life outside of the job role, particularly to one's physical and mental health. With this aspect, job satisfaction has a positive effect on the life satisfaction of employees. Based on these explanations, examining the relationship between income inequality and job satisfaction is also related to expanding the economics literature in the context of economic happiness (Banjoko, 2002). Income distribution, which should not be considered only in economic terms in terms of its causes and consequences, is also directly related to the applied social policies, traditional relations, culture, and the participation of the people in political processes. Income inequality is primarily affected by a series of socioeconomic developments such as the distribution of production factors in the country, gender differences, age structure of the population, education level, employee happiness, job satisfaction, wealth distribution, inflation, taxes, and informal employment (Turgut, 2019).

I have seen some studies in the literature examining the relationships between income, income inequality, and job satisfaction. For example,

Dau-Schmid and Mukhopadhaya (1999) investigated the effect of material and moral benefits obtained by legal professionals on job satisfaction. Gao and Smyth (2010) examined the effects of relative income distribution on job satisfaction and status within the organization. Medgyesi and Zólyomi (2016) investigated the effects of financial satisfaction on job satisfaction and happiness. O'Donnell (2015) investigated the impact of individual factors, work-related factors, and income on job satisfaction. Wunder and Schwarze (2006) conducted studies on how individuals determine their welfare level by making social comparisons. This study, unlike the previous ones, tries to contribute to the literature by looking at the relationships between income inequality and job satisfaction from a more theoretical perspective. Based on the fact that a better understanding of the determinants of job satisfaction can lead to improved labor market policies and its consequences, the aim of this study, which was prepared using the literature review model, is to examine the theoretical and conceptual framework of the relationships between income inequality and job satisfaction.

Conceptual Framework

Income, Income Distribution, and Income Inequality Concepts

Income is the sum of payments made to factors of production in return for the production of final goods within a country's borders in a year (Wildman, 2021). It can be said that the greater the gross national product, or in other words, the national income, which is the monetary expression of the sum of the values of the goods and services produced in a country in a given period of time, the greater the consumption opportunities (or in other words, the possibilities of benefiting from public services) of the inhabitants of that country (TUIK, 2008: 55). Income distribution, on the other hand, is defined as the division of national income generated in a country over a certain period of time among individuals, groups, or factors of production. When it comes to income distribution in a country, what should be understood is the extent to which the income generated in the economy in a certain period of time is distributed by the decision units in the economy. It can be said that it is impossible to find an equal and fair distribution schedule, even if the income distributions between countries differ (Bilan, Mishchuk, Samoliuk, and Yurchyk, 2021). In addition, a large national income does not indicate that the income distribution is egalitarian. Therefore, if there are inequalities in income distribution, this does not mean that the consumption level of the society is high as a whole or that everyone (individuals in the lower- and upper-income brackets) benefits from public services at a high level. The economic theory is concerned with the problem of distribution of national income to whom, how, and in what way, rather than the acquisition of national income. In other words, income distribution enables the determination of the relationship between income inequality and social and economic institutions (TK, 2008: 55). Today, it is undisputedly accepted that income distribution will not be fair as a result of a self-functioning market economy without government intervention, especially in underdeveloped and developing countries. In countries where the market conditions are left to their own devices, in other words, production, consumption, and distribution balances are determined according to the price mechanism and market conditions, it is not expected that the income distribution will be fair as long as the ownership distribution, that is, the degree of ownership of the production factors and the demand for the production factors, is different. Through fiscal policy tools, the government can realize the redistribution of income by influencing the distribution of the benefits of public expenditures and the tax burden (Song, Xie, Tan, and Wang, 2020).

Income inequality, on the other hand, is an economic policy change that can improve the welfare of an individual without adversely affecting the welfare of other individuals. This necessitates an effective functioning in the fair distribution of the increasing income in an economic structure. In addition, it is thought that an economic policy change that raises the income level of individuals in a certain income group without reducing the income level of other individuals in the society, and thus can be described as suboptimal, will also lead to income inequality (Bilan et al., 2021). Because at least a group whose income does not change, noticing an individual whose welfare level rises with increasing income in the social system is interpreted as income inequality. Such an imbalance in the economic structure, on the one hand, brings with its positive factors such as increased productivity, rising entrepreneurship level, increased job performance of the labor force working with high wages, and a decrease in the cost of capital (Feldstein, 1998). On the other hand, increasing income inequality has negative effects for a large part of the society by decreasing investment opportunities due to the loss in savings volume, decreasing the marginal rate of return on labor and capital, slowing down capital accumulation, decreasing the level of output due to free market failures, and increasing poverty (Solt et al., 2020). Another explanation for the concept of income inequality was made by the economist Amartya Sen, who won the Nobel Prize in Economics for his Capacity Poverty Approach. According to Sen (1997), the concepts of economic inequality and income inequality mean different things, although they are used interchangeably. Even if giving a larger share of income to someone who needs more because of disability is thought to be against the principle of income equality, the greater need for economic resources due to disability should be taken into account when assessing economic equality needs.

Identifying inequalities in income distribution has not been easy. Until the 1990s, no economist dealt with this issue. However, after the 1990s, economists thought that income inequality was due to the decrease in the economic growth rate (Fields, 1989; Persson and Tabellini, 1991). The distribution of income is affected by some factors. Distribution of production factors in the country, demographic distributions such as gender, age, and education level, wealth distribution, inflation, informal employment, and taxes are factors that affect income distribution (Medgyesi and Zólyomi, 2016). Income inequality occurs when income distribution is not done fairly. Fair income distribution is one of the basic conditions of being a developed country. Equality is the favorite and most inspiring phrase of contemporary citizenship. In societies with inequalities, people's health and well-being are threatened (UNDP, 2016). Egalitarian societies perform better in mental and physical health, education system, sustainability, employee happiness and satisfaction (Bapuji, 2015; Hurrelman, Rathman, and Richter, 2010). Income distribution inequality has been tried to be measured by some methods; Gini Coefficient, Lorenz Curve, Percentage Analysis (P80/20), Percentage Household/Individual Groups, and Purchasing Power Parity. However, these measurement methods are rich in content but not sufficient measurement tools. Income distribution inequality affects many factors, and these factors also affect income distribution inequality (OECD, 2021).

General Theoretical Approaches to Income Distribution

Since individuals' knowledge and skills or innate abilities and financial opportunities are different from each other, this situation causes income inequality. For this reason, the explanation of this situation differs in terms of economics schools. These schools act independently of each other, even though they are diverse and influenced by one another in some ways in terms of ideas or in terms of interaction. The methods of explaining the negative situations in the economy are different from each other. In this section, it is possible to elaborate on how some of the economic theories explain this unequal distribution in income distribution and provide a multifaceted perspective by deepening the subject (table 1.1).

Job Satisfaction

Job satisfaction is a subject on which many studies have been carried out in the management literature (Dixit and Dean, 2018; Lee and Chelladurai, 2018; Luthans, 2005; Navajas-Romero, Díaz-Carrión, and Casas-Rosal, 2020). The most frequently cited definition of job satisfaction was made by Locke (1976), who defined job satisfaction as "a positive or positive emotional state resulting from the evaluation of one's work and work experiences." Job satisfaction is

TABLE 1.1
Major Theories Showing the Effects of Economic Policies on Income Distribution in Broad Terms

Physiocracy Approach (Quesnay)	With the physiocracy that developed in France in the second half of the eighteenth century, it is stated that the "school age" began in economic thought. In physiocratic thought, distribution was based on agriculture, as the agricultural sector was considered the only productive sector. Here, the views on distribution belong to Quesnay, one of the leading thinkers of the school. Accordingly, the only productive activity is agriculture, and in society, there are producers in agriculture (productive class) and landlord class, trade and craftsman class (barren class) (Steiner, 2003). Dr. Quesnay shows how goods reenter the economy in each period and how they go to consumption by various classes. He tried to reveal that economic activities are in a continuous cycle; a social product is created with this continuous cycle and this is shared among the classes in the society. According to this approach, the productive class is those who produce on the land using labor and capital. They give a part of the product to the sterile class, and this class cannot add anything to the value of the product and cannot create value. In the exchange of goods between the productive and sterile classes, what the productive class gives will always return to itself. Thus, the net product will eventually go to another class, the landlords. This approach can be easily explained with the help of the input-output table developed by Leontief (Eren, 2015: 16).
Classical Distribution Approach	The classics' approach to income distribution in the triangle of interest, rent, and wage reveals the functional distribution approach. Later, with Schumpeter adding entrepreneurial profit to it, the functional distribution was completed (Mills, 2002: 72).
Neoclassical Approach to Distribution	The neoclassical approach formulates the problem of distribution at two levels: distribution among individuals and among factors. This means that the distribution of income among individuals depends on factor prices and the distribution of production factors among individuals. As there is no class distribution, the issue of factors of production, which is the basic element that determines the distribution among individuals, is also left aside. This pricing issue is handled independently of social and institutional factors and is resolved depending on the objective conditions of production (Storesletten, Zhao, and Zilibotti, 2019). The views of neoclassical economists on distribution are examined under the titles of distribution based on marginal productivity theory and distribution theory based on production function. The distribution theory based on the marginal productivity principle was first proposed by John Bates Clark in 1899 and later developed by Wicksell and Wicksteed. Although it is possible to find some basic and general principles of the application of marginal analysis for factor pricing in Menger, neoclassical distribution theory reached its most mature level in the late nineteenth century with Wicksteed and Clark. This theory states that the factors of production should receive a share in proportion to their contribution to production, and thus a fair distribution will be ensured by distributing the entire product without leaving a residue among the factors (Haseeb, Suryanto, Hartani, and Jermsittipart, 2020).

(continued)

TABLE 1.1
(Continued)

Neoclassical Distribution Approach Based on Production Function	The conceptual tool developed by neoclassical economists for factor shares and distribution problems is the marginal productivity and elasticity of factors that are the subject of productivity analysis. Since the production function is a whole consisting of productivity and coproduct analysis, the neoclassical theory of production and distribution appears to be intertwined. Thus, it is possible to obtain all the results related to the distribution from the production function (Kazgan, 2006).
Keynesian Approach	Keynes also focused on distribution and emphasized that the two main problems of capitalist economy are full employment and income distribution, but he mostly dealt with solving the first problem. The analysis methods he brought were the starting point for long-term growth and distribution theories by the economists who came after him (Fisunoğlu and Tan, 2009).
Synthetic Approaches	Synthetic views have also been tried to be put forward by trying to mutually complement the deficiencies of the neoclassical and Keynesian income distribution models. The main ones are Weintraub, Ferguson, Findlay, and Robinson models (Lesson and Palm, 2020).

Source: Calculated by authors.

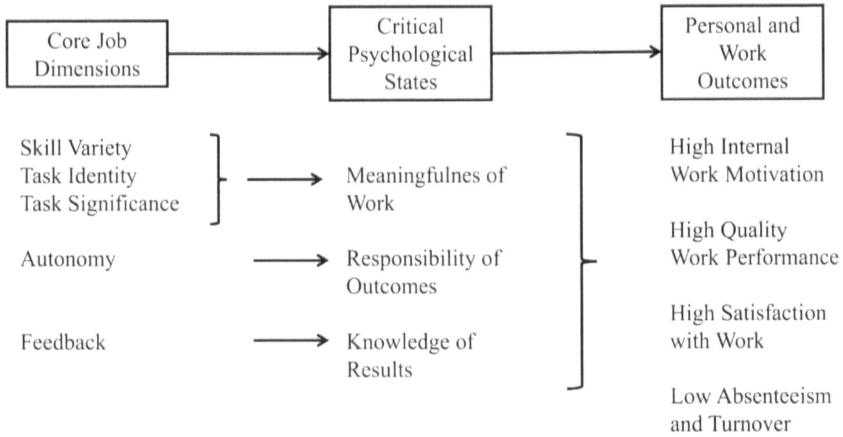

FIGURE 1.1
Job Characteristics Model.

considered as the mental, physical, and environmental pleasure that members get from the workplace. It can also be defined as an employee's emotional and cognitive reactions to his job at work (Huang Lee, McFadden, Murphy, Robertson, and Cheung, 2016). Job satisfaction not only affects the productivity and performance of employees affected by organizational events such as organizational change but also affects the perceived service quality, customer loyalty and satisfaction, and brand image improvement while a business achieves its goals (O'Donoghue and Tsui, 2013). Considering the central role it plays in the success of employees, job satisfaction is an indispensable element for businesses to gain competitive advantage in all sectors (Kramar, 2014). Navajas-Romero et al. (2020) highlight four factors as a determinant of job satisfaction: professional development, interpersonal relationships, economic expectations, and working conditions.

Job satisfaction is a multidimensional and complex concept because there are many factors that affect job satisfaction, including individual, organizational, and environmental (Özsoy and Ardıç, 2017). In general, most definitions include an employee's emotional state of being toward his job. This could be their attitudes toward certain aspects of the individual, such as working conditions in general, work or coworkers, or wages. However, it can be said that the degree of meeting the expectations of the employees can determine their job satisfaction levels. In addition, job satisfaction is not just about how much the employee enjoys the job (Lu, While, and Barriball, 2005). Hassard, Teoh, and Cox (2007) conducted a study in an educational institution in the United States; when it was evaluated how much the employees enjoyed the individual tasks related to their roles, it was moderately related to the satisfaction of the job itself and these tasks. They stated that there is a higher correlation between global job satisfaction and these tasks, and that factors such as the importance of the task and the concentration and level of control displayed while doing the job did not have any effect on job satisfaction.

Classification of the Job Satisfaction Theories

Job satisfaction theories and motivation theories are strongly interrelated. The most emphasized theories on this subject are Equity theory (Adams, 1963); Maslow's hierarchy of needs theory (Maslow, 1970); Herzberg's motivation-hygiene theory (Herzberg, 1966); the job characteristics model (Hackman and Oldham, 1975); and the dispositional approach (Judge and Lanen, 2001).

Hierarchy of Needs

Maslow's hierarchy of needs theory is one of the important theories that enables one to understand job satisfaction. According to the theory, human needs consist of a hierarchy of five levels: physiological needs, security, belonging/love, esteem, and self-actualization (Johns and Saks, 2001; Luthans, 1992; Maslow, 1970). In the hierarchy in question, the needs are not listed randomly but are placed from the base of the pyramid to the top. This approach has two main assumptions: According to the first assumption, every behavior that a person shows is aimed at meeting certain needs that the person has. The person acts in certain directions to meet his needs. Therefore, needs are an important factor determining behavior. The second assumption concerns the order of needs. Accordingly, people have needs that show a certain hierarchical order. Until the lower-level needs are met, the higher-level needs cannot motivate the person to act (Onaran, 1981). According to Maslow (1970), once a need is satisfied, it no longer has a motivating feature. Thus, man tends toward the satisfaction of other needs that he wants to be satisfied.

Equity Theory

Equity theory is a theory that examines whether equality is fair in terms of access to resources and interpersonal relations. In the system, where employees are seen simply as black boxes, they try to keep the relationship between what employees give and what they receive. Accordingly, employees give some inputs to the workplace and in return they get some benefits from the workplace, and they also perceive these benefits in different ways (Adams, 1963).

In terms of motivation of employees, how they perceive this ratio of received/given and the sense of justice in this perception play an important role. Equity theory, like other motivation theories in the literature (e.g., Maslow's hierarchy of needs), accepts that individual perceptions are a factor that affects communication with other people in the community (McCormick and İlgen, 1980). According to Adams, being paid less than deserved is one of the main factors that cause anger, and being paid more than deserved is one of the main factors that cause guilt (Spector, 2008).

Hezberg's Two-Factor Theories

The two-factor theory put forward by Herzberg is one of the most well-known motivation theories, and it is also accepted as one of the most important theories developed about job satisfaction. In the theory, the needs of the employee in the business environment are listed under the name of the situation protection factors that cause dissatisfaction and the motivation factors that provide satisfaction. Situation maintenance factors are mostly environmental related outside the job; they are environmental oriented. The factors are the company's policy, supervision, wage, interpersonal relations, and working conditions. While they do not provide job satisfaction, they prevent dissatisfaction (Greenberg and Baron, 2003: 153). Motivational factors are directly related to the job itself, the success of the employee at work, job satisfaction, and development. The factors are success, recognition, taking responsibility, giving the opportunity to be promoted, and the job itself. According to the theory, satisfaction is not the opposite of dissatisfaction, and the employee can work without being satisfied but also dissatisfied with his job. If an enterprise meets the requirements of the situational protection factors but cannot provide the requirements of the motivational factors, the employee can continue his/her job without getting satisfaction from his/her job (Başaran, 2000: 217; Doğan and Kılıç, 2008).

The Job Characteristics Model

Hackman and Oldham introduced the job characteristics approach in 1975 that explains the causes of job satisfaction. This approach is based on the dimensions of skill variety, task integrity, task importance, autonomy, and feedback, which researchers describe as the five core characteristics of the job. Accordingly, these characteristics lead to three psychological states in individuals, and these situations create important results in job satisfaction and motivation of individuals. To the extent that the job requires a variety of skills, the tasks contain integrity and are important, and the individual feels that his job is meaningful. Hackman and Oldham also developed the Job Diagnostic Survey to measure all these variables (Beck, 2004: 408).

Dispositional Approach

One of the theories used to explain job satisfaction is the dispositional approach. This approach states that some relatively stable characteristics of a person affect job satisfaction independently of job characteristics and status (Judge, Heller, and Mount, 2002). This approach provides evidence of a stable relationship between job satisfaction, career, overtime, and tasks.

If I briefly summarize the theories given earlier, Herzberg's motivation-hygiene theory and Maslow's hierarchy of needs enjoy less empirical support in the shadow of their past reputations. Empirical support for the dispositional approach and job characteristics model is increasing. However, it can be said that the work environment is affected by motivating factors and has an effect on the job satisfaction of the employees, and the job characteristics model or personality can be used to explain job satisfaction. As a result, Furnham et al. (2009) tried to understand the common effect of such different variables on job satisfaction by adding Herzberg's motivation-hygiene theory alongside personality. As a result of their studies, they found that the five major personality traits and demographic variables commonly used in the literature constitute an important part of job satisfaction.

The Relationship between Income Inequality and Job Satisfaction

Researchers like Hamermesh (1977) and Borjas (1979) and economists seem to be interested in job satisfaction in the 1970s. Recently, interest in job satisfaction has started to intensify with the studies of economists such as Clark and Uysal (1996) and Clark, Kristensen, and Westergard-Nielsen (2009). Borjas (1979) describes how union membership affects job satisfaction; Bender, Donohue, and Heywood (2005), on the other hand, conducted some studies investigating the effect of gender difference on job satisfaction. In addition, one of the issues that economists are interested in is the effect of income on job and life satisfaction (Appleton and Song, 2009; Clark et al., 2009; Donald and Siu, 2001; Panos and Theodossiou 2007; Senik, 2004). A common result of these studies is that if the income of an employee's colleagues increases relative to his own income, then that employee's job satisfaction also increases. In traditional microeconomic models of the labor supply, job benefit relates to the income one receives from the job and the hours of work required to secure a given level of income. Studies in this area indicate that working hours and wages will be the antecedents of job satisfaction. Sociologists argue that the antecedents of job satisfaction should be viewed from a broader perspective (Medgyesi and Zólyomi, 2016). In Kalleberg's (1977) study, job satisfaction is directly related to job values and job characteristics. Kalleberg (1977) mentions that there are six dimensions that people consider important in their work. These are financial value (level of pay and benefits), career value (promotion opportunities), convenience (short commute, convenient working hours), intrinsic value (whether the job task is interesting), relationships with coworkers and resource adequacy (employment) (whether the necessary resources have been given). Satisfaction with a job results from comparing the actual characteristics of the job with a person's views on what the job should have. Therefore, differences in job satisfaction may not only be the results of different job-related rewards but also result from different work values (Ehrenberg and Smith, 2009). Hammermesh (1999) stated that job satisfaction will show itself for a short time, and it will be more vulnerable to wage distribution. Considering the inequalities that occurred in the markets in the 1990s, it is naturally possible to experience a decrease in job satisfaction levels. A comparison of the International Society of Political Psychology's (ISPP) work-related attitude surveys in 1989 and 1997 shows a certain decrease in the percentage of fully satisfied workers in Norway and Germany. When both periods are compared, the same trend is observed in England, the United States, and the Netherlands, which are countries with a significant deterioration in income distribution, but the satisfaction indices do not decrease. In any case, these changes may not be visible in aggregated analyses, as we work with mean values. As changes in the functional income distribution affect all employees, this will not be the case exactly as will appear in average values of satisfaction (if they affect job satisfaction). The 1980s and 1990s saw a decline in the share of total wages to total income in both the United States and Europe, which must have negatively affected job satisfaction (Hassard et al., 2013). Spector (1997) concluded, based on different comparative analyzes of job satisfaction, that differences in job satisfaction between countries seem likely to be real. Specifically, it refers to four countries, the Dominican Republic, Hong Kong, Singapore, and the United States, whose satisfaction values range from 133.3 in Hong Kong to 160.9 in the Dominican Republic.

In addition, economists have long been concerned with the possibility that individuals care about both their absolute income and their income relative to others. Relative income concerns have important implications for micro and macroeconomic policy and are important for understanding the impact of income inequality. Studies in this area have proven a systematic correlation between relative income and brain activity associated with job satisfaction, happiness, health, longevity, and reward (Card, Mas, Moretti, and Saez, 2010). In other words, an employee's thinking that he is paid less than his colleague for the same job or learning that a manager working in the same business receives a very high salary from him affects the job satisfaction of the employee negatively. Especially in large companies, senior managers earn several hundred times the income of an average worker, and the share of these managers continues to increase despite the decrease in the company's performance (Piketty, 2014). The worst part of this situation is that the restructuring of company operations under the name of shareholder value comes with low wages and job losses, losses in workers' social rights. Therefore, this process led to the emergence of a dual labor market. On the one hand, senior executives receive income and job satisfaction far beyond their contribution to society. On the other hand, unqualified labor force settles for low wages due to the decrease in bargaining power in the process of wage determination and distribution of economic surplus (Lin and Tomaskovic-Devey, 2013). This situation has a negative effect on the job satisfaction of the employees.

Conclusion

There are many reasons for inequalities in income distribution. The difference between living conditions and living standards of various social classes can be defined as inequality. Income inequality, on the other hand, shows the difference between the share of a certain population segment from the national income and the share of another population segment at the same rate from the national income. Structural formations in the country (population structure, unemployment, informal economy, inflation, etc.) and policies produced (tax, social security, agriculture, price policies, etc.) may cause deterioration in income distribution. It is possible to get a share from the income generated, first of all, by working in a job. In this context, job satisfaction is of great importance in terms of people, businesses, and social welfare. Job satisfaction is related to the enjoyment one gets from life. This can be seen as the key to success and competitive advantage for businesses. Because while high job satisfaction is accepted as an indicator that the organization is well managed, the most important sign of deterioration in organizational conditions is the decrease in employee satisfaction. On the other hand, the effect of income on employee satisfaction is indirect, and income is generally seen as a source of dissatisfaction for employees (O'Donnell, 2015). In this sense, it is also important whether the income obtained is perceived as fair by the employee, and unfair wages can create dissatisfaction in the employee. When the literature is examined, it is stated that organizations should understand the factors affecting job satisfaction in order to increase job satisfaction of their employees. In the public sector, the employment-increasing and unemployment-preventing policies and investment policies of the governments should be at the top of the priority targets. After all these explanations, it is thought that this study, which was prepared within the framework of the theoretical ground, will fill the gap in the literature to some extent in explaining the relationships between income distribution and job satisfaction.

References

Adams, J. S. (1963). Toward an Understanding of Inequity. *Journal of Abnormal and, Social Psychology, 67*(5), 422–436.

Appleton, S. and Song, L. (2008). Life Satisfaction in Urban China: Components and Determinants. *World Development, 36*, 2325–2340.

Banjoko, S.A. (2002). *Human Resource Management: An Expository Approach*. Lagos: Pumark Press.

Bapuji, H. (2015). Individuals, Interactions and Institutions: How Economic Inequality Affects Organizations. *Human Relations, 68*(7), 1059–1083. doi:10.1177/0018726715584804.

Başaran, İ.E. (2000). *Örgütsel Davranış-İnsanın Üretim Gücü*. Ankara: Feryal Matbaası.

Beck, R.C. (2004). *Motivation Theories and Principles*. New Jersey: Prentice Hall.

Bender, K.A., Donohue, S. and Heywood, J.S. (2005). Job Satisfaction and Gender Segregation. *Oxford Economic Papers 57*, 479–496.

Bilan, Y., Mishchuk, H., Samoliuk, N., and Yurchyk, H. (2020). Impact of Income Distribution on Social and Economic Well-Being of the State. *Sustainability, 12(1)*, 429. doi:10.3390/su12010429.

Booth, P. (Ed.). (2012). *And the pursuit of happiness: Wellbeing and the role of Government*. London: The Institute of Economic Affairs.

Borjas, G. (1979). Job Satisfaction, Wages and Unions. *Journal of Human Resources, 14*, 21–40.

Card, D., Mas, A., Moretti, E., and Saez, E. (2010). Inequalıty at Work: The Effect of Peer Salarıes on Job Satısfactıon. NBER *Workıng Paper Serıes*, No: 16396. Natıonal Bureau of Economıc Research.

Çelik, A.H. (2015). Buaziz'den Rabia'ya, Trablustan Şam'a Arap Baharının Sonuçları Üzerine Bir Değerlendirme. *Akademik Yaklaşımlar Dergisi*, 6(2), 34–53.

Chahal, H. and Mehta, S. (2010). Antecedents and Consequences of Organisational Citizenship Behaviour (OCB): A Conceptual Framework in Reference to Health Care Sector. *Journal of Services Research, 10*(2), 25–44.

Clark, A.E. and Oswald, A. (1996). Satisfaction and Comparison İncome. *Journal of Public Economics, 65*, 359–381.

Clark, A.E., Kristensen, N., and Westergard-Nielsen, N. (2009). Job Satisfaction and Co-Worker Wages: Status or Signal? *Economic Journal, 119*, 430–447.

Dau-Schmidt, K.G. and Mukhopadhaya, K. (1999) The Fruits of Our Labors: An Empirical Study of the Distribution of Income and Job Satisfaction Across the Legal Profession. *Articles by Maurer Faculty*, 520. https://www.repository.law.indiana.edu/facpub/520.

Dessler, G. and Varrkey, B. (2005). *Human Resource Management, 15 e*. Pearson Education India.

Dixit, S. and Arrawatia, M. (2018), The Impact of Talent Management on Job Satisfaction and Employee Performance in Public Sector Banks of Rajasthan, *International Journal of Creative Research Thoughts*, 6(1), 425–435.

Doğan, S. and Kılıç, S. (2008). Örgütsel Bağlılığın Sağlanmasında Personel Güçlendirmenin Yeri ve Önemi. *Erciyes Üniversitesi İktisadi ve İdari Bilimler Fakültesi Dergisi*, 29, 37–61.

Donald, I. and Siu, O.L. (2001). Moderating the Stress Impact of Environmental Conditions: The Effect of Organizational Commitment in Hong Kong and China. *Journal of Environmental Psychology 21*, 353–368.

Ehrenberg, R.G. and Smith, R.S. (2009). *Modern Labor Economics: Theory and Public Policy*. 11th ed. Prentice Hall.

Eren, G. (2015). Tarımsal Kapitalizm: Fizyokrasi, *Atılım Sosyal Bilimler Dergisi, Hitit Üniversitesi İİBF*, *5*(2), 16.

Feldstein, M. (1998). Income Inequality and Poverty. *NBER Working Paper*, No: 6770, doı:10.3386/w6770.

Fields, G.S. (1989). Changes in Poverty and Inequalıty in Developıng Countrıes. *The World Bank Research Observer*, *4*(2), 167–185. doi:10.1093/wbro/4.2.167.

Fisunoğlu, M. and Tan, B.K. (2009). Keynes Devrimi ve Keynesyen İktisat. *Ekonomik Yaklaşım*, *20*(70), 36.

Furnham, A., Eracleous, A. and Chamorro-Premuzic, T. (2009). Personality, Motivation and Job Satisfaction: Hertzberg Meets the Big Five. *Journal of Managerial Psychology*, *24*(8), 765.

Gao, W. and Smyth, R (2010). Job Satisfaction and Relative Income in Economic Transition: Status or Signal? The Case of Urban China. *China Economic Review*, *21*, 442–455.

Greenberg, J. and Baron, R.A. (2003). *Behavior in Organizations: Understanding and Managing The Human Side of Work*. New Jersey: Prentice Hall.

Hackman, J.R. and Oldham, G.R. (1975). Development of the Job Diagnostic Survey, *Journal of Applied Psychology*, *60*, 161.

Hamermesh, D.S. (1999). The Changing Distribution of Job Satisfaction. NBER Working Paper 7332, Cambridge, MA.

Haseeb, M., Suryanto, T., Hartani, N.H., and Jermsittipart, K. (2020). Nexus Between Globalization, Income Inequality and Human Development in Indonesian Economy: Evidence from Application of Partial and Multiple Wavelet Coherence. *Social Indicators Research*, *147*, 723–745.

Hassard, J., Teoh, K., and Cox, T. (2013). Job Satisfaction and Psychosocial Issues: Definitions and Theories, *Occupational Safety & Health Wikipedia - European Agency for Safety & Health at Work*. Available at: http://oshwiki.eu/wiki/.

Herzberg, F. (1966). *Work and the Nature of Man*. Cleveland: World Publishing Company.

Huang, Y.H., Lee, J., McFadden, A.C., Murphy, L.A., Robertson, M.M., and Cheung, J.H., (2016). Beyond Safety Outcomes: An Investigation of the Impact of Safety Climate on Job Satisfaction, Employee Engagement and Turnover Using Social Exchange Theory as the Theoretical Framework, *Applied Ergonomics*, *55*, 248–257.

Hurrelmann, K., Rathmann, K., and Richter, M. (2010). Health Inequalities and Welfare State Regimes: A Research Note. *Journal of Public Health*, *19*(1), 3–13. doi:10.1007/s10389-010-0359-1.

ILO. (2015). *Wages and Income Inequality*. Global Wage Report 2014/15.

Johns, G. and Saks, A.M. (2001). *Organizational Behaviour: Understanding and Managing Life at Work*. 5th ed. USA: Addison Wesley Longman (Toronto: Pearson Education Inc.).

Judge, T.A. and Lanen. R.J. (2001). Dispositional Affect and Job Satisfaction: A Review and Theoretical Extension. *Organizational Behavior and Human Decision Processes, 8*(6), 67.

Judge, T.A., Heller, D., and Mount, M.K. (2002). Five-Factor Model of Personality and job satisfaction: A Meta-Analysis. *Journal of Applied Psychology, 87*, 530–541.

Kalleberg, A.L. (1977): Work Values and Job Rewards: A Theory of Job Satisfaction. American *Sociological Review, 42*, 124–143.

Kazgan, G. (2006). *İktisadi Düşünce veya Politik İktisadın Evrimi,* Remzi Kitabevi, 12 .bs, İstanbul.

Kramar, R. (2013). Beyond Strategic Human Resource Management: İs Sustainable Human Resource Management the Next Approach? *The International Journal of Human Resource Management, 25*(8), 1069–1089. doi:10.1080/09585192.2013.816863.

Lee, Y.H. and Chelladurai, P. (2017). Emotional İntelligence, Emotional Labor, Coach Burnout, Job Satisfaction, and Turnover İntention in Sport Leadership. *European Sport Management Quarterly, 18*(4), 393–412. doi:10.1080/16184742.2017.1406971.

Lesson, R. and Palm, C. G. (2020). *Milton Friedman on Freedom: Selections from the Collected Works of Milton Friedman.* The Hoover Institution Press. Originally published: Milton, Friedman. (1970). One and Only Social Responsibility of Business. *New York Times Magazine.*

Lin, K.-H. and Tomaskovic-Devey, D. (2013). Financialization and US Income Inequality, 1970– 2008. *American Journal of Sociology, 118*(5), 1284–1329.

Locke, E.A. (1976). The Nature and Causes of Job Satisfaction. In Dunnette, M.D. (ed.), *Handbook of industrial and organizational Psychology.* Chicago: Rand McNally.

Loke, J.C.F. (2001). Leadership Behaviours: Effects on Job Satisfaction, Productivity and Organizational Commitment, *Journal of Nursing Management, 9*, 191–204. doı:10.1046/j.1365-2834.2001.00231.x.

Lu, H., While, A.E., and Barriball, K.L. (2005). Job Satisfaction Among Nurses: A Literature Review. *International Journal of Nursing Studies, 42*(2), 211.

Luthans, F. (2005). Organizational Behavior. 10th ed. McGraw-Hill.

Maslow, A.H. (1970). *Motivation and Personality.* 2nd ed. New York: Harper & Row.

McCormick, E.J. and Ilgen, D.R. (1980) *Industrial Psychology.* 7th ed. Prentice-Hall: Englewood Cliffs.

McShane, S. (1984). Job Satisfaction and Absenteeism: A Meta-Analytic Re-examination, Canadian *Journal of Administrative Sciences, 1*(1), 61–77. doı:10.1111/j.1936-4490.1984.tb00721.x

Medgyesi, M. and Zolyomi, E. (2016). Job Satisfaction and Satisfaction in Financial Situation and Their İmpact on Life Satisfaction. *Social Situation Monitor Research Note* 6/2016. Directorate-General for Employment, Social Affairs and Inclusion.

Mills, J. (2002). *A Critical History of Economics.* New York: Palgrave Macmillan, p. 72.

Navajas-Romero, V., Díaz-Carrión, R., and Casas-Rosal, J.C. (2020). Comparing Working Conditions and Job Satisfaction in Hospitality Workers Across Europe.

International Journal of Hospitality Management, 90, *102631.* doi:10.1016/j.ijhm.2020.102631.
O'Donnell, P. (2015). *The Effect of Income and Working Conditions on Job Satisfaction.* Available at: https://business.tcnj.edu/wp-content/uploads/sites/219/2015/08/ECO-495-2015_Patrick-ODonnell.pdf (accessed October 10, 2021).
O'Donoghue, K. and Tsui, M. (2013). Social Work Supervision Research (1970-2010): The Way We Were and the Way Ahead. *British Journal of Social Work, 45*(2), 616–633. doi:10.1093/bjsw/bct115.
OECD. (2021). *Income İnequality (İndicator).* doi: 10.1787/459aa7f1-en (accessed December 15, 2021).
Onaran, O. (1981). *Çalışma Yaşamında Güdülenme Kuramları.* Ankara: Sevinç Matbaası.
Özsoy, E. and Ardıç, K. (2017). Karanlık Üçlü'nün (Narsizm, Makyavelizm ve Psikopati) İş Tatminine Etisinin İncelenmesi. *Yönetim ve Ekonomi, 24*(2), 391–406. doi:10.18657/yonveek.297733.
Panos, G.A. and Theodossiou, I. (2007). Earnings Aspirations and Job Satisfaction: The Affective and Cognitive İmpact of Earnings Comparisons. *Centre for European Labour Market Research, Discussion Paper* 2007-01.
Persson, T. and Tabellini, G. (1991). Is Inequality Harmful for Growth? Theory and Evidence. *Working Paper No: 91-155.* doi:10.3386/w3599.
Piketty, Thomas. (2014). *Capital in the Twenty-First Century.* Translated by Arthur Goldhammer. Cambridge, MA, and London: The Belknap Press of Harvard University Press.
Sen, A. (1997). From Income Inequality to Economic Inequality. *Southern Economic Journal, 64*(2), 383–401.
Senik, C. (2004). When Information Dominates Comparison: A Panel Data Analysis Using Russian Subjective Data. *Journal of Public Economics, 88,* 2099–2133.
Solt, F. (2020). Measuring Income Inequality Across Countries and Over Time: The Standardized World Income Inequality Database. *Social Science Quarterly, 101*(3), 1183–1199. doi:10.1111/ssqu.12795.
Song, M., Xie, Q., Tan, K. H., and Wang, J. (2020). A Fair Distribution and Transfer Mechanism of Forest Tourism Benefits in China. *China Economic Review,101542.* doi:10.1016/j.chieco.2020.101542.
Spector, P.E. (1997). *Job Satisfaction. In: Application, Assessment Causes and Consequences.* London: Sage.
Spector, P.E. (2008). *Industrial and Organizational Behavior.* 5th ed. Hoboken, NJ: Wiley.
Steiner, P. (2003). Physiocracy and French Pre-Classical Political Economy. In Samuels, W.J., Bıddle, E.J. and Davıs, J.B. (eds.), *The History of Economic Thought.* New Jersey, USA: Blackwell Publishing, Ltd.
Storesletten, K., Zhao, B., and Zilibotti, F. (2019). Business Cycle during Structural Change: Arthur Lewis' Theory from a Neoclassical *Perspective. NBER Working Paper* No: 26181/ doi:10.3386/w26181.
Temin, P. (2017). *The Vanishing Middle Class: Prejudice and Power in a Dual Economy.* Cambridge: The MIT Press.

TUIK. (2008). Tüketim Harcamaları, *Yoksulluk ve Gelir Dağılımı Sorularla Resmi İstatistikler Dizisi* – 6, Ankara.

Turgut, A.S. (2019). Türkiye'deki Gelir Eşitsizliğinin Toplumsal Cinsiyet, Kadının İstihdamı ve Kadın Yoksulluğu Açısından Değerlendirilmesi, *KOSBED, 38*, 315–329. doı:10.35343/kosbed.581637.

UNDP. (2016). *Regional Development Report: The Case Study on Income and Social Inequalities in Turkey.* Ankara: Birleşmiş Milletler Kalkınma Programı Türkiye Ülke Ofisi.

United Nations Millennium Declaration. (2000). United Nations General Assembly Resolution 55/2. New York: United Nations. www.un.org/ millennium/declaration/ares552e.pdf (accessed October 8, 2021).

Uztopal, D. (2017). Kapital'in Yazılma Tarihi. (Erişim Tarihi: October 7, 2021). https://teoriveeylem.net/2017/10/ kapitalin-yazilma-tarihi/.

Wildman, J. (2021). COVID–19 and Income Inequality in OECD Countries. *The European Journal of Health Economics, 22,* 455–462. doi:10.1007/s10198-021-01266-4.

Wunder, C. and Schwarze, J. (2006). Income Inequality and Job Satisfaction of Full-Time Employees in Germany. *IZA Discussion Papers,* No. 2084.

2

The Health Resilience and Welfare Inequality of the Turkish Population in Response to the Syrian Refugee Inflow

Berna TUNCAY and İlhan Can ÖZEN

Introduction

Turkey is located adjacent to the regions of the Syrian war, the ensuing humanitarian crisis, that started in 2011. After the outbreak of conflicts in Syria on March 2011, over 4.5 million people have been forced to leave their country and over 3,750,000 of them moved to Turkey until the end of 2016 (AFAD 2017). The Turkish government has implemented "open-door policy" for the reception of these populations and consequently shouldered a significant load collaborating with nongovernmental organizations and spent nearly $12 billion for caring refugee population, with the records suggesting that $3 billion was spent in the early reception period (until the start of 2015) on the health operation, health service, and health reception specifically. Refugees were first met at border crossing points, and they were registered and given identity cards that document the status of "temporary protection." The vaccination drive and healthcare access were provided to the refugee population using these identity cards. A significant population was able to access the Turkish health system, completely free of fee, through this access channel. The open access system, creating an important flexibility in keeping the health level of the vulnerable Syrian population constant, or limiting the war effect that these populations have suffered, is at the same time leading the health shock effect to be much more immediately reflected through the general healthcare system. This significant process of integration has created certain opportunities for health research, because the effect of this significant and sizeable integration on the processes and outputs of the health system is well worth to be investigated, for the domestic population as well as for the Syrians. This study focuses on the welfare of the domestic population in terms of health outputs, in addition to the work on the health of Syrians that we have already carried out (Tuncay et al. 2022). The opportunity for identification arises from the fact that although the health effect was sizeable, it was by no means geographically homogenous, with a specific region affected more significantly than the rest of the Turkish geography, which is creating a nice local health equilibrium-national health equilibrium contrast that we can exploit for identification (Card 1990).

The pitfalls of the analysis are that the region under question had specific health system and health outcome challenges before the Syrian arrival; the underestimation of these historical and regional characteristics must mean that the specific inequalities and lower capacities of the region can be clouding the estimates for the effect we can generate for the Syrian shock. So novel strategies are needed in order to control the historical and geographical characteristics that drive health processes and health outcomes.

Syrian refugee shock and historical data of Turkish health coverage system constitute very important results in terms of public health and welfare context. Therefore, our goal in this research is to identify the initial effect of the Syrian group, and also measure the resilience of the health system afterward. The problem is that the adaptation and shock processes are evolving over time, and the datasets need to be analyzed carefully to interpret these processes and how they are coevolving. This research is the first systematic effort to not only analyze the functionings and outputs of the Turkish health system (measured at the level of the Turkish patients and health demanders) but to do it with the latest statistical methodologies for a cleaner identification. The results suggest that the Syrian arrival has not significantly affected the functioning of the Turkish health system (as measured for instance by the bed turnover ratios, hospital bed occupancy rates, physician to population ratios, and how the aggregate applications are divided among the different stages of the health system). The picture for the health system outputs and health outcomes is a little bit more nuanced, with an initial period of negative effect in many important health outcomes reversed by the period's end (2016), when a more mature integration of the Syrians to the health system is achieved.

Literature Review

The literature on the consequences of forced migration for public health and welfare can be classified into two categories: studies that examine the effects of forced migration on native population and studies focusing on the effects of forced migration on migrants. This section focuses on the native population effect. In the literature, which studies the effects of forced migrants on the well-being of native people in host societies, there are findings with mixed results; migrants can affect both positively and negatively the welfare and health outcomes of refugee-hosting societies. Among those papers, Alix-Garcia and Saah (2010) explore the effect of refugee influx to the regions in Western Tanzania from Burundi and Rwanda in the early 1990s. They use various price indices for agricultural goods and the household data that comes from two separate Demographic and Health Surveys (DHS) performed in 1991–1992 and 1996, and they show positive effects of the refugee camps on the wealth of rural households. The authors first use variation in refugee influx over different periods of time to investigate the effects of proximity to refugee camps on prices of agricultural goods in Tanzania. They show significant increases in the prices of some agricultural products in regions near the refugee camps. The authors then use a difference-in-difference (DID) approach for the treatment effect to vary with distance from the refugee camps to measure the wealth effect of the migration on receiving societies. They employ various welfare indicators at a household expenditure level (electricity, television, radios, refrigerators, bicycles, etc.) and find that the welfare indicators in rural regions near the refugee camps increase following the arrival of Rwandan migrants while those indicators decrease for households living in urban regions. They provide a suggestive evidence that host country households living in rural regions close to the refugee camps may have generated more income from selling their agricultural products at higher prices and consumed more durable products increasing their wealth level. Household data also indicates decreased incidence of wealth indicators in urban areas. In another paper, studying the relationship between the refugee presence and the welfare, Maystadt and Verwimp (2014) look at the distance of the local residents to refugee camps in Kagera to explore the impact of the refugee inflow on local people consumption. The paper employs the Kagera Health and Development Survey (KHDS) dataset from Economic Development Initiatives (EDI) and the World Bank for years between 1991 and 1994 and uses refugee impact (an average of the refugee population weighted by an exponential distance function) as a treatment variable that explains to what extent each local resident is affected by the refugee inflow. In other words, they proxy the impact of a refugee camp by the distance between any region and the refugee camps and the refugee population of those camps. Controlling for the effects on economic activities, they show that the closer a local person is or the more crowded the refugee camp is, the more likely that his welfare will increase. They find that the workers in nonagricultural sector and self-employed farmers are positively affected by the refugee inflow, only if they are located near the refugee camps and if the refugee inflow is very intense. On the contrary, the agricultural workers are negatively affected in regions close to the refugee camps due to a labor market competition and higher prices on the commodity markets. The agricultural and political environment in refugee-hosting regions is important in determining the well-being of refugees, and refugees are better off when they have access to local employment opportunities particularly in an agricultural sector in those regions. They also report that health and sanitation services improved in refugee-hosting regions and approximately 30% of the healthcare services are received by local population. Similarly, Alix-Garcia et al. (2018) examine the effect of refugee inflows on the welfare of the host population in Kakuma region in Kenya. The authors use both nighttime lights data and household survey data with prices, refugee, and food deliveries to investigate the effects of the refugee camps on consumption in the host region. They estimate the sensitivity of the nighttime lights to the interaction between time-varying refugee population and proximitiy to Kakuma. They employ spatial and intertemporal variation for the density of nighttime lights and parametric and semi-parametric estimations for proximity to the refugee camps in order to interact with refugee population for each year. They found that local households in refugee-hosting societies get benefits from living near the refugee camps; their level of consumption increases as the intensity of refugee population increases in those regions. Moreover, recently, using the KHDS, new research on the impact of civil war on the host population measures the distance to the closest hospitals and health centers in refugee-affected regions in Kagera and shows that refugee influx does not have any effect on the accessibility of health services (Maystadt and Verwimp 2014).

Differently from the studies summarized earlier, few other studies show negative effects of the refugee inflow on host population focusing on the impact of forced migration due to civil wars on the health outcome of local residents. For instance, Montalvo and Reynal-Querol (2007) show an increase in the transmission of several diseases in the refugee-hosting population. The authors use a panel data estimation of 135 countries between 1962 and 1997. They use different datasets including the number of diagnosed malaria cases from WHO, the health data from the World Development Indicators of the World Bank, and the data on refugees from the United Nation High Commission for the Refugees (UNHRC 2016). They proxy two groups of factors where the determinants of malaria incidence are included in the fixed effect panel data estimation regressions—geographical conditions and social conditions. Geographical conditions are country specific but time invariant, which are included in the country-specific effect of their regression. They employ two main instruments—a civil war in the refugee country of origin and the estimated number of refugees. They structured an empirical model to explain bilateral refugees based on various geographical specifications such as distance between countries, and sizes; then, they employ the estimated number of refugees as an instrument variable for the actual size of refugees. Their instrumental variables estimates show that every 1,000 refugees cause approximately 2,000 and 2,700 additional cases of malaria in refugee-hosting countries. The authors conclude that the size of the mass population movement (due to civil war) from a country with a high volume of malaria has a significant impact on the number of malaria cases in the refugee-hosting countries. In a similar empirical design, large refugee inflows from poor living conditions have also been associated with the spread of infectious diseases such as malaria in other studies (Kalipeni and Oppong 1998; Kazmi and Pandit 2001). However, Gallup and Sachs (2001) outline potential econometric challenges and measurement errors to interpret the impact of large and sudden refugee influx on the spread of malaria. The authors state that the measurement of malaria incidence in a population is very difficult as there is no clear methodology to diagnose malaria.

Nevertheless, Baez (2011), employing different estimation strategies, sheds light on measuring the heavy burden of hosting a large arrival of refugees on the health outcome of host population. The author investigates the short-run and long-run health effects of massive migration in 1994 from Burundi and Rwanda to the region of Kagera in Tanzania and focuses on the causal effects of refugee intensity on health outcomes of local children. The paper uses Tanzania Demographic and Health Survey (1992 and 1996) for a household level cross-sectional data and KHDS (between 1991 and 1994, and 2004) to investigate the short-run and long-run effects of the forced migrants on three health outcomes of native children living close to the refugee camps; nutrition, morbidity, and infant mortality, particularly focusing on children aged between zero and four years old for nutrition, and morbidity outcomes and children aged between zero and five years old for infant mortality. The author employs a natural experiment design to eliminate the effect of data limitations on estimations and the difficulty of using right control groups for refugee-hosting native population. Moreover, the author uses intra- and inter-cohort variation to investigate the long-run effects of refugee influx on child health outcomes. All empirical strategies are employed by double and triple difference analysis on pre- and post-refugee influx data. Importantly, the author defines the degree of refugee intensity with respect to historical and geographic specifications to exploit the exogenous arrival of refugees in Kagera and uses the distance of native population to the border with Rwanda to characterize the burden of refugees in those regions. The results show that there is a significant negative effect of high refugee intensity on the health outcomes of native children for both short run and long run (10 years following the arrival of migrants); mortality rates for children under five years old increase compared to pre-refugee influx period; and native children living in regions close to refugees have various infectious diseases such as diarrhea and fever, and they are subject to an increase in childhood malnutrition (reduced height at early ages).

More tragically, the refugee influx in Goma, Tanzania, in 1994 was extremely intense with approximately 1,000,000 Rwandans crossing the border (Damme 1995). The government was not able to cope with the spread of infectious diseases, particularly cholera. Because of this massive population movement, local people living in these regions were under the risk of cholera epidemic as well. The public policy makers decided to move all refugees to the north of Tanzania, which was even more threatening for the refugees and other populations. The lack of medical treatment and clean water caused many refugees to die on the way. On the other hand, the refugee shock with more than 500,000 people in the early 1990s in Guinea had important implications as well (Damme 1995). In that case, the government did not build any refugee camps, but local residents welcomed all refugees in their living regions. Moreover, the Ministry of Health in Guinea did not build any refugee healthcare facilities, but all refugees were entitled to have free access to existing healthcare services at the local health centers and hospitals. United Nations High Commissioner for Refugees (UNHRC 2016) was paying a fee for each visit which was the same as the one local resident in Guinea pay. In the host regions with intense refugee inflow, supplemental healthcare providers were employed for all refugees. Consequently, offering free healthcare to refugees increased the workload in the local healthcare facilities, and hosting refugees in local regions introduced the risk of several epidemic diseases such as cholera, measles, and meningitis for both refugees and refugee-hosting local residents. Similarly, Porignon et al. (1995) and Goyens et al. (1996) discuss the role of host health services in Goma region that was exposed to a heavy refugee influx from Rwanda in 1994. The authors state that Rwandan refugees seeking treatments with their poor health profiles had caused a work overload for the local hospitals and health centers affecting the local residents.[1] Overwhelmed healthcare facilities caused serious public health risks for the host population including a decrease in healthcare quality, disruption in preventive healthcare, and financial capacity problems. Studying the effects of refugees on host populations and on their health services capacity, Whitaker (2002) conducts a series of different interviews with people in regions at different distances from the refugee camps and collects more data in government meetings and NGO activities as well. The author uses different research strategies including cost and benefit rankings, map drawing, and time use surveys. The results suggest that the refugee influx in Tanzania had a significant impact on the government's healthcare infrastructure. Healthcare utilization of refugees at hospitals was very intense putting high pressure on the local health facilities; refugees used more beds than local residents at many hospitals causing shortage of drugs. Poor local residents living near the refugee-affected regions were given limited access to healthcare facilities near the camps as outpatients. The author also reports that refugees had caused several diseases including malaria, HIV/AIDS, dysentery to spread out among local residents, and skin diseases among Tanzanian children. Moreover, comparing the access to healthcare services between refugees and local residents living in rural regions in the late 1990s, Orach et al. (2005) show that the number of obstetric operations was higher for refugee women compared to the host population living in rural areas in Uganda, and interestingly, maternal mortality was significantly higher in the refugee-hosting society than the rates in the refugee population. Healthcare facilities in Uganda are better equipped for refugees than for the host population suggesting that refugees have a better healthcare utilization particularly in obstetric services than the rural host population due to potential geographic and financial reasons.[2] It is inevitable that refugees are likely to affect the native population of the host country due to the risk of introducing several diseases and particularly the risk of local health service capacity constraints. Kreibaum (2016), using various household survey data (2002–2003, 2005–2006, and 2009–2010) and employing DID models, examines the effect of heavy refugee inflow on the local residents in Uganda. The author identifies the impact of an increase in refugee population by constructing a natural experiment and relying on a common trend assumption.[3] The identification strategy also assumes that the composition between treated and untreated clusters remains stable in a repeated cross-sectional analysis. Accordingly, the author finds that excessive demand in healthcare facilities has created a high level of workload in public health centers, and refugee-hosting population are less likely to have access to healthcare services. Finally, Rennert (1994) explores the effects of 1989–1992 Russian immigration on mortality patterns in Israel. This paper compares official mortality statistics from Israel and the Soviet Union to investigate differences in significant causes of death and calculates overall age-adjusted mortality rates in Israel, considering the Russian mortality rates, Israeli population, and the relative size of the immigrant population following the forced migration. The results indicate that mortality rates in the European republics of the former Soviet Union were reported about 40% higher than mortality rates in Israel. And, the results show that massive immigration has the potential to change the overall health profile of the host country. Apparently, in developing countries hosting most of the world's refugee population, refugee-hosting societies residing in refugee-affected regions are disadvantaged population particularly in terms of health outcomes; therefore, public health authorities should give attention to the local residents' access to healthcare services, strengthening the capacity of local healthcare facilities, and thus welfare. Overall, forced migration to a large extent is an important source of an increase in the incidence of serious diseases and of a high pressure on the country's healthcare infrastructure affecting public health and society's welfare.

Data and Methodology

The data on the Turkish health system is long and extensive, and well tabulated in a yearly fashion by the Turkish health ministry, and the data on the health outputs is collected from the 2013 and 2018 rounds of the Turkish DHS, undertaken by the Hacettepe Population Studies Institute. The health system level variables (e.g., the bed turnover ratios, hospital bed occupancy rates, and physician to population ratios) are captured at the province level, to be used as controls for the health outcome determination process. The capacity of the health system (C_{it}) at the personnel level[4] (C_{itp}), at the technology level[5] (C_{itt}), and at the bed level[6] (C_{itb}) is defined in the regression framework, to capture health output both before the Syrian shock (2009–2012) and after the Syrian shock (2013–2016). The data is collected at the aggregate level assuming that province-level health system is representative and a meaningful classification. The shock variable is measured by looking at the health level applications of the Syrians and aggregated at the system level from E-Nabiz Data to the level of the province, and from the Turkish internal ministry (Directorate General of Migration Management-DGMM), collecting internal movement statistics of the 3.3 million Syrians who have arrived in the country.

The DHS 2013–2018 is the main data source used for the health output part of the regression, on the mortality and life expectancy dimensions, aggregated for the province level.[7] The main analysis is undertaken on the total 20,000 mother-birth matches that are summarized in the DHS data. Information about the number of deaths occurring among 1,000 births, under-5 mortality, and expectation of average livelihoods is undertaken from this sample, for the years between 2009 and 2016.

In terms of the provinces, we focus on the 9 provinces among the top 10 refugee receiving province list from 2012 to 2016 (see figure 2.1). The reason why Istanbul is excluded from the analysis is that it is an outlier province and the city with the highest level of development, population, and also the highest capacity in terms of health system development, where the selection issues would also be the most glaring.

We look at the influence of these health shocks on a different and holistic set of health outcomes, from mortality to life expectancy.

The geography we are focusing on is the area that is specifically influenced by the shock, as measured by the size of the migrant health demanders,

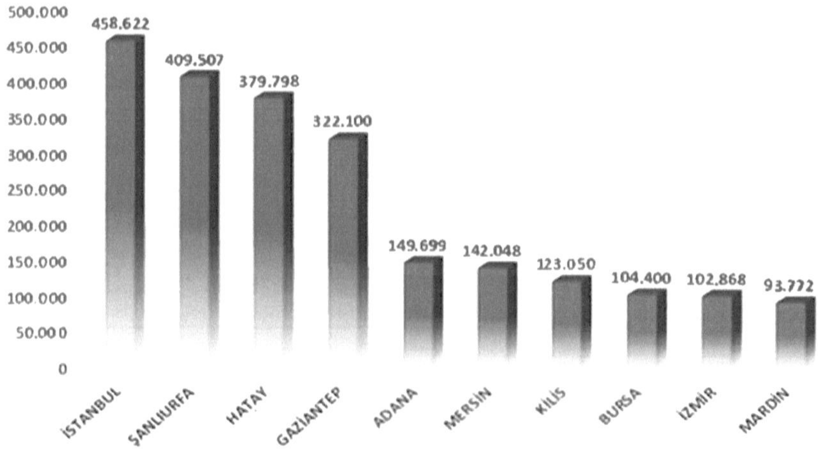

FIGURE 2.1
The Top 10 Turkish Provinces Receiving Syrian Refugees under Temporary Protected Status. *Source*: Created by authors.

divided by the total health demand in the public healthcare sector. You can see in figure 2.1, what are these fundamental provinces where we target and pinpoint to see if indeed there is a health outcome effect in these targeted geographies.

Methodology of Identification

The health outcomes that we focus on are infant mortality, early age mortality, and life expectancy, as these will be most affected by the health shock that is observed in this specific sub-geography. The problem is that this region that has received the Syrians does not have homogenous characteristics with the rest of the Turkish geography (Tuncay et al. 2022), which would create certain problems, and the recent historical trend that existed prior to the Syrians' arrival can cloud and pollute our estimation for the Syrian effect, when focusing fundamentally on these regions. The problem of identification can be specified as finding control units that are similar enough to the treated geographical units, such that the changes in the fundamental variables can truly be identified as the effect of the treatment (Syrian local shock) that is under question. Otherwise, pretreatment differential trends and different levels at the historical level for the treatment and control units can bias our results.

For the identification methodology, we follow two novel methodologies for this question and this challenge, the synthetic control methodology and the DID methodology. The synthetic control methodology, recently developed by Abadie et al. (2010), uses weighted combinations among the control units to replicate the pretreatment trends for the crucial variable and the covariates and shows the comparison of the levels and trends of the actual treatment units against these historically comparable synthetic control units. The pretreatment data is available for all 81 provinces, and the 9 separate provinces are proxied by the remaining 72 provinces, in order to create a meaningful potential outcome, which estimates the situation in the affected provinces if the Syrian shock did not occur. We also employ DID methodology to use the fixed characteristics of the units, and the historical time tends to focus on the within unit, through time differences (different than the historical national trend) that have been introduced as a result of the treatment (Doudchenko and Imbens 2016).

In the simple statistical language, the exogenous change (through time as denoted by the subscript t) in the outcome variable we are trying to estimate (Y), when we divide our geography (using the subscript s) to affected geographies denoted with T (treatment group), and unaffected geographies denoted with C (control group), is equal to:

$$\delta = E\left[Y_{ist} | s = T, t = 2016\right] - E\left[Y_{ist} | s = T, t = 2009\right]$$
$$- E\left[Y_{ist} | s = C, t = 2016\right] - E\left[Y_{ist} | s = C, t = 2009\right]$$

The treated group of provinces are observed before and after the period of treatment and a difference is created by taking the values after and before ($A = E[Y_{ist} | s = T, t = 2016] - E[Y_{ist} | s = T, t = 2009]$), and the same method is followed through for the untreated (control) group of observations ($B = E[Y_{ist} | s = C, t = 2016] - E[Y_{ist} | s = C, t = 2009]$), with a crucial difference and difference (A-B) being equal to δ which is the crucial causal effect of interest. The assignment of the groups into the treated and control categories is exogenized by using the distance to the border variable, which is a common approach in the literature (Altındağ and Kaushal 2021, Aksu et al. 2018, Aygun et al. 2021, Tumen 2016).

In the absence of a randomized assignment, these approaches are the best we can do under the non-randomized, nonexperimental setting.

Method for Shock Differentiation

On selection of provinces, we aim to differentiate between the provinces which have been affected in terms of the scale of effect, and the degree of shock they have suffered. From the shock and health shock literature, it is clear that the shock's effect is proportional to the relative size of the shock (compared to "normal" reactions of the health system), and inversely proportional to the overall size of the local health system. (We normalize the shock variable as a percentage of total

FIGURE 2.2
The Affected and Unaffected Provinces and the Differentiated Effect. *Source*: Created by authors.

size of the provincial healthcare system.) We capture the year-to-year increase in the health applications prior to the treatment (before the 2013 integration of the Syrian groups) as Δc, and the size of the shock is conceptualized as the number of Syrians that are applying to the local (provincial) health system of the country after treatment Δt, so our relative shock variable (H_t) can be measured by Δt/Δc, and we are showing the provinces' relative shock in figure 2.2. Looking at this differentiation we are able to differentiate the most affected three provinces (Kilis, Sanliurfa, and Kahramanmaras) from the other six provinces that have affected with a more manageable shock level. The regression and matching strategies are employed to see whether the effect on the health system is graded by this relative shock effect.

The shock dimensions are conceptualized as H_t and allow for a differentiation of the Turkish geography, as can be seen in figure 2.2. After this first-stage instrument being created, we look at the effect of this shock on the crucial health outcome variables, first in an OLS setting.

Empirical Results

OLS Regression Results

The OLS regression for our health output Y is defined as follows:

$$Y_{it} = = \alpha_1 t_i + \alpha_2 P_i + \alpha_3 C_i + \alpha_4 H_i + \Omega_i$$

where t_i is the time trend, P_i is the province specific fixed effects, and C_i is the health capacity at the province level that we want to control for.

The OLS results in tables 2.1 and 2.2 confirm three sets of results:

1. Significant health shocks in the first period, remaining significant until 2014 and 2015.
2. All the health outcome shocks and setbacks are cleared by the end of the period.
3. The effect is graded, with three provinces with the largest shock having a significantly larger and longer setback in its health outcomes (as can be seen in table 2.1).

The results substantiate both a significant health shock (as measured by the unexpected relative supply overuse) that can be observed on the input and output dimension and the health resilience that allows the health outputs to return to their pre-shock levels and trends. Since this pattern of rebounding health outputs (as measured in life expectancy, infant mortality, and under-5 mortality) is observed as the shock is still in the Turkish health system (the arrival and further integration of the Syrian population are accomplished in this 2015–2016 period), we feel confident that we are observing truly increased capabilities, and not the simple return to earlier health functions.

TABLE 2.1
The Under-5 Mortality Regression for Shock Differentiation (2012–2014)

Variables	*Coeff.*	*st-dev.*	*t-stat*
Syrian Migration Effect	0.0664	0.0234	2.84^{**}
3 Provinces	0.00196	0.000655	3.00^{***}
Time Effect	−0.0504	0.0101	-4.96^{***}
Physician Per Population	−0.00405	0.0175	0.23
Number of Beds	−0.365	0.0132	-2.75^{**}
Health Institution Per Population	−2.67	1.47	-1.82^{*}
Growth Rate Population	4.446	5.672	0.78
Intercept	77.92	(0.735)	106.01^{***}

Source: Calculated by authors.

TABLE 2.2
Fixed-Effect Estimates of the Syrian Effect for 2015 and 2016

<table>
<tr><th>Variables</th><th>2015(β|t-stat|pr.)</th><th>2016(β|t-stat|pr.)</th></tr>
<tr><td>Life Expectancy Effect</td><td>−.0144|| −1.79||0.07</td><td>−.0005||−0.06||0.951</td></tr>
<tr><td>Infant Mortality Effect</td><td>.0626|| 3.23 ||0.001</td><td>0.014 ||0.83 ||0.405</td></tr>
<tr><td>Under-5 Mortality Effect</td><td>.0451|| 2.02||0.044</td><td>.0008|| 0.04 ||0.969</td></tr>
</table>

Source: Calculated by authors.

Differences-in-Differences Approach to Exogeneity

In terms of establishing clear causality, we first utilize the DID approach to focus on the time effects that are becoming operational through the shock effects we are thinking about. The identification strategy is controlling for the time-invariant characteristics, as those are subtracted out of both the treated and the control geographical units. The process of defining the treated group (Group T) in an exogenous manner is achieved by differentiating between the provinces which are within 100 kilometers of the Syrian border as the treatment group and the remaining provinces which are not (Group C). As we stated before, the distance to the Syrian border is used as an exogenous instrument of treatment in a lot of the Syrian effect literature, and we follow the same methodology here. The pre-period for this analysis is from 2009 to 2012, where there is no clear presence of Syrian influx in the Turkish geography and the Turkish health system. The post-period of this analysis is from 2013 to 2016.

As can be seen from table 2.3, the initial significant negative shock is substantiated for the health outcomes for the treated region, when we define the treated region in an exogenous manner, using the minimization of the travel distance assumption. It must be noted that none of the process variables of health show any significant effect from the shock, as substantiated by the DID methodology.

Synthetic Control Approach to Exogenous Change

The synthetic control approach creates the ideal control group to compare the situation with our specific treatment group. The 72 remaining provinces are differentiated and weighted to create the synthetic group average, to create the counterfactual time trend for the treatment group if treatment

TABLE 2.3
Diff-and-Diff Approach for Exogenous Estimation of the Syrian Effect (2009–2015)

Diff-and-Diff Approach For Main Health Outcome Variables	*Coeff.*	*Std. Err.*	*t-stat*
$(\beta_T^{*post1} - \beta_T^{*pre}) - (\beta_C^{*post} - \beta_C^{*pre})$	0.000067	0.000020	3.35^{***}
$(\beta_T^{**post2} - \beta_T^{**pre}) - (\beta_C^{**post} - \beta_C^{**pre})$	−0.027	0.009	-2.82^{***}

Note: ***, **, * denote the significance levels at 1%, 5%, and 10% respectively. Values in parentheses show probability values.
Source: Calculated by authors.
[1]This coefficient collects data on the diff-and-diff methodology where we are looking at infant mortality for the Turkish population.
[2]This coefficient collects data on the diff-and-diff methodology where we are looking at life expectancy for the Turkish population.

did not occur. Our approach uses 72 potential control units, with $T_0 = 4$ as the number of pretreatment periods and $T_1 = 4$ as the number of posttreatment periods. The visual results suggest that especially the top 3 provinces represent a significant shock, with an initial divergence between actual and synthetic control starting in 2013, and the difference is crucially closing for all units by the year 2016. For the six less affected provinces (whose values are bunched together), the divergence of values (with the affected provinces suffering from lower life expectancy and higher mortality) occurs at a lower level, and the divergence opens much later and closes much before (figures 2.6, 2.10, and 2.14). For the three affected provinces (as can be seen in figures 2.3–2.5 for the life expectancy, and in figures 2.7–2.9 for the infant mortality, and in figures 2.11–2.13 for the under-5 mortality) the divergence between the synthetic control and actual units (which used to be non-existent before 2013) is much larger in the health outcome values and stays around in the system much longer. In figure 2.6, which is representative of the six provinces that are among the less affected group, in terms of its effect on life expectancy it shows a much smaller effect initially that disappears by 2014.

Another health outcome variable that is much more responsive to shocks would be the mortality measures, especially the infant mortality and under-5 mortality that are mortality levels in which successful health system functionality can minimize. When we analyze these dimensions and the affected

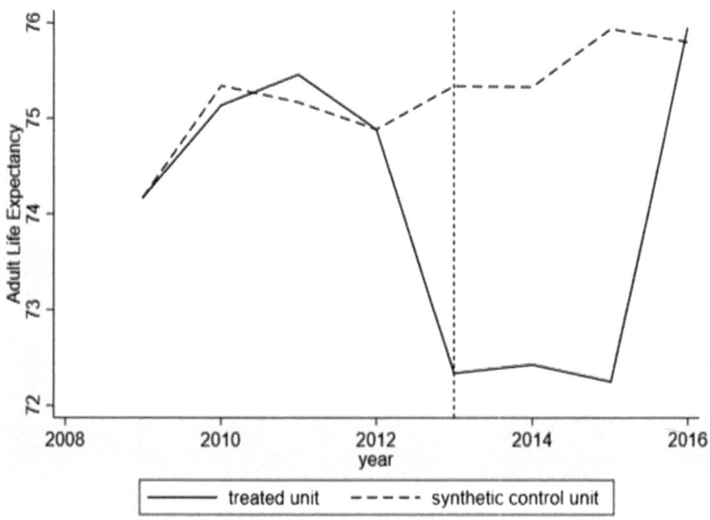

FIGURE 2.3
Most Affected Province and Its Synthetic Control—Life Expectancy Analysis. *Source*: Created by authors.

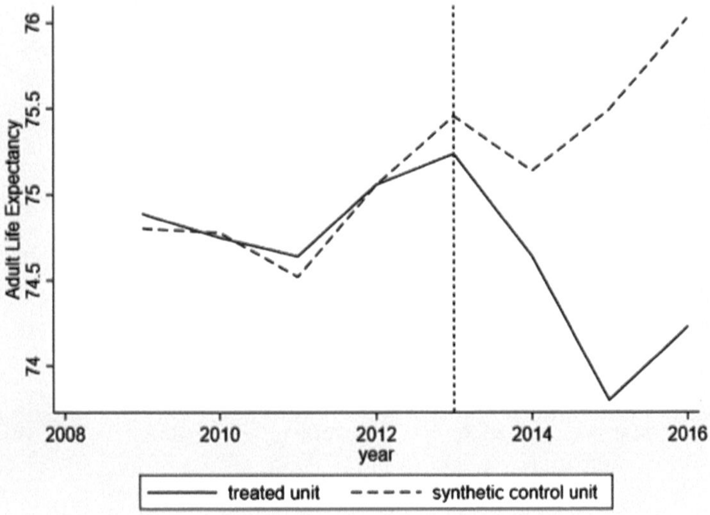

FIGURE 2.4
Second Most Affected Province and Its Synthetic Control—Life Expectancy Analysis.
Source: Created by authors.

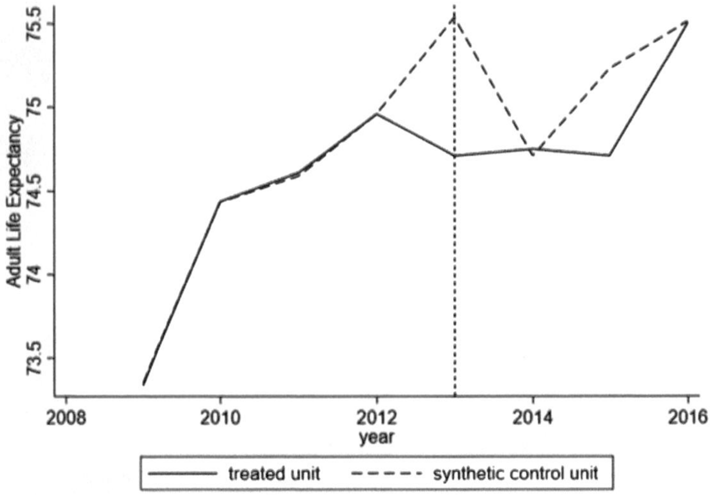

FIGURE 2.5
Third Most Affected Province and Its Synthetic Control—Life Expectancy Analysis.
Source: Created by authors.

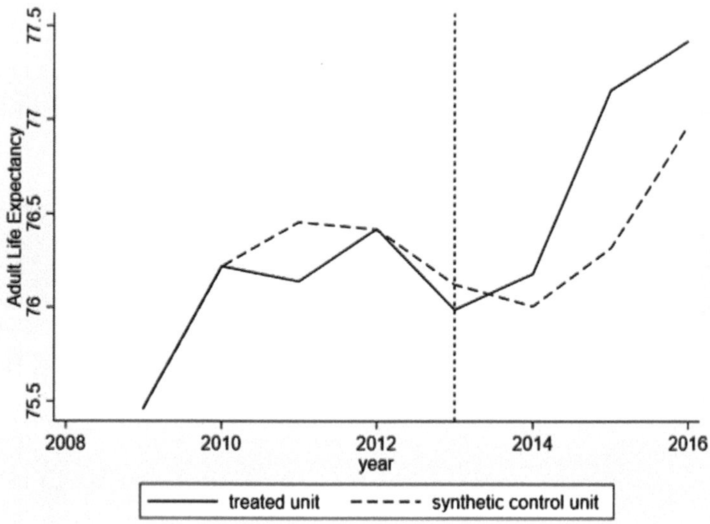

FIGURE 2.6
Least Affected Province among the Destinations and Its Synthetic Control—Life Expectancy Analysis. *Source*: Created by authors.

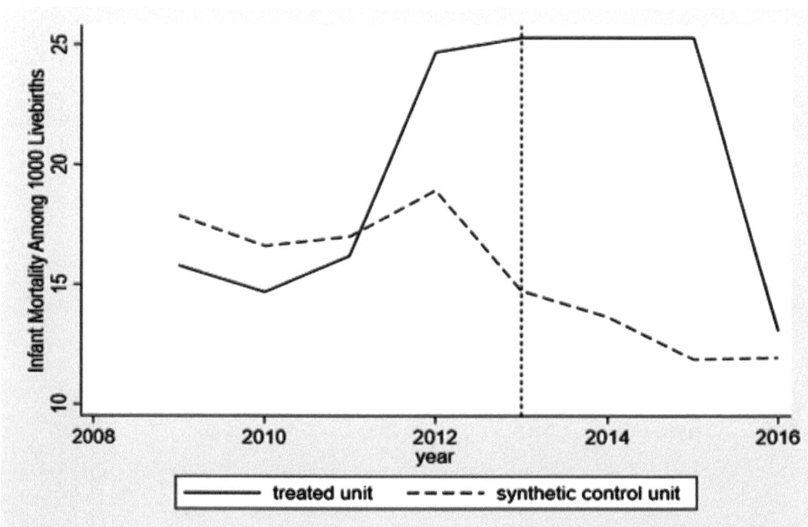

FIGURE 2.7
Most Affected Province and Its Synthetic Control—Infant Mortality Analysis. *Source*: Created by authors.

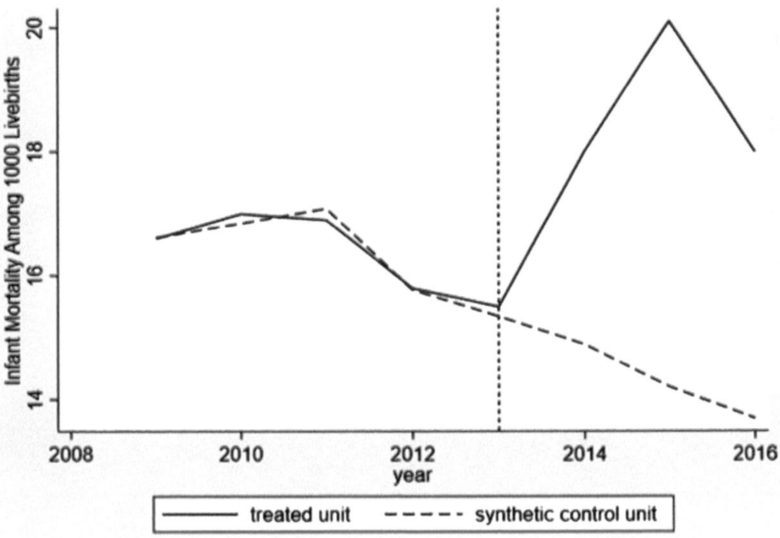

FIGURE 2.8
Second Most Affected Province and Its Synthetic Control—Infant Mortality Analysis.
Source: Created by authors.

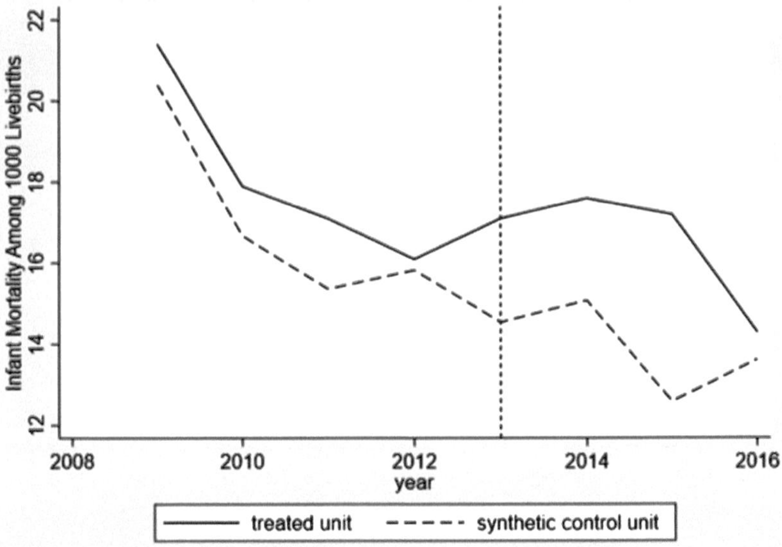

FIGURE 2.9
Third Most Affected Province and Its Synthetic Control—Infant Mortality Analysis.
Source: Created by authors.

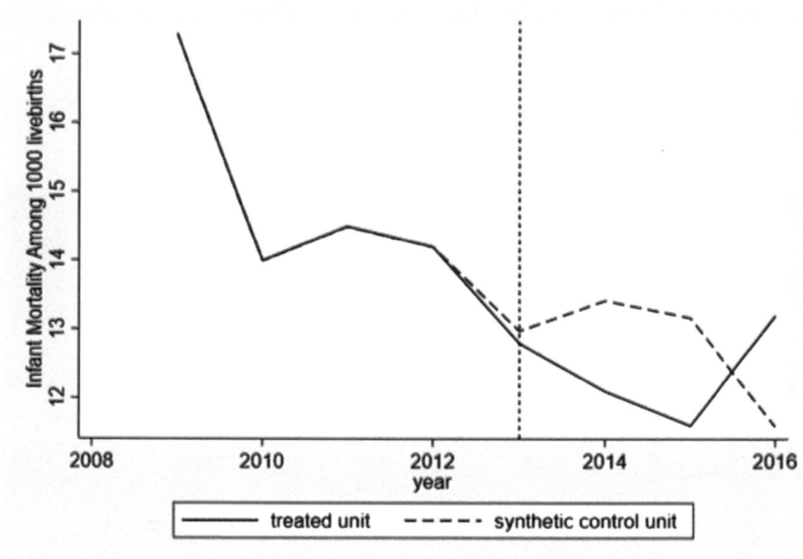

FIGURE 2.10
Least Affected Province among the Destinations and Its Synthetic Control—Infant Mortality Analysis. *Source*: Created by authors.

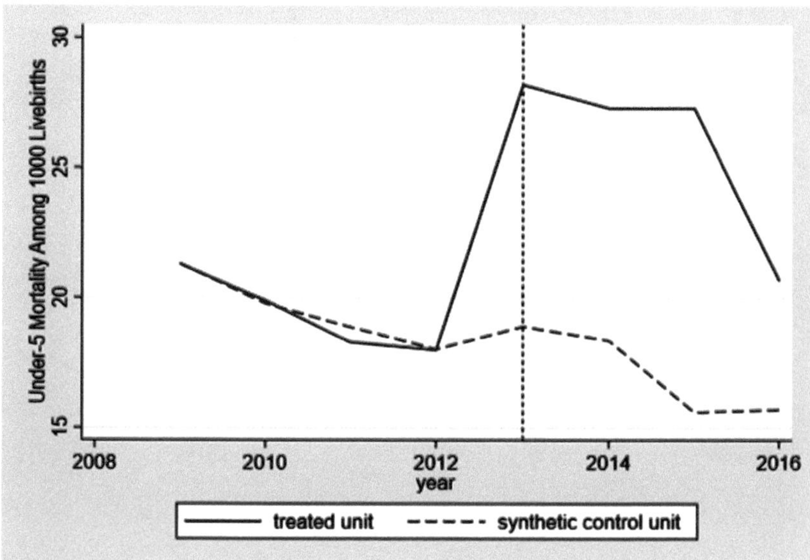

FIGURE 2.11
Most Affected Province and Its Synthetic Control—Under-5 Mortality Analysis. *Source*: Created by authors.

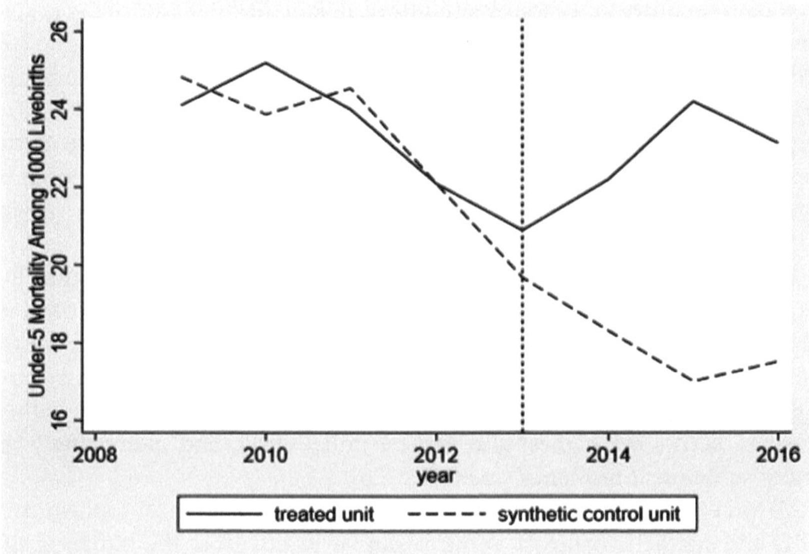

FIGURE 2.12
Second Most Affected Province and Its Synthetic Control—Under-5 Mortality Analysis.
Source: Created by authors.

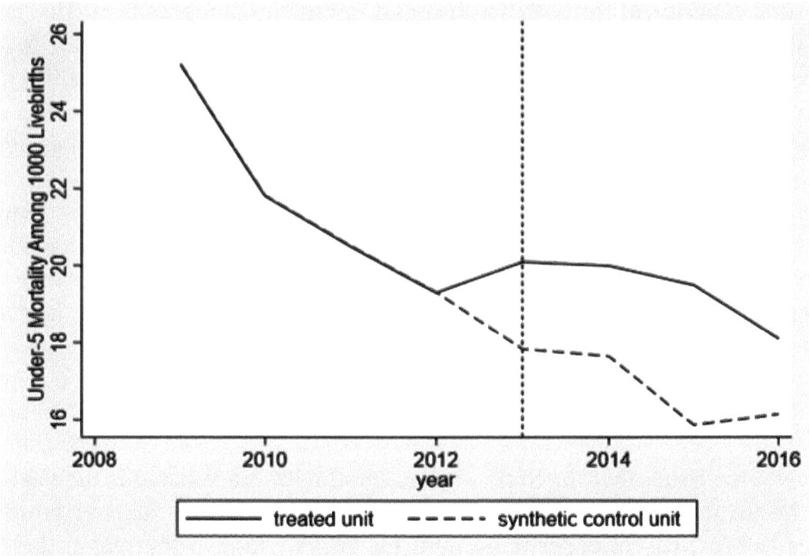

FIGURE 2.13
Third Most Affected Province and Its Synthetic Control—Under-5 Mortality Analysis.
Source: Created by authors.

provinces (in order to see the magnitude of shock) the infant mortality graphs for three of the most affected provinces show the same picture (figure 2.7–2.9), with a mortality divergence (and even reversal) observed for the period 2012–2014, with increased convergence in values for the period 2015–2016, suggesting that the affected provinces are returning to the national trend, after a medium term prolonged shock effect. The same path analysis can be confirmed with the under-5 mortality figures in figures 2.11–2.13, for the three most affected provinces.

The graded approach we are using, which is clearly shown in figure 2.2, is confirmed to be important in deriving the results. In the regressions (see table 2.1), the three province core is affected significantly different from the remaining six provinces,[8] and even among the three, the synthetic control approach substantiates that the worst affected province with the highest shock H_t shows the highest and earliest initial effect, and interestingly the largest subsequent resilience (see figure 2.3).

All three approaches, from the most naive (OLS) to the most sophisticated (DID and synthetic control), confirm similar results from the initial significant shock that is significantly localized (9 among the 81, and 3 among the 9), and a later (in 2015 and more pronounced in 2016) increased resilience allows the affected locality to converge to the natural trend, even in the presence of continuing shock to the healthcare system.[9]

This integration of a large body of Syrian refugees constitutes a significant natural experiment for both Turkish and international researchers. This is a first study, using a very valuable health outcomes survey, looking at it from the macro-health perspective, asking which part of the Turkish health system seems to have a health system stress that has led to an observation of stagnation of localized health outcomes. And, results indicate that the same provinces showing increased health resilience (Kruk et al. 2015) return to their natural trend, in terms of the ability to protect the health of its domestic population. For the successful integration of refugees, in a middle income-developed health system context, this research underlines the importance of identifying the points of health demand vulnerability, and also the importance of building up health system resilience at the local level.

Regional Welfare Inequality Effects

One of the issues that the Syrian influx could have exacerbated is the degree of health inequality in the Turkish geography, which was already noticeable before 2013. In order to account for this, we look at the region that is affected and compare it with the average in the Turkish geography. Looking at the region and dividing into two groups, we see that an overall story of initial shock and subsequent resilience is confirmed for infant mortality (figures 2.15 and 2.16), under-5 mortality (figures 2.17 and 2.18), and life expectancy (figures 2.19 and 2.20).

In figures 2.15 and 2.16 and in figures 2.17, 2.18, 2.19, and 2.20, we can observe that the health inequalities between the specific regions have mostly stayed in position with respect to the country average. The movements, at the initial stage, and the later stage cancel out, which suggests that in the shock period (2012–2016), there is no regional divergence in terms of the different health outcomes.

In terms of overall regional inequality in these crucial health outcomes, the lowest value of health inequality for infant mortality differences is measured in 2016, for the entire period of the Syrian population influx,[10] as can be seen in table 2.4. Similarly, the lowest values of health inequality for under-5 mortality differences (see table 2.5) and for life expectancy differences (see table 2.6) are measured in 2016 suggesting that the welfare shock for the domestic population[11] has shown a rebound in the 2015–2016 period.

The main concern is that the specific domestic population in the region defined by figure 2.2 was already vulnerable to health shocks and welfare loss, and health supply problems would be more vulnerable after the Syrian influx. The results show both initial support for this concern and a later health resilience, as resilience of the health system being able to take a greater pressure, due to a supply drop (Sardo et al. 2019), or a sudden and/or sustained

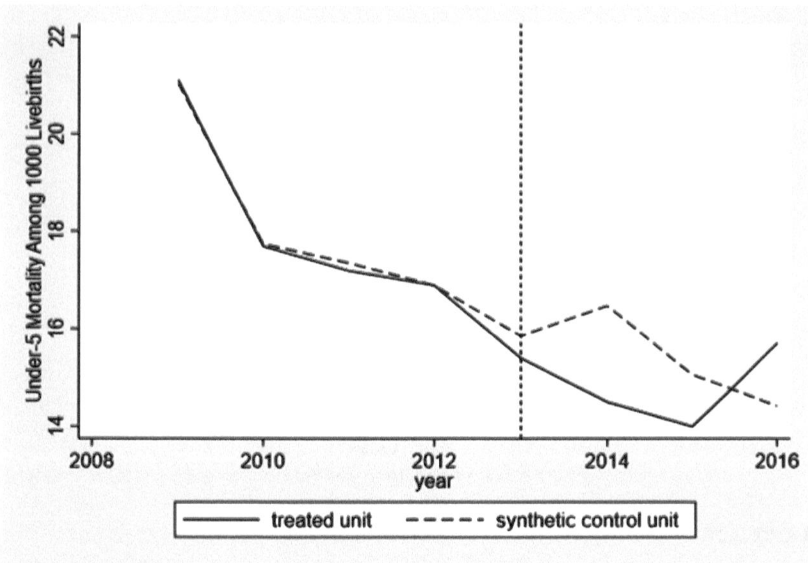

FIGURE 2.14
Least Affected Province among the Destinations and Its Synthetic Control—Under-5 Mortality Analysis. *Source*: Created by authors.

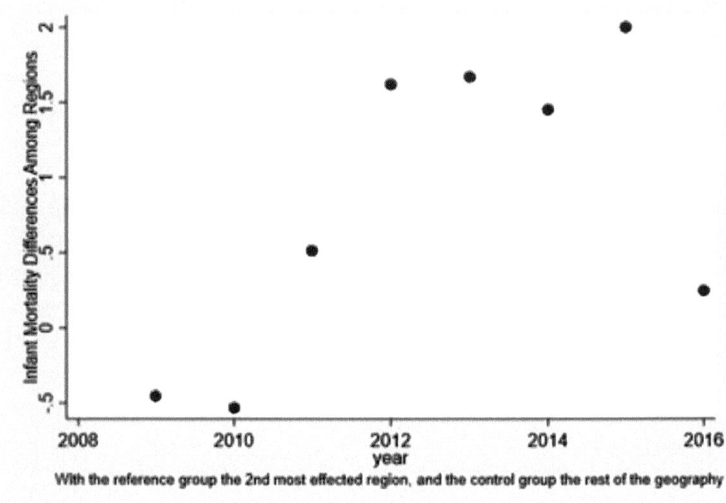

FIGURE 2.15
Second Most Affected Region and the Rest of Turkish Geography (Infant Mortality Difference) *Source*: Created by authors.

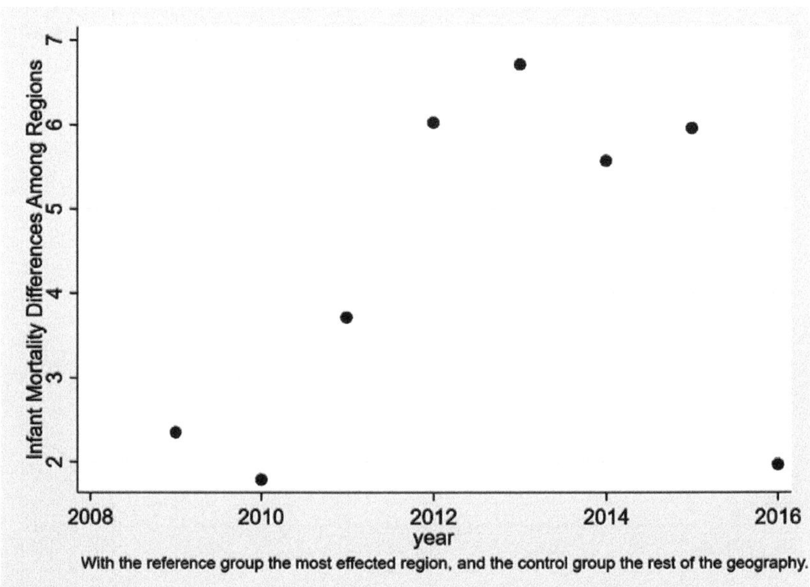

FIGURE 2.16
Most Affected Region and the Rest of Turkish Geography (Infant Mortality Difference). *Source*: Created by authors.

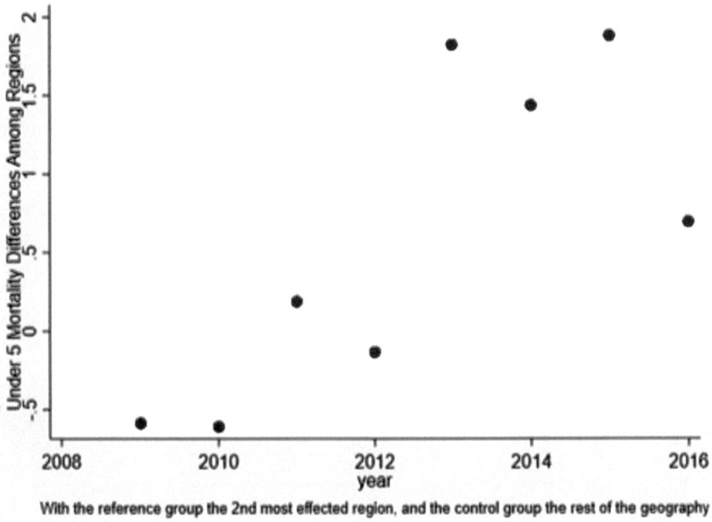

FIGURE 2.17
Second Most Affected Region and the Rest of Turkish Geography (Under-5 Mortality Difference). *Source*: Created by authors.

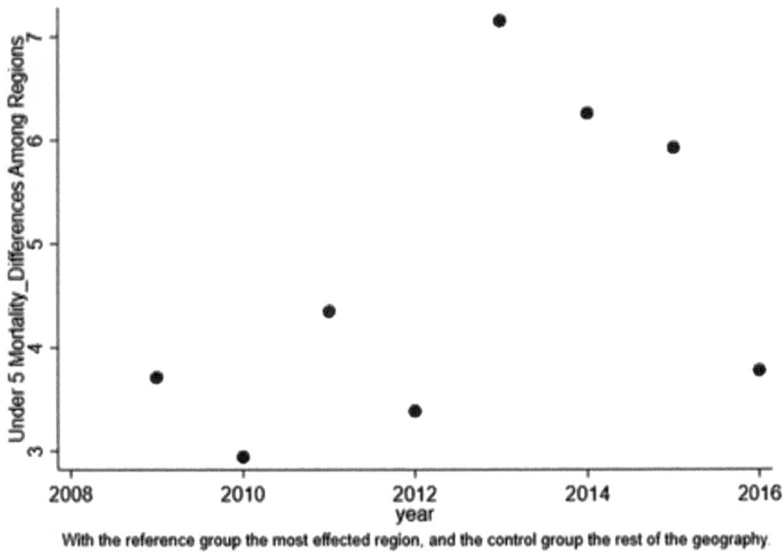

FIGURE 2.18
Most Affected Region and the Rest of Turkish Geography (Under-5 Mortality Difference). *Source*: Created by authors.

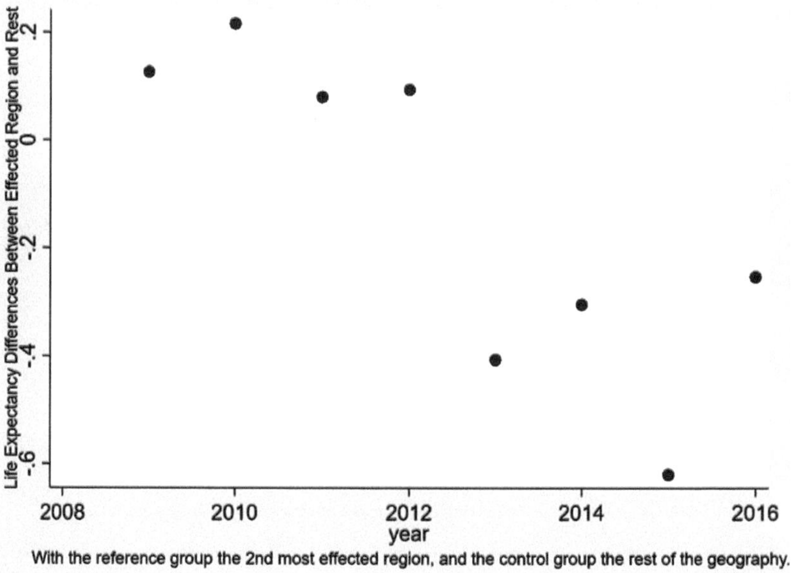

FIGURE 2.19
Second Most Affected Region and the Rest of Turkish Geography (Life Expectancy Difference). *Source*: Created by authors.

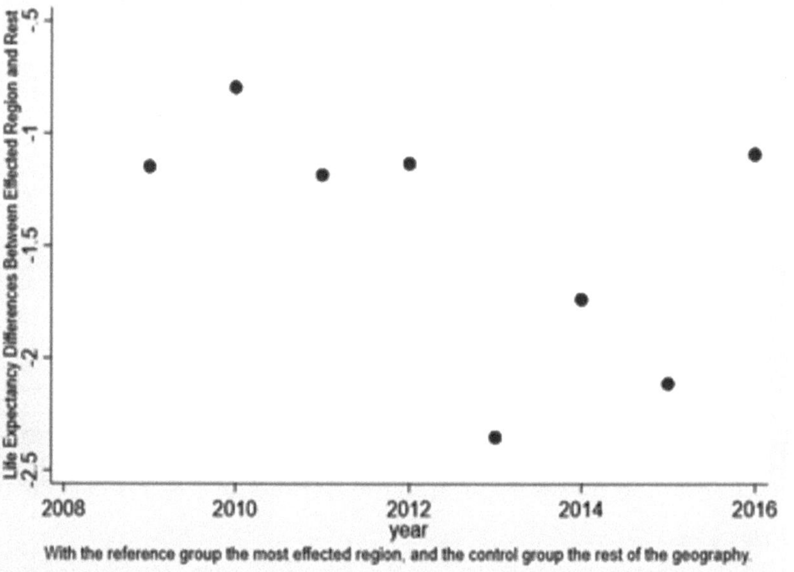

FIGURE 2.20
Most Affected Region and the Rest of Turkish Geography (Life Expectancy Difference). *Source*: Created by authors.

TABLE 2.4
Health Inequality in Infant Mortality at the Regional Level[1] (IBBS2[2] Regions)

Year	GE(−1)	GE(0)	GE(1)	GE(2)	Gini
2012	0.02578	0.02451	0.02494	0.02540	0.12398
2013	0.02622	0.02704	0.02836	0.03026	0.13020
2014	0.02417	0.02511	0.02655	0.02860	0.12407
2015	0.02923	0.02960	0.03067	0.03252	0.13726
2016	0.02421	0.02438	0.02499	0.02608	0.12370

Source: Calculated by authors.
[1]The first four columns represent Generalized Entropy class score GE(a) for a = −1, 0, 1, 2. The last column represents the inequality measure that is calculated with the typical gini inequality coefficient calculation.
[2]IBBS2 is a spatial statistical classification that divides the Turkish geography into 26 sections.

TABLE 2.5
Health Inequality in Under-5 Mortality at the Regional Level[1] (IBBS2 Regions)

Year	GE(−1)	GE(0)	GE(1)	GE(2)	Gini
2012	0.02413	0.02400	0.02428	0.02500	0.12418
2013	0.02794	0.02901	0.03063	0.03288	0.13335
2014	0.02601	0.02698	0.02849	0.03065	0.12882
2015	0.02947	0.02997	0.03113	0.03304	0.13756
2016	0.02276	0.02360	0.02489	0.02669	0.12045

Source: Calculated by authors.
[1]The first four columns represent Generalized Entropy class score GE(a) for a = −1, 0, 1, 2. The last column represents the inequality measure that is calculated with the typical gini inequality coefficient calculation.

TABLE 2.6
Health Inequality in Life Expectancy at the Regional Level[1] (IBBS2 Regions)

Year	GE(−1)	GE(0)	GE(1)	GE(2)	Gini
2012	0.00006	0.00006	0.00006	0.00006	0.00616
2013	0.00010	0.00010	0.00010	0.00010	0.00755
2014	0.00008	0.00008	0.00008	0.00008	0.00712
2015	0.00011	0.00011	0.00011	0.00011	0.00838
2016	0.00007	0.00007	0.00007	0.00007	0.00615

Source: Calculated by authors.
[1]The first four columns represent Generalized Entropy class score GE(a) for a = −1, 0, 1, 2. The last column represents the inequality measure that is calculated with the typical gini inequality coefficient calculation.

demand increase (Burke et al. 2021). We also note that the sources of health resilience at the level of domestic population health behavior and corresponding changes in healthcare capacity and adaptation of the regional healthcare system are important topics to be analyzed in a further study.

Conclusion

A country's economic and social welfare does not only depend on its own institutional setup but also depends on what happens in its neighboring countries. Low-quality institutions in neighboring countries increase the possibility of armed conflicts and extensive refugee flows. Therefore, government authorities should consider possible direct and indirect channels through which neighboring institutions may affect the welfare of other countries. Movements of refugees in large numbers due to military conflicts within their country of origin are increasing all over the world. Forced migration has important implications for the people that move and for the societies that host the migrants. Forced migrants are typically displaced from poor economic conditions, and they arrive in the host country with low health profiles as a result of poverty. Health issues associated with migration are very extensive including infectious diseases, chronic diseases, injuries, and mental problems. The impact of forced migration on the health of immigrants and host societies can have serious consequences due to a changing profile of morbidity and mortality rates. There is a related growing body of literature that has comprehensively studied the effect of forced migration on different population groups. Most of the current literature about the effect of refugee arrivals on native population health outcomes is qualitative highlighting the importance of context, and there are just a very few studies providing quantitative evidence on the welfare in terms of the health outcomes of forced migration on host societies in developing countries. The scarcity of data and the difficulty of measuring the potential effects and referring those results to a causal impact of refugees are the major obstacles (Ruiz et al. 2017). However, it is obvious that massive refugee influx and settlements are likely to have important effects on the refugee-hosting societies, particularly in developing countries. These effects are generally considered negative due to the fact that forced migrants arrive in the host country with their poor economic and health conditions during military conflicts. The sudden and massive movement of refugees, particularly as a result of civil wars, can significantly increase the risks of epidemic disease and affect the health profile of the host country negatively. The countries neighboring Syria (ACTED 2013) report that local residents in refugee-hosting societies were exposed to food insecurity due to the intensity of forced migrants increasing pressures on goods market, labor market, and particularly on healthcare market. But these reports do not provide any counterfactual results (Maystadt and Verwimp 2014). Therefore, more research is needed to better understand the health effects of hosting forced migrants especially on the healthcare capacity of the hosting country to manage a sudden and heavy refugee influx, and the impact on welfare in terms of health outcomes of the native population. The host country's structural capacity to handle the sudden and significant increase in the demand for healthcare due to refugee shock identifies the effects on healthcare market testing the existing healthcare system and policy from the public health point of view (Porignon et al. 1995, Goyens et al. 1996, Whitaker 2002). Moreover, there is a need to clarify the complexity of the channels through which large inflows of refugees affect hosting population particularly in developing countries. Therefore, we aim to quantify this impact on the capacity of the hosting country to manage a sudden refugee shock to its healthcare market and identify the effects of additional healthcare burden on the health outcomes of refugee-hosting population.

The empirical analysis in this study supports three important conclusions. First, there was a significant shock; second, this shock was quite regional in nature; and third, we can observe an equally regional resilience buildup that brought the health system outputs back to their pre-shock levels. The differentiated shock has been found to be a proportional integration effect (total number of new provincial health system integrants/total provincial healthcare system size), as the shock effect is most observable, and most prolonged in three provinces where this differentiated shock has been greatest. In all nine of the most affected provinces, 2014 is the clearest period for the observation of the shock, and 2015 and most importantly 2016 is the most important period for building up the resilience in the health system. The welfare results suggest that a significant increase in the welfare of the Syrian refugee population is not gained at the expense of the welfare of the Turkish domestic population in the catchment areas as a whole. The welfare results are corroborated at the level of infant mortality, and under-5 mortality for the young age group, and for the whole population at the level of the life expectancy. These conclusions are consistent with a resilient health system, meeting the challenge of the health influx, in stages, and as it builds capabilities. The results are confirmed with the DHS data (aggregated at the provincial level) and for the health outcomes pinpointed at the dimensions of life expectancy, infant mortality, and under-5 mortality.

Notes

1. Rwandan refugees had an access to the health services with free of charge where each visit had its own cost. The average rise in the number of patient visits was approximately 300%.

2. UNHRC pays the healthcare costs for refugees. Approximately, a third of the total population consists of refugees, two-thirds of the healthcare facilities are settled for refugees, remaining are settled for the rural host population.

3. According to the common trend assumption, refugee-hosting regions and regions with free of refugees are likely to have an economic development in a parallel extent in the absence of refugee influx.

4. The number of doctors, nurses, and technical personnel is normalized by the province populations.

5. The usage of diagnostic services, and the number of specialized clinics, the number of ICU's (intensive care units), and the number of technology intensive health units are normalized by the province populations.

6. The number of beds and the number of ICU (intensive care units) beds are normalized by the province populations.

7. As it is an individual level data projected to the province level, there is a confidence interval for the minimum and maximum values, $x^m \pm z \times \frac{s}{\sqrt{n}}$, but we use the x^m (predicted) for every province for all the different time periods (2009–2016).

8. Graphically the same difference is observed when we compare figure 2.6 with figures 2.3–2.5, figure 2.10 with figures 2.7–2.9, and figure 2.14 with figures 2.11–2.13.

9. The Syrian population that is registered under the temporary protected status increased from 2.1 million to 3.3 million in this period (Internal Ministry MGMM Data).

10. The Syrian Civil war had started in 2011, but as the first refugees started entering Turkish territory in December 2011, it means that we can use 2012 as our starting period for the shock analysis.

11. DHS (2013–2018) collects data on the Syrian population (under temporary protected status) and the Turkish domestic population separately, and as we are using the Turkish dataset only, we are capturing in this study how the health situation of the Turkish population is changing in the affected region, and in the rest of the Turkish geography.

References

Abadie A, Diamond A, and Hainmueller, J. 2010. Synthetic control methods for comparative case studies: Estimating the effect of California's tobacco control program. *Journal of the American Statistical Association*, 105(490), 493–505.

AFAD. 2017. *Population Influx from Syria to Turkey, Life in Turkey As A Syrian Guest.* Retrieved from https://www.afad.gov.tr/kurumlar/afad.gov.tr/17933/xfiles/population_influx_1_.pdf.

Aksu E, Erzan R, and Kırdar MG. 2022. The impact of mass migration of Syrians on the Turkish labor market. *Labour Economics*, 76, 102183.

Alix-Garcia J and Saah D. 2010. The effect of refugee ınflows on host communities: Evidence from Tanzania. *The World Bank Economic Review*, 24(1), 148–170.

Alix-Garcia J, Walker S, Bartlett A, Onder H, and Sanghi A. 2018. Do refugee camps help or hurt hosts? The case of Kakuma, Kenya. *Journal of Development Economics*, 130, 66–83.

Altındağ O and Kaushal N. 2021. Do refugees impact voting behavior in the host country? Evidence from Syrian refugee inflows to Turkey. *Public Choice*, 186(1), 149–178.

Aygun A, Kırdar M, and Tuncay B. 2021. The effect of hosting 3.4 million refugees on native population mortality. *Journal of Health Economics*, 80, 102534.
Baez J. 2011. Civil wars beyond their borders: The human capital and health consequences of hosting refugees. *Journal of Development Economics*, 96, 391–408.
Burke S, Parker S, Fleming P, Barry S, and Thomas S. 2021. Building health system resilience through policy development in response to COVID-19 in Ireland: From shock to reform. *The Lancet Regional Health – Europe*, 9, 100223.
Card D. 1990. The impact of the Mariel boatlift on the Miami labor market. *ILR Review*, 43(2), 245–257.
Damme WV. 1995. Do refugees belong in camps? Experiences from Goma and Guinea. *Lancet*, 346(8971), 360–362.
Doudchenko N and Imbens GW. 2016. Balancing, regression, difference-in-differences and synthetic control methods: A synthesis. No. w22791. National Bureau of Economic Research.
Gallup JL and Sachs JD. 2001. The economic burden of malaria. *American Journal of Tropical Medicine and Hygiene*, 64(1–2 Suppl), 85–96.
Goyens P, Porignon D, Soron'gane EM, and Tonglet R. 1996. Humanitarian aid and health services in Eastern Kivu, Zaïre: Collaboration or competition? *Journal of Refugee Studies*, 9(3), 268–280.
Kalipeni E and Oppong J. 1998. The refugee crisis in Africa and implications for health and disease: a political ecology approach. *Social Science and Medicine*, 46(12), 1637–1653.
Kazmi JH and Pandit K. 2001. Disease and dislocation: the impact of refugee movements on the geography of malaria in NWFP, Pakistan. *Social Science and Medicine*, 52(7), 1043–1055.
Kreibaum M. 2016. Their suffering, our burden? How congolese refugees affect the Ugandan population. *World Development*, 78, 262–287.
Kruk ME, Myers M, Varpilah ST, and Dahn BT. 2015. What is a resilient health system? Lessons from Ebola. *The Lancet*, 385(9980), 1910–1912.
Maystadt JF and Verwimp P. 2014. Winners and losers among a refugee-hosting population. *Economic Development and Cultural Change*, 62(4), 769–809.
Ministry of Health. Retrieved from http://www.istanbulsaglik.gov.tr/w/sb/saggel/belge/Av_Elif_Selen_AY.pdf.
Montalvo J and Reynal-Querol M. 2007. Fighting against Malaria: Prevent wars while waiting for the 'miraculous' vaccine. *The Review of Economics and Statistics*, 89(1), 165–177.
Orach CG and Brouwere VD. 2005. *Integrating Refugee and Host Health Services in West Nile Districts, Uganda*. Oxford University Press.
Porignon D, Noterman JP, Hennart P, Tonglet R, Soron G, and Lokombe TE. 1995. The role of the Zairian health services in the Rwandan refugee crisis. *Disasters*, 19(4), 356–360.
Rennert G. 1994. Implications of Russian immigration on mortality patterns in Israel. *International Journal of Epidemiology*, 23(4), 751–756.
Ruiz I and Vargas-Silva C. 2017. The Consequences of forced migration for host communities in Africa. *Revue d'économie du développement*, 25, 135 à 154.

Sardo DR, Thurner S, Sorger J, Duftschmide G, Endelf G, and Klimek P. 2019. Quantification of the resilience of primary care networks by stress testing the health care system. *PNAS*, 116(48), 23930–23935. doi:10.1073/pnas.1904826116.

Tumen, S. 2016. The economic impact of Syrian refugees on host countries: Quasi-experimental evidence from Turkey. *American Economic Review*, 106(5), 456–460.

Tuncay, B., Özen, İ.C. & Bump, J.B. Shelter from the storm: health service access and utilization among Syrian refugees in Turkey. *J Public Health (Berl.)* (2022). https://doi.org/10.1007/s10389-022-01697-0.

United Nations Human Rights Council (UNHRC) Report in Egypt. 2016. Available from: http://reliefweb.int/sites/reliefweb.int/files/resources/Egypt-%E2%80%93-Regional-Refugee-Resilience-Plan-2016-2017.pdf.

United Nations Human Rights Council (UNHRC) Report in Egypt. 2016. Retrieved from https://data2.unhcr.org/en/documents/download/44067.

Whitaker BE. 2002. Refugees in WesternTanzania: The distribution of burdens and benefits among local hosts. *Journal of Refugee Studies*, 15(4), 339–358.

3

The Effect of COVID-19 Pandemic on Poverty in Emerging Countries

Pınar Fulya GEBEŞOĞLU

Introduction[1]

The COVID-19 pandemic, known as the coronavirus pandemic, is an ongoing pandemic of coronavirus disease 2019 (COVID-19) caused by severe acute respiratory syndrome coronavirus 2 (SARS-CoV-2). It was first identified in December 2019 in Wuhan, China, and rapidly transmitted all over the globe. The administrative efforts to slow down the spread of the COVID-19 virus inevitably led to an unprecedented economic recession. The lockdown measures, social isolation, temporary factory closures, and so on, resulted in major reallocation and redistribution issues in the global economy.

In addition to the direct economic cost resulting from labor loss, the cycle-induced contraction in demand is expected to result in repercussion effects. Unfortunately, more vulnerable groups such as the poor and the less educated segments of the population have been affected more adversely during the pandemic. For instance, sharp decline in service sector activities translated into comparatively low-paying job losses and pandemic induced shift to working from home hit the unskilled workers harder. Sumner et al. (2020) argue that COVID-19 threatens the United Nations Sustainable Development Goal of ending poverty by 2030 and estimate that the economic impact may result in a retraction of approximately a decade in the world's progress toward reducing poverty.

Most governments around the globe have immediately responded with various policy tools that aim to countervail the negative economic effects of the pandemic. Yet the effectiveness of these measures and policy implications in terms of income distribution remains to be ambiguous. More empirical research and further in-depth discussion are needed to identify good policy practices. This chapter investigates the effect of the COVID-19 pandemic on income distribution and poverty in emerging countries and attempts to assess the effectiveness of the recent measures taken by the governments to protect more vulnerable segments from the adverse effects of the pandemic.

The chapter is organized as follows. Following a brief introduction to the subject in the first section, the second section presents literature review regarding the most relevant studies on the COVID-19 pandemic's effect on income distribution and poverty. The third section presents analysis of data and comparative graphics. The fourth section summarizes economic and social protection policies introduced by selected emerging economies in response to the COVID-19 pandemic. The fifth section concludes.

Literature Survey

Hoogeveen and Lopez-Acevedo (2021) argue that COVID-19 increased poverty and led to greater inequality while creating new poor defined as "those who were not poor in the first quarter of 2020 but have become poor since" in the Middle East and North Africa (MENA) Region. Even the economic recovery is argued to deepen inequality because the informal sector which often employs vulnerable groups tends to recover more slowly (Hoogeveen and Lopez-Acevedo, 2021).

Nguyen et al. (2021) analyze microdata compiled from high-frequency phone surveys conducted in selected countries of the MENA region and indicate that the households in the bottom 40% are more severely affected by the COVID-19 pandemic and also are less likely to fully recover.

Vitenu-Sackey and Barfi (2021) employ econometric panel data techniques such as Ordinary Least Squares Regression (OLS) and robust least square regression for 170 countries and conclude that the stringency measures and the number of COVID-19 cases recorded have an adverse impact on poverty alleviation efforts. The authors used stringency index, total cases, and total number of deaths as the pandemic impact variables and gross domestic product per capita to represent economic growth and human development index as a proxy for poverty alleviation.

Darvas (2021) argue that large-scale employment protection schemes may have prevented the total employment decline but not its adverse distributional consequences in Europe.

Eurofound (2021) studied employment shifts by job-wage quintiles in the European Union from 2019Q2 to 2020Q2 and found that the largest increase in employment is observed in the highest-paid jobs, and the largest loss in employment is observed in the lowest-paid jobs, implying inequality increase in wage earnings.

Sumner et al. (2020) estimate the poverty headcount through per capita household income or consumption contraction scenarios and estimate that poverty headcount rate at US$1.9 per day could increase by 1 percentage point even under the most optimistic scenario of 5% contraction in per capita income. In other words, a scenario of 5% contraction may as well translate into an increase of 85 to 135 million in the number of people living in poverty, 180–280 million under a 10% contraction and 420 to 580 million under a 20% contraction scenario, respectively.

Han et al. (2020) use Basic Monthly Current Population Survey for a large representative sample of the US families and conclude that the US government policy has been effective in declining poverty because of the pandemic via various tools such as the unemployment insurance payments, Economic Impact Payments, and other forms of government assistance although the benefit was unevenly distributed across different states.

Gentilini et al. (2020) identify cash transfers, wage subsidies, subsidized sick leave, and other forms of subsidized social security contributions and unemployment insurance as most widely introduced set of tools to mitigate the adverse economic effects of the pandemic. Although the stimulus packages helped millions to survive the crisis, direct and indirect subsidies may either have arrived late or been insufficient to replace lost income as many households with little savings to draw on had to bear the burden of indebtness (OECD, 2021). Chetty et al. (2020) argue that the stimulus payments for COVID-19 that increased consumer spending had limited impact on increasing employment because they did not flow to businesses most affected by COVID-19.

Hill and Narayan (2020) indicate that although the impact of the COVID-19 pandemic on income distribution is yet uncertain, the longer-term risks to equality are less dubious considering the past evidence. The previous empirical literature estimated income inequality impacts of pandemic although the estimates carried some identification problems such as the effect of the 2008–2009 Global Financial Crises that complicate the interpretations of empirical findings. Still the empirical literature provides sufficient conclusive evidence on the asymmetrical distributional effects of recessions in general.

Data

Unemployment

The unemployment rate in emerging economies increased on average by 24.8% in the first year of the pandemic. This annual increase in unemployment rates is unprecedented before the COVID-19 pandemic. Although the International Labour Organization (ILO) estimates are subject to uncertainty, the global economy is estimated to recover quickly. Despite the comparatively fast pace of recovery, unemployment rates are expected to stay well above the prepandemic levels for the next couple of years (figure 3.1).

The increase in unemployment has certain adverse implications on income distribution and poverty in emerging economies. The distribution of unemployment across various age groups, education levels, and genders also highlights the vulnerability of certain subgroups due to the negative effects of the pandemic. For instance, the unemployment rates for the age groups 25 and above have increased by 36.6% which accounts for more than 50% of the increase in unemployment for the rest of the population and also for the subgroup of 15–24 ages.

As the COVID-19 virus is observed to disproportionately affect older age, the labor market is also expected to present asymmetric distortion with respect to the nature of the jobs performed. For instance, some jobs are more convenient for remote work, whereas others require face-to-face interaction. Hence, the sectors and specific jobs that are more adversely affected by the pandemic threaten more vulnerable groups based on age, gender, and education levels. According to the ILO estimates, the change in working hours relative to 2019Q4 declined the most for the low-income and lower-middle-income country groups compared to the higher-income country groups. Swinnen (2020) argues that COVID-19 hit the poorest particularly hard because it directly affects physical labor which is often their most important, if not only productive, asset.

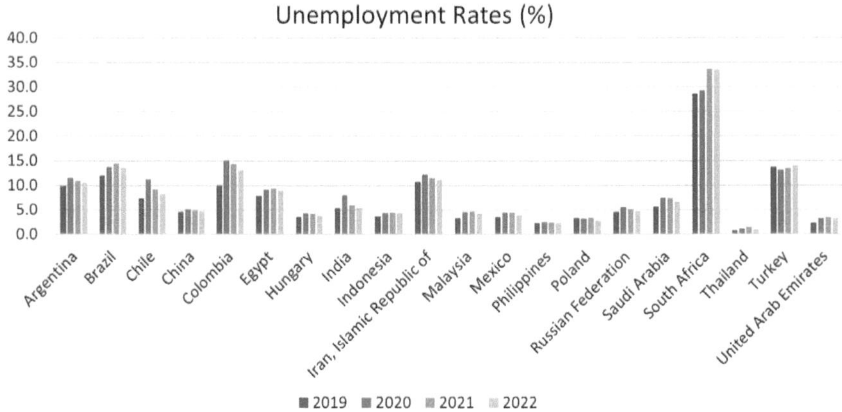

FIGURE 3.1
Unemployment Rates in Selected Emerging Economies. *Source*: Created by authors based on the data downloaded from ILOSTAT (ILO modeled estimates as of November 2021, Unemployment rates for 2020 are real values).

GDP Per Capita

The GDP per capita declined on average by 4.90% for emerging economies in 2020. The graph in figure 3.2 shows that the GDP per capita declined for most of the countries analyzed except for the slight increase in Turkey, Iran, Egypt, and China.

Prices and Cost of Living

In addition to the direct economic effect of the pandemic via loss of jobs and incomes, the increase in prices indirectly contributes to the welfare loss by increasing cost of living. A variety of disruptions in food value chains caused by labor market shocks in production, distribution, food service industry, and so on along with initial trade restrictions escalated food prices all over the world. Food prices increased more than 10% on average for emerging economies in 2020. The highest increase in food prices was observed in Iran, Argentina, Turkey, and Brazil. Although the increase in food prices may affect various households differently depending on their situation as being net buyers or sellers of food items, empirical literature provides ample evidence on the impact of general food price increases on poverty and household welfare in developing countries (Martin and Ivanic, 2016). As the increase in consumer price indices of food prices is higher than the increase in general prices, food prices inflation has more pronounced welfare effects on the poor who tend to spend a larger share of their income on food (figures 3.3 and 3.4).

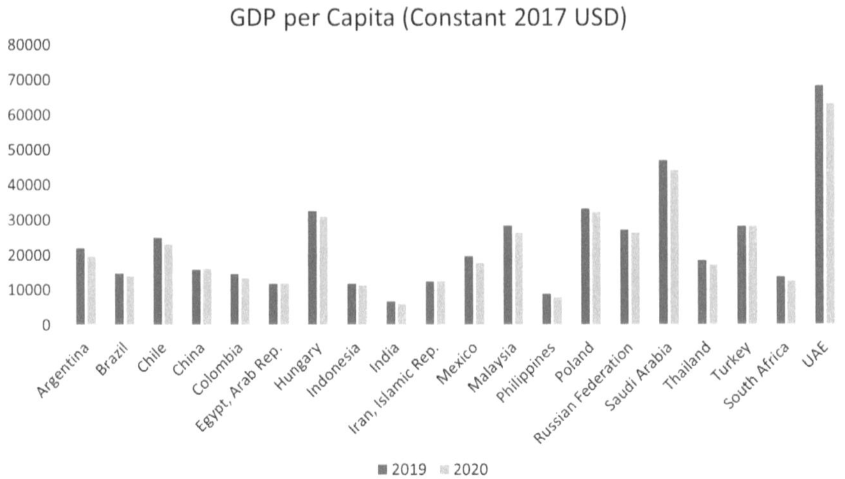

FIGURE 3.2
GDP Per Capita in Selected Emerging Economies. *Source*: Created by authors based on the data downloaded from World Bank https://data.worldbank.org/indicator/NY.GDP.PCAP.PP.KD?name_desc=false&view=chart.

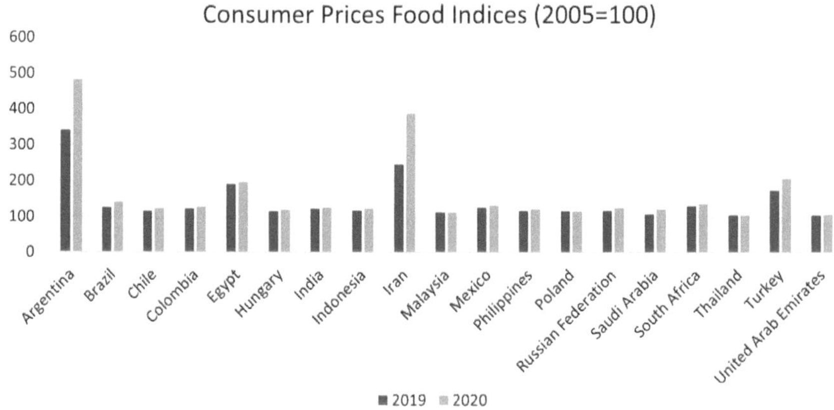

FIGURE 3.3

Consumer Prices Food Indices in Emerging Economies. *Source*: Created by authors based on the data downloaded from the Food and Agriculture Organization of the United Nations https://www.fao.org/faostat/en/#data/CP.

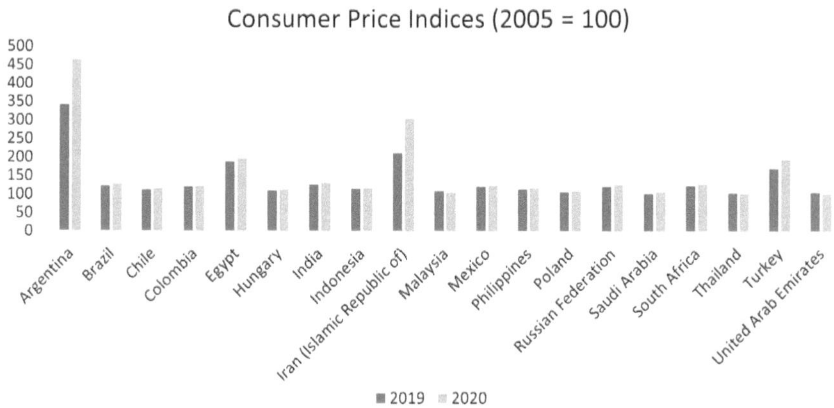

FIGURE 3.4

Consumer Price Indices in Emerging Economies. *Source*: Author's calculations based on the data downloaded from the Food and Agriculture Organization of the United Nations https://www.fao.org/faostat/en/#data/CP.

Economic and Social Protection Policies in Response to COVID-19

Many governments introduced mitigative precautions such as unemployment insurance benefits, unpaid leave subsidies, and increase in social transfers. As the policy responses launched by the authorities have multidimensional targets and tools, presenting an exhaustive list of precautions and policies in response to COVID-19 is beyond the aim and scope of this chapter. Main macroeconomic measures that directly target to mitigate poverty and alleviate the welfare effects of unemployment and deterioration in income distribution are presented in this chapter. The precautions and policy changes mentioned here do not constitute an exhaustive list of policy responses to COVID-19 pandemic, nor the subsidies announced by the governments are fully realized as the pandemic is still going on and the policies can be tailored with respect to the changing needs and priorities term. According to this result, a positive and significant relationship has been obtained between the United States and China in the short term.

Argentina

Argentina designated certain beneficiaries a lump sum benefit of up to 3,000 pesos such as those who receive the minimum pension, poor with children, and women receiving maternity benefit. The Emergency Assistance Program for Work and Production to cover more companies and activities has been expanded to provide subsidies for businesses as of May 2020. Also direct income support was provided for employers and workers affected by the COVID-19 emergency under the Emergency Assistance Program for Work and Production. Emergency Family Income has been created to compensate the loss or serious decrease in the income of people employed in the informal sector. In addition to the direct and indirect subsidies, tax-related policy changes are introduced such as tax and contribution deferrals for specific groups, tax exemption of Emergency Family Income, Universal Child Allowance, and the Complementary Salary. Also the sectors that are critically affected by the coronavirus pandemic are temporarily exempted from the payment of employment contributions. The Central Bank of Argentina (BCRA) provided incentives, so banks grant credits at preferential rates to small and medium companies for the payment of salaries. The credit line established for the Emergency Assistance for Work and Production Program is a subsidized credit line that is guaranteed by the Argentine Guarantee Fund and the National Fund for Productive Development.

Brazil

The government in Brazil approved a financial support program for 2020 that is approximately 8.6% of the GDP. A temporary income support to self-employed and informal sector employees is provided for three months, and tax payments are also postponed temporarily. The Central Bank of Brazil responded to the COVID-19 crises by cutting back the policy rate to a record low level of 2.20% as of June 2020. Yet additional monetary loosening is expected to be less effective as the policy rate is already below the neutral rate (World Bank, 2020). Subsidies to finance wages and wage subsidies to maintain labor contracts are introduced especially for small- and medium-size enterprises. Also an emergency aid program is launched to grant three monthly transfers of R$600 to families with income levels below half a minimum wage per capita for informal and own-account workers, as well as the unemployed who do not receive any unemployment insurance payment. Other measures to reduce shock for formal sector employees are also taken such as enhancing flexibility for remote work and leave policies, extra wage subsidies, temporary suspension of mortgage payments, and so on.

Chile

A set of fiscal measures up to 4.7% of the GDP included enhanced subsidies and unemployment benefits, liquidity provision to SMEs, tax deferrals, and so on. An additional fiscal package was later announced in July of 2020 in order to support the middle-income households suffering severe income losses, through loans from the treasury, mortgage payment delays, and subsidies for rentals. A constitutional amendment that allowed withdrawal of up to 10% of the accumulated funds in the personal retirement accounts in order to mitigate poverty caused by the pandemic is put in force. Existing measures were expanded for the middle-income households and vulnerable groups with a cost of up to 3.3% of the GDP (IMF, 2020). The Central Bank of Chile implemented the Financial Facility Conditional on Increased Lending that can be defined as a four-year lending facility at the monetary policy rate at its effective lower bound, which is assessed to be 0.5%. The Chilean government transformed the Small Business Guarantee Fund that has already been used for the funding of SMEs into a massive guarantee program designed for the COVID-19 crisis. Regulatory and prudential measures concerning banks were adopted, and the implementation of the Basel III was suspended for a year. The Central Bank of Chile announced to purchase government treasuries in the secondary market, to face conditions of stress and financial instability (Silva, 2021).

China

Discretionary fiscal measures up to 4.7% of the GDP were taken such as acceleration in disbursement of unemployment insurance and extension of unemployment insurance to migrant workers. Local governments also increased coverage of benefits provided to households in poverty. The Central Bank of China injected liquidity via open market operations in order to maintain financial stability and introduced an expansive set of new tools to ease lending to micro- and small-sized enterprises such as initiating a zero-interest "funding-for-lending" scheme (RMB 400 billion) to finance new unsecured loans of local banks and provide incentives to further extend payment holidays for eligible loans (IMF, 2020). Guofeng (2021) argues that improvements in the structural monetary policy tool system contributed to the financing of the micro and small businesses that increased in volume and decreased in costs. The issuance of the combined additional government bonds to fight COVID-19 and supplement increased fiscal deficits amounted to RMB 3.6 trillion in 2020. Small- and medium-sized enterprises are temporarily exempted from paying employer contributions to pension, unemployment, and work-related injury insurance schemes (Gentilini et al., 2020).

Colombia

Colombian government launched a transfer program of value added tax (VAT), planning a transfer of 3% of the funds collected as VAT to the most vulnerable households which includes approximately 1 million people. Also water service is provided free of charge to the designated vulnerable households. New credit lines for payroll and loan payments for small- and medium-sized enterprises and specific sectors most affected by the pandemic are introduced. A subsidy equivalent to the half of the minimum wage per employee is provided for businesses that lost more than 20% in revenues in the three months following the pandemic. The Central Bank of Colombia increased liquidity by reducing benchmark interest rates five times since the beginning of the pandemic from 2.75% to 1.75% (IMF, 2020). Informal sector workers who constitute more than half of the economically active population in Colombia were entitled to unconditional cash transfers of US$45 per month until the end of 2020 (Acosta et al., 2021).

India

The fiscal support measures in India focused primarily on social protection and healthcare. Lower-income households and low-wage workers are specifically targeted, and direct cash support and in-kind transfers such as food and cooking gas are provided. Temporary measures to ease the tax burden are introduced. Financial sector measures in terms of easing credit flows to micro-, small-, and medium-scale enterprises, as well as agricultural sector, are taken. The Reserve Bank of India reduced the repo and reverse repo rates and announced various liquidity measures. Banks were allowed to use countercyclical provision buffers to allocate specific provisions for nonperforming loans until the end of March 2022 (IMF, 2020). Migrant worker tragedy that drew attention during the chaos created by the COVID-19 pandemic lockdown measures proved the necessity for social protection policies, decent work standards for the informal sectors and rural social protection schemes (Sengupta and Jha, 2020).

Indonesia

Indonesian government initiated an economic recovery program totaling 3.8% of the GDP in 2020 including direct subsidies to low-income households such as food aid, conditional cash transfers, and electricity subsidies. Also, unemployment benefits are increased both in magnitude and scope extending to the informal sector employees. The Central Bank of Indonesia (BI) was given the authority to purchase long-term government securities in order to finance the increasing fiscal burden due to the fiscal stimulus package provided for the COVID-19 pandemic. The BI carried out a number of interest rate reductions in a measured and gradual manner in 2020 (Waryijo, 2021). The stimulus packages also attempted to remove restrictions on imports and exports, in order to alleviate the adverse affects of global supply-chain disruptions caused by the virus (IMF, 2020).

Russia

Certain unemployment benefits were enhanced both in amount and duration for certain eligible groups temporarily. Unconditional direct cash payments of US$150 to all households with children under 16, subsidized mortgage rates for younger families, and major tax exemptions for IT companies were introduced. The Central Bank of Russia eased regulatory requirements to provide incentives to the banks to enable more favorable treatment for FX loans issued to certain sectors, as well as increasing credit flow to corporate borrowers. The Bank of Russia adopted a broad range of policy mix as both to direct monetary policy and also supervise and regulate bank and nonbank financial sectors.

South Africa

The Unemployment Insurance Fund Benefits were expanded by the government as an initial response for those who lost their jobs due to the pandemic. The most vulnerable households temporarily received higher social grants. Additional temporary COVID-19 subsidies are granted for the unemployed who do not receive Unemployment Insurance Fund Benefits. Also funds were enabled to assist small- and medium-sized enterprises that are in financial hardship due to COVID-19 lockdown measures. The SMEs in certain sectors were granted to defer tax liabilities (IMF, 2020). The Central Bank of South Africa (SARB) responded to COVID-19 crisis with liquidity injections starting March 2020. According to Loewald (2021), the approach of the SARB focused on declining dysfunctionality in the market rather than determining prices, by using interventions to inject liquidity into the market and ensuring its smooth functioning, rather than for economic stimulus purposes.

Turkey

The fiscal stimulus package announced by the authorities was estimated to be around 12.7% of the GDP including a grant package for tradesmen and small businesses and loan deferrals for farmers, Credit Guarantee Fund-backed lending scheme for SMEs, and so on. Certain debt enforcement and bankruptcy proceedings were temporarily suspended, and restrictions on dividend payments by banks and firms were introduced in 2020 (IMF, 2020). The Central Bank of the Republic of Turkey initiated a policy mix of monetary easing including direct bond purchases, injections of credit through public banks, and intensive use of foreign exchange reserves to manage depreciation pressures on the domestic currency (Kara, 2021). Incentives were provided for further credit expansion via supervisory regulations of the Banking Regulation and Supervision Agency (BRSA) such as the "asset ratio," which put pressure on banks either to enlarge their credit portfolios despite the concentration in risks or to engage in swap transactions with the Central Bank.

Conclusion

The COVID-19 pandemic increased poverty and inequality. Self-employed, informal sector employees, and service sector employees suffered either loss of jobs or decline in income. In addition to the income channel that directly affected welfare, indirect effects via consumption such as the surge in prices in general and food prices in particular, increasing healthcare costs due to sickness and other disruptions in the service sector, and so on, deepened the welfare loss observed by the poor and the vulnerable.

Although high-frequency phone surveys and COVID-19 Household Monitoring Dashboard of the World Bank contribute to gaining some insight regarding the economic consequences of the pandemic, the data available are still far from enabling a standardized comparative analysis for emerging economies. Further research is required to derive empirical evidence on the extent of the impact of the COVID-19 pandemic on poverty, income distribution, and inequality. Most of the countries designed various policy responses to alleviate poverty caused by the pandemic, yet the efficiency of these macroeconomic policies depends on the operational and institutional capacity of the governments. Developing political support for a broad set of policy mix combining both large fiscal stimulus packages and balancing monetary policy tools is perhaps the least of the challenges that governments face considering the lack of prior experience and data unavailability to aid the decision-making process in the face of an unprecedented global pandemic. Hence one of the most important problems in macroeconomic policy design to mitigate the adverse effects of a pandemic is the limitations associated with reaching timely, reliable, and categorizable data.

The COVID-19 pandemic is not over yet. Most of the crucial data required to analyze the economic effects of the pandemic is not yet available, and country comparisons cannot be conducted due to data limitations. Nevertheless, distributional impacts of the pandemic should be investigated thoroughly to be able to design more efficient and timely policy responses for future pandemic. Timely data collection and access to more detailed data are essential to make decisions based on priorities, vulnerabilities, risks, and exposures of subgroup of populations in the society.

Note

1. This chapter should not be reported as representing the views of the Ministry of Treasury and Finance. The views expressed herein are those of the author and do not necessarily represent those of the Ministry of Treasury and Finance of Turkey.

References

Acosta, C., M. Uribe-Gómez, and D. Velandia-Naranjo. 2021. "Colombia's Response to COVID-19 Pragmatic Command, Social Contention, and Political Challenges." In *Coronavirus Politics: The Comparative Politics and Policy of COVID 19*, editors: Scott L. Greer, Elizabeth J. King, Elize Massard da Fonseca, and André Peralta-Santos, University of Michigan Press, Ann Arbor. ISBN: 978-0-472-90246-0 (OA). https://doi.org/10.3998/mpub.11927713.

Chetty, Raj, John N. Friedman, Nathaniel Hendren, Michael Stepner, and The Opportunity Insights Team. 2020. "Real-Time Economics: A New Platform to Track the Impacts of COVID-19 on People, Businesses, and Communities Using Private Sector Data." Working Paper, May.

Darvas, Zsolt M. 2021. "The Unequal İnequality İmpact of the COVID-19 Pandemic." Bruegel Working Paper, No. 2021/06, Bruegel, Brussels.

Eurofound. 2021. *COVID-19: Implications for Employment and Working Life*, COVID-19 Series, Publications Office of the European Union, Luxembourg. https://www.eurofound.europa.eu/publications/report/2021/covid-19-implications-for-employmentand-working-life.

Gentilini, U., M. Almenfi, and I. Orton. 2020. "Social Protection and Jobs Responses to COVID-19: A Real-Time Review of Country Measures." Downloaded at 9 http://www.ugogentilini.net/wpcontent/uploads/2020/03/global-review-of-socialprotection-responses-to-COVID-19-2.pdf.

Gerszon, Mahler Daniel, Yonzan Nishant, Lakner Christoph, Aguilar R. Andres Castaneda, and Wu Haoyu. 2021. "Updated Estimates of the Impact of COVID-19 on Global Poverty: Turning the Corner on the Pandemic in 2021?" *Data Blog*, June 24, 2021. https://blogs.worldbank.org/opendata/updated-estimates-impact-covid-19-global-poverty-turning-corner-pandemic-2021.

Guofeng, S. 2021. "The People's Bank of China Adhered to Normal Monetary Policy and Enhanced Support to the Real Economy to Offset the İmpact of Covid-19." İn *Monetary Policy and Central Banking in the Covid Era*, editors: Bill English, Kristin Forbes, Ángel Ubide, and Center for Economic Policy Research. ISBN: 978-1-912179-44-2, CEPR Press.

Hill, Ruth, and Ambar Narayan. 2020. "Covid-19 and Inequality: A Review of the Evidence on Likely Impact and Policy Options." Working Paper. Centre for Disaster Protection, London.

Hoogeveen, Johannes G., and Gladys Lopez-Acevedo. 2021. "Distributional Impacts of COVID-19 in the Middle East and North Africa Region." *MENA Development Report*. World Bank, Washington, DC. https://openknowledge.worldbank.org/handle/10986/36618. License: CC BY 3.0 IGO.

IMF. 2020. "Policy Responses to COVID 19." https://www.imf.org/en/Topics/imf-and-covid19/Policy-Responses-to-COVID-19#C.

Jeehoon, Han, Bruce D. Meyer, and James X. Sullivan. 2020. "Income and Poverty in the COVID-19 Pandemic." *Brookings Papers on Economic Activity*, Vol. 2020(2), pp. 85–118.

Kara, H. 2021. "Monetary Policy in the Covid Era: The Turkish Experience." İn *Monetary Policy and Central Banking in the Covid Era*, editors: Bill English, Kristin Forbes, Ángel Ubide, and Center for Economic Policy Research. ISBN: 978-1-912179-44-2, CEPR Press.

Loewald, C. 2021. "Weathering Covid: South Africa's Central Bank Policy in 2020 and 2021." İn *Monetary Policy and Central Banking in the Covid Era*, editors: Bill English, Kristin Forbes, Ángel Ubide, and Center for Economic Policy Research. ISBN: 978-1-912179-44-2, CEPR Press.

Nguyen, M. C., G. B. Deudibe, and R. J. Gansey. 2021. "Unequal Impact of COVID-19 on MENA Households." İn *Distributional Impacts of COVID-19 in the Middle East and North Africa Region*, editors: Johannes G. Hoogeveen and Gladys Lopez-Acevedo. MENA Development Report. World Bank, Washington, DC. https://openknowledge.worldbank.org/handle/10986/36618.

OECD. 2021. "Inequalities in Household Wealth and Financial Insecurity of Households, Policy Brief, Centre on Well- being, Inclusion, Sustainability and Equal Opportunity (WISE)." https://www.oecd.org/wise/Inequalities-in-Household-Wealth-and-Financial-Insecurity-of-Households-Policy-Brief-July-2021.pdf.

Sengupta, Sohini, and Manish K. Jha. 2020. "Social Policy, COVID-19 and Impoverished Migrants: Challenges and Prospects in Locked Down India." *The International Journal of Community and Social Development*, Vol. 2(2), pp. 152–172. in.sagepub.com/journals-permissions-india. https://doi.org/10.1177/2516602620933715.

Silva, Pablo Garcia. 2021. "The Central Bank of Chile's Policy Response to the Covid-19 Crisis." İn *Monetary Policy and Central Banking in the Covid Era,* editors: Bill English, Kristin Forbes, Ángel Ubide, and Center for Economic Policy Research. ISBN: 978-1-912179-44-2, CEPR Press.

Sumner, A., C. Hoy, and E. Ortiz-Juarez. 2020. "Estimates of the İmpact of COVID-19 on Global Poverty." United Nations University World Institute for Development Economics Research Publication (UNU-WINDER) Working Paper, April, 2020/43. https://www.wider.unu.edu/sites/default/files /Publications/Working-paper/PDF/wp2020-43.pdf. Accessed on: 5/4/2020.

Swinnen, J. 2020. "Covid-19 is Exacerbating İnequalities in Food İnsecurity." In *COVID-19 and Global Food Security*, editors: J. Swinnen and J. McDermott (pp. 20–22). International Food Policy Research Institute, Washington, DC. https://doi.org/10.2499/p15738coll2.133762_03.

Swinnen, J., and R. Vos. 2021. "COVID-19 and Impacts on Global Food Systems and Household Welfare: Introduction to a Special Issue." *Agricultural Economics*, Vol. 52, pp. 365–374. https://doi.org/10.1111/agec.12623.

Vitenu-Sackey, P. A., and R. Barfi. 2021. "The Impact of COVID-19 Pandemic on the Global Economy: Emphasis on Poverty Alleviation and Economic Growth." *The Economics and Finance Letters*, Vol. 8, No. 1, pp. 32–43. ISSN(e): 2312-430X ISSN(p): 2312-6310. https://doi.org/10.18488/journal.29.2021.81.32.43.

Warjiyo, P. 2021. "Bank Indonesia's Response to Covid-19: Synergise to Build Optimism for Economic Recovery." İn *Monetary Policy and Central Banking in the Covid Era,* editors: Bill English, Kristin Forbes, Ángel Ubide, and Center for Economic Policy Research. ISBN: 978-1-912179-44-2, CEPR Press.

Will, Martin, and Maros Ivanic. 2016. "Food Price Changes, Price Insulation, and Their Impacts on Global and Domestic Poverty." İn *Food Price Volatility and Its Implications for Food Security and Policy*, editors: Matthias Kalkuhl, Joachim von Braun, and Maximo Torero, SpringerOpen. https://doi.org/10.1007/978-3-319-28201-5.

World Bank. 2020. "Covid 19 in Brazil: Impacts and Policy Responses." https://www.worldbank.org/en/country/brazil/publication/covid-19-in-brazil-impacts-policy-responses.

4

The Relationship between Income Inequality and Economic Growth in Developing Economies

Mehmet ŞENGÜR

Introduction

In the economic processes, each factor of production has a specific role, along with individuals. The basic production and distribution processes are carried out through task distribution among economic units. While some individuals participate in production with labor, others take part in the production process through capital or enterprise. This simple operation is the same regardless of the development status of countries. However, it is inevitable that there are some differences such as the share of the actors involved in the production process.

In the past, countries that industrialized early have enjoyed greater economic and social development. Over time, the differences in countries in basic macroeconomic indicators have led to different development stages as developed or developing countries. There have been hypotheses that countries lagging behind in economic and social development would catch up with countries that have industrialized and developed early. History has not fully confirmed this because it is not a realistic assumption that different countries will follow a similar development process. The internal dynamics of countries contradict the assumption that any country will imitate the growth and development process of a developed country in the same way. In fact, this is the main factor that leads to the classification of countries in terms of the development stage.

Countries differ in many macroeconomic aspects such as economic growth, inflation, unemployment, per capita income, and fair distribution of income. It is an important question in what way the revenue obtained as a result of the production of goods and services will be distributed. The answers given to this question or the equal distribution of income as a result of the answers also vary. As a result of all these differences, income inequality figures, as other macroeconomic indicators, are not the same in different countries around the world.

Income inequality is simply the result of unequal distribution of the revenue generated as a result of production to the members of the society. If there is income inequality, this means that there is also unfair income distribution. There are many factors that affect income inequality, such as education level, age, gender, globalization, economic growth, and the structure of labor markets. The subject that forms the basis of our study is the investigation of the relationship between economic growth and income inequality in developing countries. Kuznets (1946, 1955) conducted the first study on this subject and provided a basis for subsequent research. After Kuznets found that there is an inverted U-shaped relationship between economic growth and income inequality, studies have been conducted in different countries and datasets examining this relationship have been generated.

At first, the study conceptually discusses Kuznets's inverted-U hypothesis. Then, it examines the empirical research on the relationship between economic growth and income inequality. After the examination of empirical research, the study reveals the main macroeconomic indicators of developing countries based on data obtained from the World Bank (WB). Finally, the study empirically analyzes the relationship between economic growth and income inequality in developing countries through models.

Theoretical Framework

Disposable income, or simply income, is found by subtracting taxes from personal income. And income earned in a certain period is among flow variables. It is more accurate to consider the income that does not include taxes or transfers. Because the income earned by individuals before tax will not reflect a real purchasing power. The income generated from the assets individuals own provides benefits to individuals or households. The income used by economic units is simply categorized as wage income, interest income, rental income, and profit income (Rycroft, 2014; Brian, 2015). And how much income will be obtained by whom is a question that needs to be answered for the society. When everyone is involved in the production, this will result in more or less income earned. However, it is clear that income will not be accessible to everyone when not all individuals have a means of production. This will lead to differences in income and wealth among the members of the society.

Wealth consists of assets you own and can use to make a profit. Your house is an asset, and it gives you shelter, status, and satisfaction. If you have a Picasso painting, hanging on your wall, you'll enjoy it, because looking at it will make you happy. It is also an asset if you own a car, which is a convenient resource for transportation. Most people have an instinctive feeling about what fortune (wealth) is, such as money in the bank, land, stocks, jewelry, artwork, pension rights, and life insurance. However, our wealth, like our savings, also has obligations such as loans and mortgages besides our assets. In this respect, wealth is not only a positive thing; it has also negative aspects. Wealth is important in terms of supporting people in difficult times and when they are unemployed. In addition, deposits and stocks in the bank may also be a source of income. These allow individuals to make one-time or large-scale investments such as education and property. Wealthy people earning income will enable them to make faster positive contributions in terms of income. Here, the income-generating capacity of wealth should not be overlooked. The access of rich people to investment opportunities or to the necessary tools for investment will accelerate their income generation. In this case, rich people will have an advantage over others, that is, the poor. This situation that results from the inequality between the rich and the poor will get worse over time. This income inequality will also limit the equality of opportunity among the members of the society (Brain, 2015; Rycroft, 2014; McKay, 2002). It is desirable for any country to reach equality in income distribution for all individuals. However, it is a well-known fact that economic functioning cannot be built on this equality. Therefore, income inequality emerges as an inevitable consequence of people getting different levels of income share in society.

Even though we simply define income inequality, there is a lot of conceptual debate on inequality. Even if it starts with a simple definition, it is a very complex situation that has a different meaning to each person. While inequality has a material dimension such as wealth and income, it also has an abstract welfare aspect. Income inequality can be identified by examining the living standards of the individuals living in the society. Income inequality is related to access to economic and social opportunities in society. Income inequality negatively affects access to opportunities and results in poverty for individuals (Atkinson and Bourguignon, 2014; McKay, 2002). Inequality is not only about the fairness of income distribution; it also affects the social areas of society. Income inequality leads to limited access and exclusion for some individuals in many economic and social areas.

Identifying and measuring income inequality is also important for policy purposes. Common criteria applicable to different subgroups of the population and different geographic areas can be used. Inequality may differ across the country, in terms of regions, and sometimes even within regions themselves. For this reason, a clear determination of the situation will be inevitable for the policies to be implemented in the fight against inequality. Because the causes of inequality can be more than one, such as age, gender, geography, education, economic development, living in an urban or rural region, and occupation. The development level of the country is also an important element of inequality. Inequality is closely related to many factors such as employment, education, health, nutrition, housing, and access to basic services. While these factors are sometimes a direct cause of inequality, they can also be an indirect cause of inequality (Haughton and Khandker, 2009; Odekon, 2006).

Income inequality is related to the imbalance in the distribution of income or economic resources among the members of the society. It is not possible to explain the distribution of inequality with a single number, and different studies can be conducted on this subject. Inequality is a multidimensional concept as it can be defined in a different way for each individual. It is also possible to divide the measurement methods of inequality into two categories, objective and subjective. There are multiple tools to identify income inequality, but the Gini coefficient developed by Corrado Gini is the most well-known one (Sen, 1997; Atkinson and Bourguignon, 2014; Brain, 2015). It is also quite natural that there is more than one measurement method to explain a multidimensional situation. Methods such as the Gini coefficient, Pareto Coefficient, Theil Inequality Index, Kuznets's Curve, and Atkinson Inequality Criterion are used.

Pioneering work on the study of economic growth and income inequality has been carried out by Simon Kuznets. In the absolute income hypothesis, it is assumed that the average consumption of individuals decreases as a result of a long-term increase in disposable income. However, Kuznets found that consumption does not decrease with a long-term increase in disposable income. In his work, he started with the assumption that increasing income does not affect the consumption tendency of individuals in the long run. Kuznets focused on the reasons behind this situation and examined early industrializers such as the United States, Germany, and England. Kuznets basically studied the direction of the relationship between income inequality and economic growth. As a result of the analysis made with the data from the United States, Germany, and England, it was found that income inequality increased in the first periods of economic growth. However, in the latter stages of the study, it was observed that the relationship between income inequality and economic growth reversed after a certain point. Based on this result on the economies of developed countries, it was stated that the relationship between economic growth and income inequality has an inverted-U shape graph (Kuznets, 1946, 1955).

Literature Review

In a 1973 study on economically developed and developing countries, it was found that developed countries have more income inequality. The finding that income inequality is higher in developed countries than in undeveloped countries is compatible with the first step of Kuznets's inverted-U hypothesis (Paukert, 1973). Kuznets's hypothesis has been tested in developed and developing countries. In the analyses in which functions of different orders were used, it was seen that the inverse-U hypothesis was invalid (Matyas et al., 1998). The effect of economic growth on income inequality has been investigated by List and Gallet in 71 countries. Although there are some differences between developing and developed countries, the result was found to be compatible with the inverted-U hypothesis (List and Gallet, 1999). Barro determined that the Kuznets hypothesis is valid, although it falls short in explaining the income inequality differences between developed and developing countries over time (Barro, 2000). Ongan (2004) investigated the relationship between income inequality and foreign capital investments in developed and developing countries. However, according to the findings obtained from the analysis, it was observed that the relationship between income inequality and economic growth followed an increasing and then decreasing course. Khasru and Jalil (2004) tested the inverted-U hypothesis in developed and developing countries. It has been found that the inverted-U hypothesis is generally valid, but there are differences among countries. These differences were seen in developed countries, and it has been seen that Kuznets's hypothesis is not valid for some developed countries. Deutsch and Silber (2004) analyzed economic growth and income inequality by considering individual income and factor income, which refer to different income distributions. Although it is seen that there are different results for different types of income, the Kuznets hypothesis was found to be valid in general. Anand and Kanbur examined the relationship between income inequality and economic growth in developing countries. As a result of the cross-section analysis for 1953–1976, Kuznets's hypothesis was found to be invalid (Anand and Kanbur, 1993).

According to the results of the analysis for developed countries, it was determined by Ram that Kuznets's inverted-U hypothesis was valid. Income inequality was observed to increase in the first period but tended to decrease in the second period (Ram, 1997). In the study in which the Kuznets hypothesis was tested with the assumption of a two-sector economy, an increase in income inequality was observed in the long term by considering the change in the population structures of the sectors (Robinson, 1976). Kuznets's hypothesis was tested by using enough countries to cover 85% of the world's population through the Theil index. The analysis results were found to be compatible with the Kuznets hypothesis (Ram, 1989). As opposed to

Kuznets's hypothesis, Clarke found that there is a significant but negative relationship between income inequality and economic growth. Another result of this study, which is similar to the findings of Anand and Kanbur, is that the scope of the relationship is limited (Clarke, 1995).

In the analysis carried out by using the Gini coefficient, it was concluded that the relationship between economic growth and income inequality is similar to Kuznets's theory (Thornton, 2001). Bleaney and Nishiyama (2002) examined the relationship between economic growth and income inequality in multiple countries with data from 1960 to 1990. With the finding that income inequality increased with a high level of economic growth, Kuznets's hypothesis was supported.

Nel (2003) found that the relationship between income inequality and economic growth was weak but consistent with the Kuznets hypothesis in the study conducted for the countries in Africa. Chen (2003) found that although the analysis results on various countries vary in the long run, income inequality tends to first increase and then decrease, similar to Kuznets's assumption. Deininger and Squire (1997) analyzed a 30-year dataset for sub-Saharan Arctic, Latin America, and OECD countries. The results of the analysis revealed that the inverted-U hypothesis is not valid in all countries included in the study.

Desbordes and Verardi (2012) analyzed the relationship between income inequality and economic growth with data from more than 100 countries. It has been found that the relationship between economic growth and income inequality supports Kuznets's hypothesis, but this relationship is only one-way. Huang (2004) examined the relationship between income inequality and economic growth in 75 countries with a nonlinear model. The relationship between individual income and income inequality supported Kuznets's hypothesis. Rehman et al. (2008) conducted research with panel data analysis in 51 countries within the framework of different income group classifications. It has been observed that the results of the analysis on the causes of income inequality or the factors affecting inequality also support Kuznets's hypothesis. Zang (1998) analyzed income inequality in 60 countries with data from 1967 to 1986. According to the analysis results, the inverted-U hypothesis was found to be valid.

Gallet and Gallet (2004) tested the Kuznets hypothesis by considering different population classifications for the United States. According to the findings, it was seen that the Kuznets hypothesis for the United States is U-shaped, not inverted U-shaped. Mollick (2012) examined the economic growth and income inequality in the United States. It was concluded that Kuznets's inverted-U hypothesis is valid. Rubin and Segal (2015) found that the results of the analysis for the United States in the years 1953–2008 differ by income groups. Although some differences were detected among income groups, economic growth and income inequality were found to be compatible with Kuznets's assumption.

Malinen (2012) tested the relationship between income inequality and economic growth in Latin American countries. According to the analysis results, while the long-term relationship between income inequality and economic growth for middle and high-income countries were similar to Kuznets's assumptions, no relationship was found in low-income countries. Jalil (2012) analyzed the relationship between economic growth and income inequality in China with a dataset covering 57 years. The results of the analysis revealed that the inverted-U hypothesis is valid for China. Samy (2014) tried to identify the relationship between income inequality, industrialization, and economic growth in South Korea. The results of the analysis showed that economic growth and industrialization tend to increase income inequality. Shahbaz (2010) analyzed the relationship between economic growth and income inequality in Pakistan. According to the results of the time series analysis, the inverse-U hypothesis was found to be valid for Pakistan, but it followed an inverse S-shaped path.

Kuştepeli (2006) examined economic growth and income inequality in EU countries and candidate countries. The relationship between economic growth and income inequality for EU countries and candidate countries was observed to follow an inverted U-shaped path. Oczki et al. (2017) analyzed the relationship between GDP per capita and economic growth in European Union countries within the framework of Kuznets's hypothesis. In the study, evidence is presented that there is a U-shaped relationship in contrast to the expected inverted-U relationship. Şengür (2020) examined the relationship between income inequality and economic growth for transition economies with panel data analysis. According to the analysis results, the inverted-U hypothesis was found to be valid also for transition economies.

Tokatlıoğlu and Atan (2007) tested the Kuznets hypothesis for Turkey. As a result of the analysis carried out by using the third-order function, the economic growth and income inequality relationship in Turkey was observed to follow a U-shaped course, not an inverted U-shaped course. Ak and Altıntaş (2016) analyzed the course of income inequality in Turkey with a 26-year dataset using the border test. The analysis results revealed that in Turkey, Kuznets's hypothesis is not an inverted-U, but is U-shaped. Topuz and Dağdemir (2016) tested the Kuznets hypothesis for 94 countries using data from 1995 to 2011. According to the findings of the study, Kuznets's inverted-U hypothesis is valid although some differences were detected among countries. Akıncı and Akıncı (2016) examined income inequality and economic growth in Turkey by including financial development. The results of the analysis proved that the inverted-U hypothesis was valid for the years 1960–2014. Akalin et al. (2018) tested the Kuznets hypothesis for Turkey using cubic and quadratic models. According to the findings of the cubic model, while the economic growth in Turkey is in an inverted-N shape of the income inequality relationship, it is in an inverted-U shape according to the quadratic model.

There are many empirical studies that question the validity of Kuznets's hypothesis. While the inverted-U hypothesis is confirmed in some of these studies, no correlation was found confirming the inverted-U hypothesis in others. In addition to these two different findings, some studies have concluded that the inverted-U relationship is actually U-shaped. The analysis of Kuznets's inverted-U hypothesis using current data from developing countries is the main objective of this study.

Macroeconomic Indicators of Developing Countries

Variables such as national income, capital stock, inflation, public expenditures, unemployment, foreign trade, population, and poverty are important in terms of reflecting the macroeconomic conditions of countries. These variables, which are the main indicators for national economies, also differ in developed and developing countries. It is observed that there are differences not only between developed and developing countries but also between countries at the same development level from time to time. Comparisons between countries are made on the basis of statistical data. The classification of countries is similarly made by taking into account the per capita income figures.

Countries by WB classification (datahelpdesk.worldbank):

- Low-Income Countries: Those with a per capita income of $1,035 and below.
- Lower Middle-Income Countries: Those with a per capita income between $1,036 and $4,045.
- Upper Middle-Income Countries: Those with a per capita income between $4,046 and $12,535.
- High-Income Countries: Those with a per capita income of $12,536 or more.

In this section, the main macroeconomic indicators of developing countries are presented with tables and graphs created with the data obtained from the WB. First of all, three different graphs created with GDP per capita are included.

The GDP per capita values of Argentina, Armenia, Brazil, China, Colombia, Croatia, Egypt, and Georgia are given in figure 4.1 for the years 2004, 2011, and 2019. While Georgia had a GDP per capita of $2,203 in 2004, it reached

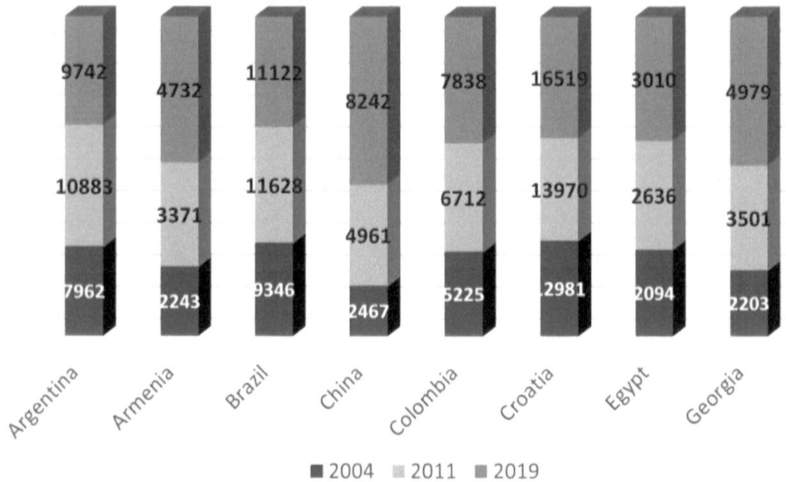

FIGURE 4.1
GDP Per Capita_1 (Constant 2010 US$). *Source*: Created by authors based on the Data from World Development Indicators (World Bank).

$4,979 in 2019. Among these eight countries, Croatia had the highest GDP per capita with $12,981 in 2004, with an increase of $3,538 to $16,519 in 2019. Although Argentina exceeded $10,000 in 2011, it decreased to $9,742 in 2019. Armenia's GDP per capita increased by more than 100% from 2004 to 2019. Except for Croatia, no other country with a per capita income of $15,000 or more over a 16-year period is among developing countries.

In figure 4.2, GDP per capita values of India, Indonesia, Iran, Kazakhstan, Kyrgyzstan, Malaysia, Mexico, and Nepal for the relevant period are given. Among the countries in the graph, the countries with more than $10,000 as of 2019 are Kazakhstan, Kyrgyzstan, Malaysia, and Mexico. Nepal, which had the lowest GDP per capita of $490 in 2004, increased to $859 in 2019. Despite the fact that Nepal achieved a 75% GDP per capita increase between 2004 and 2019, it ranks last among the developing countries. Iran's GDP per capita values of $5,624 in 2004, $6,695 in 2011, and $5,923 in 2011 remained below $6,000.

Among developing countries, India has the second-lowest GDP per capita after Nepal. The GDP per capita figures of India are $979 in 2004, $1,410 in 2011, and $2,152 in 2019. Although the GDP per capita of India increased by approximately 120% over the course of 16 years, it has a very low income compared to other countries.

When we look at figure 4.3, which includes the Philippines, Poland, Russia, South Africa, Thailand, Turkey, Ukraine, and Uruguay, it is seen that the GDP per capita figures of Poland and Turkey are above $15,000 as of 2019.

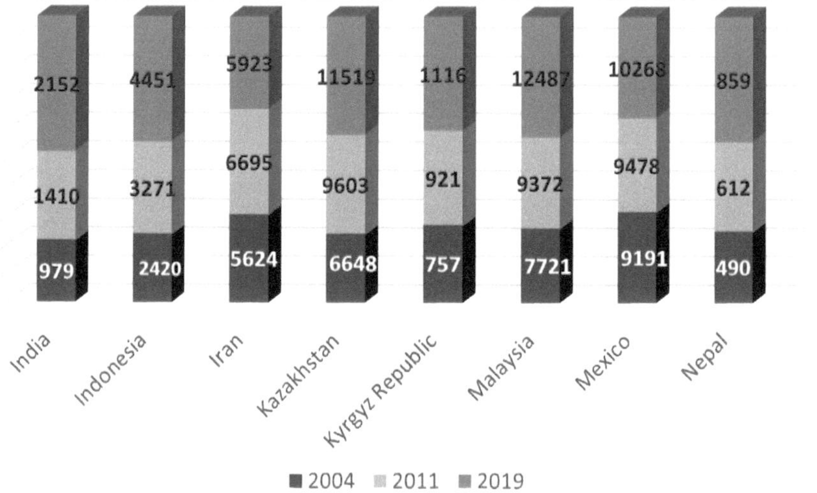

FIGURE 4.2
GDP Per Capita_2 (Constant 2010 US$). *Source*: Created by authors based on the Data from World Development Indicators (World Bank).

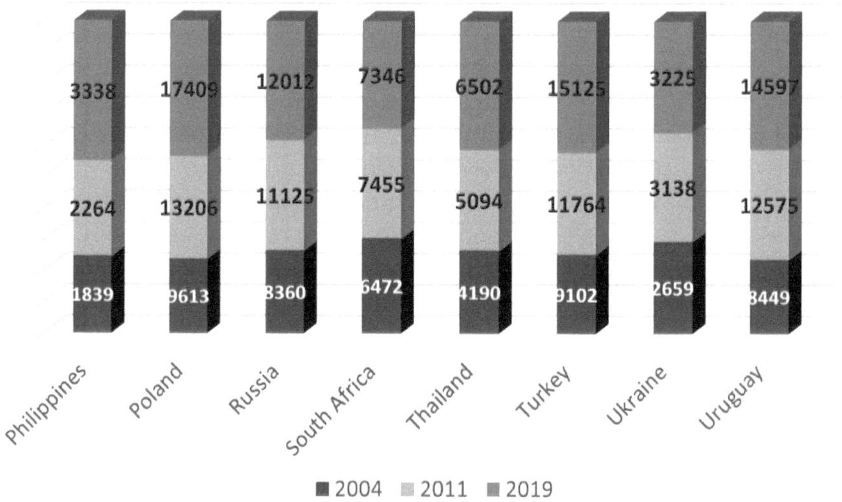

FIGURE 4.3
GDP Per Capita_3 (Constant 2010 US$). *Source*: Created by authors based on the Data from World Development Indicators (World Bank).

Among the developing countries, in 2019, Poland, Turkey, and Croatia are also among the countries with $15,000 more income. It is seen that Uruguay is close to the countries with the highest GDP per capita with $14,597. In 2004–2019, the Philippines achieved an increase of nearly 82% in GDP per

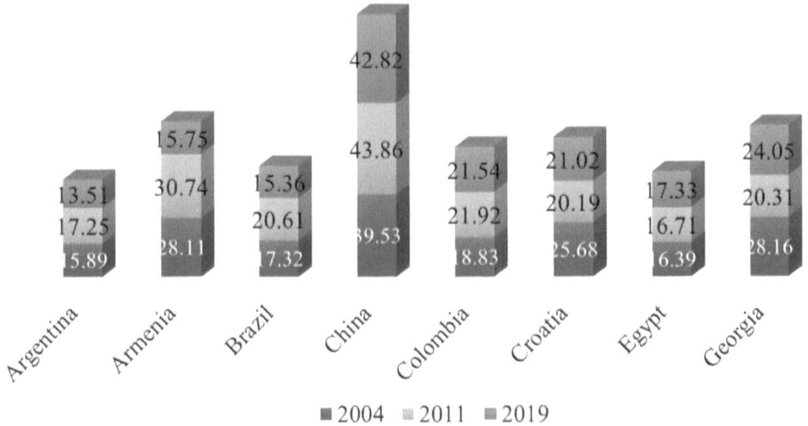

FIGURE 4.4
Gross Fixed Capital Formation_1 (% of GDP). *Source*: Created by authors based on the Data from World Development Indicators (World Bank).

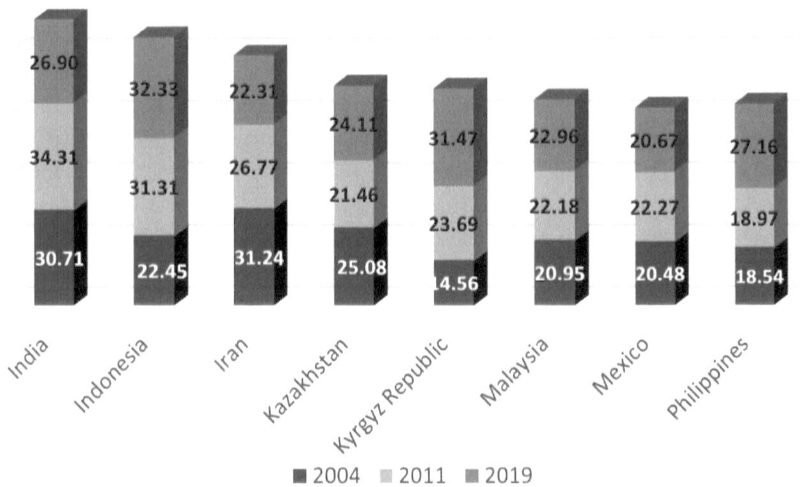

FIGURE 4.5
Gross Fixed Capital Formation_2 (% of GDP). *Source*: Created by authors based on the Data from World Development Indicators (World Bank).

capita. Despite this increase, the Philippines had the third lowest GDP per capita in 2019, after Nepal and India.

Figures 4.4–4.6 show the gross fixed capital ratios of developing countries for the years 2004, 2011, and 2019. While China had a gross fixed capital

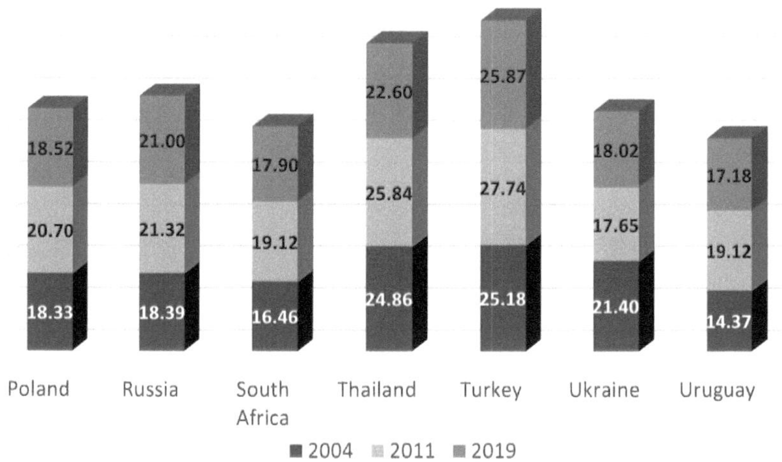

FIGURE 4.6
Gross Fixed Capital Formation_3 (% of GDP). *Source*: Created by authors based on the Data from World Development Indicators (World Bank).

ratio of 39.5% in 2004, this ratio increased to 42.82% in 2019. China ranks first among developing countries in terms of gross fixed capital ratio in the 2004–2019 period. Argentina, which is in the same graph, has a gross fixed capital ratio of 15.89%, 17.25%, and 13.51%, respectively, in the 2004–2019 period, and ranks last among developing countries. In terms of the countries included in the chart, while the gross fixed capital ratio increased for almost all of them in 2011, there was a decrease of approximately 2% in Georgia. While Armenia had a gross fixed capital ratio of 30.74% in 2011, this ratio decreased by almost half to 15.75% in 2019. In 2004–2019, Armenia ranks first in terms of decrease with a loss of approximately 50% in the gross fixed capital ratio.

Indonesia, which is included in figure 4.5, is the country with the second-highest gross fixed capital ratio after China with 32.33% in 2019. While India had a gross fixed capital ratio of more than 30% in 2004 and 2011, it decreased by approximately 7.5% to 26.9% in 2019. From 2004 to 2019, Kyrgyzstan reached 31.47% with an increase in the gross fixed capital ratio close to 120%. As of 2019, it is seen that the gross fixed capital ratios of all the countries in the chart are 20% and above.

While Turkey had a gross fixed capital ratio of 25.18% in 2004, which is shown in Graph-6, this ratio increased to 27.74% in 2011 and decreased to 25% in 2019. It is seen that Thailand, which had a gross fixed capital ratio of close to Turkey in 2004, was at the level of 22.6% in 2019. Although Poland had an increase of 2% in the 2004–2019 period, it remained at the initial level with a gross fixed capital ratio of 18.5% in 2019. Considering the 2019 figures,

South Africa and Uruguay are countries with a gross fixed capital ratio of around 17%. While Russia had a gross fixed capital ratio of 18.9% in 2004, this ratio increased to 21% in 2019 (table 4.1).

It will mean that individuals or institutions in the country do not consume a part of the income; that is, they tend to save. Increasing savings, especially investments, will increase the availability of necessary resources for economic functioning. Table 4.1 shows the savings rates of developing countries for the period 2010–2019. The country with the highest ratio of savings to GDP in 2010 was China with 51.33%. Even though China's savings rates fell to 43.82% in 2019 at the end of a 10-year period, it still maintains its position in the first place. In 2010, the Philippines had the second-highest savings rate of nearly 40% after China. The Philippines managed to stay in second place even though the savings rate fell to 31.63% within 10 years, similar to China. It is seen that India, Malaysia, Indonesia, and Kazakhstan are the other countries with savings rates above 30% in 2010. In 2010, Georgia was the developing country with the lowest savings with a rate of 10.73%. Armenia is also the country with the second-lowest savings at 13.2%. When we look at 2019, it is observed that the country with the lowest savings rate is Armenia. After Armenia, the countries with the lowest savings rates in 2019 were Brazil and Ukraine with a rate of approximately 12%. While Georgia had the lowest savings rate in 2010, it got out of this situation by increasing its savings rates to 22.04% in the 2010–2019 period.

Argentina could not increase its savings rates much in the 2004–2019 period, and it had an average of 15%. Argentina's savings rates were highest in this decade, with 17% in 2010 and 2011. Brazil was among the countries with the lowest savings rate of 12% in 2019, with a decrease of around 5% over the 10-year period. Croatia, on the other hand, was the country that increased its savings rates the most, with an increase of around 7% over the 10-year period. Malaysia was the country whose savings decreased the most in the 2010–2019 period. Malaysia's savings rates decreased by around 9% to 24.41% as of 2019. Similarly, with a decrease of 8% in the same period, the Philippines was the second country with the highest decrease, followed by China and Indonesia with a decrease of 7–7.5%.

Inflation is the main reason for the weakening purchasing power of individuals, and it affects the macroeconomic balance. Inflation data of developing countries for the 2010–2019 period are given in table 4.2. Argentina is the country with the highest inflation rate in 2010, at approximately 21%. After Argentina, the country with the second-highest inflation in 2010 was Kazakhstan (19.54%), while Russia and Georgia took third place with an inflation rate of 14%. Croatia, on the other hand, is the country with the lowest price increase in 2010 with an inflation rate of 0.92%. The country with the second-lowest inflation is Poland, followed by Colombia, in third place.

TABLE 4.1
Gross Savings (% of GDP)

	2010	*2011*	*2012*	*2013*	*2014*	*2015*	*2016*	*2017*	*2018*	*2019*
Argentina	17.31	17.35	16.06	14.95	15.75	14.14	14.64	13.08	14.42	15.80
Armenia	13.20	11.10	14.10	14.84	13.28	18.43	17.81	16.91	15.47	10.24
Brazil	17.80	18.60	17.68	18.15	16.13	14.53	13.42	13.58	12.38	12.19
China	51.33	49.23	48.67	47.38	47.62	45.52	44.48	44.96	44.39	43.82
Colombia	18.27	19.31	18.39	18.14	18.03	17.15	17.40	16.90	16.31	15.73
Croatia	18.85	18.11	16.57	17.95	19.07	23.77	23.06	25.32	25.27	25.34
Egypt	17.95	16.87	12.88	13.68	11.88	9.59	9.71	10.36	13.89	14.61
Georgia	10.73	10.01	14.46	15.43	15.28	14.47	17.70	19.24	21.34	22.04
India	36.31	35.13	35.26	34.30	33.47	32.45	30.83	31.43	31.10	29.14
Indonesia	32.73	33.22	31.99	31.12	30.67	30.12	29.92	30.88	31.80	31.01
Kazakhstan	30.39	32.79	29.75	28.99	30.14	27.64	23.90	25.93	27.79	26.96
Kyrgyz Republic	19.93	17.41	12.74	9.12	11.53	12.17	22.46	26.67	26.58	20.69
Malaysia	33.47	34.08	30.92	29.42	29.37	28.40	28.38	28.34	26.14	24.41
Mexico	23.76	23.83	23.28	20.15	21.26	21.76	22.30	23.17	23.66	23.69
Philippines	39.75	36.88	35.13	36.35	37.35	35.63	35.05	35.49	33.81	31.63
Poland	15.75	17.10	16.71	17.21	17.78	19.50	19.19	19.53	19.40	20.13
Russia	26.28	28.76	27.24	24.28	24.51	26.37	25.01	25.67	30.00	27.57
South Africa	18.01	17.54	15.10	15.36	15.66	16.48	16.53	16.14	14.88	14.95
Thailand	29.63	31.43	28.93	27.22	27.49	28.04	30.09	31.95	31.69	31.47
Turkey	21.80	23.03	23.38	23.91	24.90	25.21	24.98	26.01	27.71	26.02
Ukraine	17.55	15.77	13.07	8.77	9.90	17.69	20.28	17.79	15.21	12.06
Uruguay	17.01	17.41	12.72	14.20	13.01	14.98	14.55	12.45	11.81	12.99

Source: Calculated by author based on the data from World Development Indicators (World Bank).

TABLE 4.2
Inflation, GDP Deflator (Annual %)

	2010	2011	2012	2013	2014	2015	2016	2017	2018	2019
Argentina	20.92	23.70	22.31	23.95	40.28	26.58	41.12	26.01	40.01	50.62
Armenia	7.77	4.28	5.35	3.37	2.31	1.21	0.27	2.15	2.79	1.46
Brazil	8.42	8.32	7.94	7.50	7.85	7.57	8.10	3.64	3.29	4.15
China	6.88	8.08	2.33	2.16	1.03	0.00	1.41	4.23	3.50	1.29
Colombia	3.80	6.39	3.62	1.91	2.24	2.45	5.15	5.13	4.48	4.29
Croatia	0.92	1.65	1.48	0.75	0.14	0.08	−0.10	1.16	2.00	1.50
Egypt	10.11	11.66	19.48	8.71	11.25	9.93	6.25	22.93	21.43	13.63
Georgia	14.19	8.71	0.46	1.35	4.23	5.83	2.62	8.49	4.33	5.19
India	10.53	8.73	7.93	6.19	3.33	2.28	3.24	3.78	4.56	2.91
Indonesia	15.26	7.47	3.75	4.97	5.44	3.98	2.44	4.29	3.82	1.60
Iran	15.88	23.74	24.02	35.57	10.84	0.43	1.61	12.25	32.90	36.91
Kazakhstan	19.54	20.54	4.79	9.50	5.77	1.82	13.64	11.21	9.21	7.63
Kyrgyz Republic	10.03	22.48	8.66	3.18	8.42	3.43	6.05	6.33	3.45	−0.84
Malaysia	7.27	5.41	1.00	0.17	2.47	1.22	1.66	3.78	0.67	0.06
Mexico	4.55	5.84	4.07	1.53	4.44	2.84	5.61	6.71	4.94	3.97
Philippines	4.37	3.92	1.99	2.06	3.05	−0.72	1.28	2.32	3.74	0.76
Poland	1.65	3.27	2.36	0.30	0.52	0.97	0.31	1.86	1.20	3.15
Russia	14.19	24.46	8.91	5.32	7.49	7.25	2.84	5.35	11.10	3.78
South Africa	6.35	6.53	5.28	6.16	5.55	5.17	7.21	5.27	3.92	4.02
Thailand	4.08	3.74	1.91	1.78	1.44	0.72	2.66	1.98	1.46	0.75
Turkey	7.01	8.20	7.42	6.28	7.39	7.84	8.13	10.98	16.49	13.91
Ukraine	13.92	14.20	7.79	4.34	15.90	38.88	17.33	22.08	15.40	8.13
Uruguay	4.91	9.01	8.56	8.15	9.37	9.02	7.35	4.71	5.56	7.67

Source: Calculated by author based on the data from World Development Indicators (World Bank).

When we consider the period of 2010–2019, inflation in Argentina increased except in 2015 and 2017. Argentina reached a rate of 50.62% in 2019 with an inflation increase of around 30% at the end of the decade. In 2019, Kyrgyzstan was the country with the lowest inflation with −0.84%. In 2019, Malaysia was second in the lowest inflation ranking, while the Philippines and Thailand took third place. Argentina, Uruguay, Turkey, Poland, Iran, Egypt, Croatia, and Colombia are the countries with an increasing inflation rate in the 2010–2019 period. In other countries, on the other hand, a decreasing trend is observed in inflation rates more or less in this period. It is seen that Iran is the country with the second-highest increase in inflation with an increase of 132% in 10 years.

Access to health services, which is among the basic elements of human development, is directly related to public health expenditures and investments. Table 4.3 shows the ratios of health expenditure to GDP for 2008–2018 in developing countries. Uruguay ranks first with a health expenditure ratio of about 9% in 2008. Georgia, Argentina, and Brazil are the countries that rank second with around 8% health expenditure behind Uruguay. In the same year, Indonesia is in the last place with a health expenditure rate of 2.61%. Malaysia and Kazakhstan are the countries with the second-lowest health expenditure rates.

In 2018, the country with the highest ratio of health expenditures to GDP was Armenia with 10%. Argentina and Brazil rank after Armenia with a health expenditure ratio of around 9.5%. Despite a partial increase in health expenditures, Uruguay, which was in first place, took third place in 2018.

At the end of the 2008–2018 period, Georgia ranks first with a 1.57% decrease in health expenditure. After Georgia, there are Turkey (1.1%), Croatia (0.9%), and Mexico (0.33%), respectively. From 2008 to 2018, the ratio of health expenditures to GDP of all countries except Georgia, Turkey, Croatia, and Mexico either remained unchanged or increased, albeit slightly.

Iran and Armenia were the two countries that increased their health expenditures the most from 2008 to 2018 with a rate of 3.38%. For these two countries, the ratio of health expenditures to GDP has increased in almost all of them in the 11-year period. After 11 years, Kyrgyzstan, India, and Poland are almost the only countries that have maintained their health expenditure ratios in 2008, the start year.

Table 4.4 shows the total labor force participation rates of the developing countries for the years 2010–2019. The country with the highest labor force participation rate in 2010 was Thailand with 71.71%, while China took second place with 71.26%. The labor force participation rates of Thailand and China are almost equal, with Kazakhstan in third place with 70.36%. While Iran is the country with the lowest labor force participation rate with 42.9%, Turkey is the second country with the lowest labor force participation rate with

TABLE 4.3
Current Health Expenditure (% of GDP)

	2008	*2009*	*2010*	*2011*	*2012*	*2013*	*2014*	*2015*	*2016*	*2017*	*2018*
Argentina	8.18	9.46	9.45	9.42	9.83	9.78	9.67	10.23	9.00	10.46	9.62
Armenia	6.64	8.44	9.24	9.38	9.13	10.32	10.18	10.12	9.95	10.36	10.03
Brazil	8.02	8.40	7.95	7.79	7.74	7.98	8.40	8.87	9.21	9.47	9.51
China	3.88	4.32	4.21	4.33	4.55	4.71	4.77	4.89	4.98	5.15	5.35
Colombia	6.84	7.31	7.07	6.78	6.75	7.02	7.19	7.52	7.53	7.68	7.64
Croatia	7.73	8.18	8.10	7.79	7.80	6.53	6.70	6.79	6.83	6.78	6.83
Egypt	4.47	4.38	4.15	4.36	4.71	4.92	5.03	5.34	5.36	5.63	4.95
Georgia	8.68	9.84	9.55	8.39	8.37	8.40	8.44	7.93	8.42	7.06	7.11
India	3.51	3.49	3.27	3.25	3.33	3.75	3.62	3.60	3.51	3.54	3.54
Indonesia	2.61	2.68	2.96	2.96	2.90	2.96	3.12	2.99	3.09	2.87	2.87
Iran	5.28	6.56	6.75	6.61	6.64	5.99	6.91	7.76	8.86	8.66	8.66
Kazakhstan	3.05	3.50	2.74	2.60	3.04	2.66	2.97	3.04	3.42	3.13	2.92
Kyrgyz Republic	6.53	6.90	6.95	7.11	8.51	8.19	7.36	7.15	6.41	6.19	6.53
Malaysia	3.02	3.28	3.18	3.34	3.49	3.52	3.73	3.82	3.69	3.71	3.76
Mexico	5.70	6.13	5.98	5.70	5.84	5.94	5.63	5.80	5.62	5.52	5.37
Philippines	4.03	4.35	4.31	4.21	4.37	4.46	4.13	4.32	4.41	4.45	4.40
Poland	6.37	6.59	6.42	6.23	6.20	6.38	6.35	6.40	6.54	6.56	6.33
Russia	4.90	5.64	4.97	4.79	4.94	5.08	5.18	5.30	5.27	5.34	5.32
South Africa	6.55	7.11	7.42	7.50	7.75	7.72	7.93	8.20	8.10	8.11	8.25
Thailand	3.46	3.62	3.39	3.57	3.52	3.45	3.68	3.67	3.76	3.83	3.79
Turkey	5.22	5.49	5.02	4.65	4.44	4.37	4.33	4.12	4.28	4.18	4.12
Ukraine	5.50	6.61	6.81	6.82	7.12	6.94	7.19	7.78	7.55	7.43	7.72
Uruguay	8.83	8.64	8.59	8.64	8.76	8.82	8.77	9.01	9.42	9.52	9.20

Source: Calculated by author based on the data from World Development Indicators (World Bank).

TABLE 4.4
Labor Force Participation Rate. Total (% of Total Population Ages 15+)

	2010	*2011*	*2012*	*2013*	*2014*	*2015*	*2016*	*2017*	*2018*	*2019*
Argentina	60.40	60.63	60.50	60.22	59.69	60.02	60.31	60.59	61.39	61.61
Armenia	56.28	57.65	57.96	58.21	57.53	56.86	55.73	55.43	53.17	52.93
Brazil	64.73	63.59	64.29	64.17	63.90	64.05	63.79	64.06	64.05	64.46
China	71.26	71.06	70.84	70.59	70.30	69.98	69.61	69.19	68.72	68.24
Colombia	68.22	68.88	69.82	69.45	69.52	69.86	69.50	69.18	68.68	67.81
Croatia	52.68	51.81	51.28	50.67	52.14	52.54	51.19	51.61	51.36	51.48
Egypt	49.11	48.81	49.15	49.61	49.59	47.92	47.70	46.39	44.93	44.83
Georgia	66.32	67.31	68.27	67.74	68.53	69.26	68.44	66.74	64.31	63.61
India	54.21	53.29	52.40	51.90	51.40	50.91	50.41	49.91	49.42	49.34
Indonesia	67.19	67.27	67.73	67.05	66.81	66.50	66.18	66.80	67.44	68.01
Iran	42.90	42.48	42.10	41.73	41.34	42.44	43.94	44.87	44.95	45.16
Kazakhstan	70.36	70.38	70.48	70.61	70.87	70.89	70.13	69.25	69.10	68.81
Kyrgyz Republic	64.08	64.53	63.92	62.50	62.40	62.38	61.57	60.20	59.06	58.86
Malaysia	60.37	61.58	62.60	64.06	64.29	64.46	64.32	64.40	64.78	64.73
Mexico	60.72	60.75	61.43	61.24	60.64	60.76	60.67	60.48	60.70	61.42
Philippines	62.19	62.90	62.43	62.15	62.81	62.21	62.23	59.67	59.58	60.03
Poland	55.92	56.06	56.36	56.43	56.79	56.62	56.80	57.06	57.01	56.89
Russia	62.44	62.69	62.69	62.59	62.63	62.63	62.77	62.33	62.25	61.49
South Africa	52.48	52.54	53.04	53.73	54.05	55.38	55.52	56.18	55.99	56.08
Thailand	71.71	73.24	72.77	70.69	69.68	69.05	68.07	67.29	67.59	66.74
Turkey	47.70	48.78	48.73	49.63	50.11	50.97	51.72	52.54	52.92	52.75
Ukraine	55.03	55.29	55.00	55.66	54.44	54.76	54.56	54.52	54.35	54.16
Uruguay	65.48	65.86	65.39	64.88	65.39	64.97	64.68	64.21	63.90	63.90

Source: Calculated by author based on the data from World Development Indicators (World Bank).

47.7%. In 2010, the labor force participation rate in developing countries was 50% or more, with the exception of Iran and Turkey. Colombia, on the other hand, approached the top three countries with the highest participation rate, with a rate of 68.22%.

In 2019, Colombia was among the top three countries with the highest labor force participation rate, at 67.8%. The labor force participation rates of China, Kazakhstan, and Thailand decreased in 2019. Thailand, which was in first place among these three countries in 2010, fell to fourth place with a loss of approximately 5%. Unlike Thailand, Turkey was no longer among the lowest countries in 2019 by increasing its labor force participation rate by 5% to 52.75%. The countries with the lowest labor force participation rate below 50% in 2019 were Iran, Egypt, and India.

When we examine the 11-year period between 2009 and 2019, it is seen that Turkey, South Africa, Poland, Mexico, Malaysia, Iran, and Indonesia are the countries that have increased their labor force participation rates. Among these countries, Turkey was the country with the highest increase with an increase of 5%, while the country with the lowest increase was Mexico with an increase of 0.7%.

Population growth contributes positively to meeting the labor force needs of countries. However, as a result of rapid and unbalanced population growth, problems arise in the allocation and distribution of existing resources. Population growth rates of developing countries are given in table 4.5 for the period 2004–2019.

The Philippines and Malaysia are in the first place with a population growth rate of approximately 1.98% in 2004. In the same year, Uruguay, Ukraine, Georgia, Armenia, Russia, and Poland are countries with negative population growth rates. Croatia was the only developing country with a nearly constant population with an increase of 0.03% in 2004.

In 2019, Kyrgyzstan ranked first with a population growth rate of over 2%. While Egypt is in second place with a population growth rate of 1.98%, Colombia and the Philippines with a population growth rate of 1.36% are in third place. In 2019, the population growth rate of Uruguay and Armenia turned from negative to positive. The population growth rate of Croatia, whose population remained almost constant in 2004, took a negative value in 2019. Along with Croatia, Ukraine, Russia, Poland, and Georgia were identified as countries with negative population growth rates in 2019. In the period 2004–2019, the countries whose population growth rate was never negative are Argentina, Brazil, China, Colombia, Egypt, India, Indonesia, Iran, Kazakhstan, Kyrgyzstan, Malaysia, Mexico, Philippines, South Africa, Thailand, and Turkey.

Trade consists of the sum of imports and exports of countries. In proportion to the relationship of the country's economy with the outside world, the

TABLE 4.5
Population Growth (Annual %)

	2004	*2008*	*2012*	*2016*	*2017*	*2018*	*2019*
Argentina	1.06	0.99	1.14	1.06	1.04	1.02	0.99
Armenia	−0.57	−0.86	0.27	0.36	0.29	0.24	0.20
Brazil	1.20	0.99	0.89	0.82	0.81	0.78	0.75
China	0.59	0.51	0.49	0.54	0.56	0.46	0.36
Colombia	1.42	1.18	0.90	1.37	1.51	1.52	1.36
Croatia	0.03	−0.01	−0.31	−0.70	−1.20	−0.89	−0.55
Egypt	1.83	1.78	2.21	2.15	2.09	2.03	1.98
Georgia	−0.62	−0.30	−0.74	0.06	0.01	−0.04	−0.17
India	1.62	1.46	1.23	1.09	1.06	1.04	1.02
Indonesia	1.34	1.32	1.35	1.22	1.18	1.13	1.10
Iran	1.21	1.09	1.21	1.36	1.39	1.39	1.35
Kazakhstan	0.69	1.87	1.41	1.42	1.36	1.31	1.29
Kyrgyz Republic	1.21	0.95	1.67	2.04	1.93	1.99	2.09
Malaysia	1.97	1.91	1.45	1.36	1.36	1.35	1.33
Mexico	1.38	1.50	1.36	1.20	1.16	1.13	1.09
Philippines	1.98	1.66	1.70	1.51	1.45	1.40	1.36
Poland	−0.06	0.01	0.00	−0.04	0.01	0.00	−0.02
Russia	−0.40	−0.04	0.17	0.17	0.11	−0.01	−0.05
South Africa	1.22	1.33	1.58	1.47	1.42	1.36	1.32
Thailand	0.69	0.53	0.47	0.37	0.35	0.32	0.28
Turkey	1.38	1.20	1.63	1.63	1.59	1.49	1.34
Ukraine	−0.76	−0.54	−0.25	−0.33	−0.39	−0.47	−0.53
Uruguay	−0.07	0.25	0.30	0.35	0.36	0.37	0.36

Source: Calculated by author based on the data from World Development Indicators (World Bank).

ratio of trade to GDP will increase. The ratios of trade to GDP of developing countries are shown in table 4.6. In 2010, Malaysia ranked first with 157.94%, Kyrgyzstan ranked second with 133.23%, and Thailand ranked third with 127.25%. The country with the lowest ratio of trade to GDP in 2010 is Brazil (22.77%), followed by Colombia (34.26%) and Argentina (34.97%).

In 2019, the ratio of trade to GDP in Malaysia was 123% with a decrease of 35%. Despite this decrease, Malaysia ranks first among developing countries. After Malaysia, Georgia is in second place with a rate of 123% and Thailand is in third place with a rate of 110.39%. Brazil is the country with the lowest value in 2019 with a trade rate of 22.9%. After Brazil, Argentina and China have the lowest trade rates, respectively.

In the 2010–2019 period, Argentina, China, Egypt, India, Indonesia, Kazakhstan, Kyrgyzstan, Malaysia, Russia, Thailand, Ukraine, and Uruguay are the countries whose trade ratios decreased. Malaysia is in the first place with a decrease of 35%, while Kyrgyzstan is the country with the second-highest decrease with a decrease of 30%. Armenia, Brazil, Colombia, Croatia,

TABLE 4.6
Trade (% of GDP)

	2010	*2011*	*2012*	*2013*	*2014*	*2015*	*2016*	*2017*	*2018*	*2019*
Argentina	34.97	35.21	30.53	29.33	28.41	22.49	26.09	25.29	31.17	32.63
Armenia	64.64	69.44	75.96	77.56	75.78	71.68	76.08	87.20	92.47	95.74
Brazil	22.77	23.93	25.11	25.79	24.69	26.95	24.53	24.33	29.40	28.98
China	50.72	50.74	48.27	46.74	44.91	39.46	36.89	37.63	37.46	35.84
Colombia	34.26	39.47	38.84	37.99	37.49	38.36	36.20	35.28	36.56	37.71
Croatia	73.90	79.23	80.57	82.69	86.97	92.54	94.12	99.15	101.25	104.17
Egypt	47.94	45.26	40.71	40.37	36.92	34.85	30.25	45.13	48.28	43.27
Georgia	82.90	87.55	91.94	95.60	96.77	98.77	96.83	104.04	111.76	118.65
India	49.26	55.62	55.79	53.84	48.92	41.92	40.08	40.72	43.40	39.55
Indonesia	46.70	50.18	49.58	48.64	48.08	41.94	37.42	39.36	43.00	37.30
Iran	43.77	43.19	47.37	50.33	44.60	39.02	43.21	48.78	65.05	56.17
Kazakhstan	74.14	73.12	73.72	65.41	64.97	53.05	60.31	56.83	63.53	63.90
Kyrgyz Republic	133.23	136.18	139.68	134.03	125.13	110.96	105.82	100.62	98.88	103.08
Malaysia	157.94	154.94	147.84	142.72	138.31	131.37	126.90	133.16	130.43	123.00
Mexico	60.76	63.47	65.77	63.76	64.93	71.09	76.06	77.12	80.56	77.92
Philippines	66.10	60.80	57.84	55.82	57.47	59.14	61.78	68.17	72.16	68.61
Poland	81.93	86.95	89.27	90.56	93.47	95.43	100.08	104.55	107.42	106.36
Russia	50.36	48.04	47.15	46.29	47.80	49.36	46.52	46.88	51.13	49.07
South Africa	55.99	60.11	60.90	64.24	64.43	61.62	60.64	57.97	59.47	59.20
Thailand	127.25	139.68	137.67	132.46	130.91	124.84	120.56	120.91	120.90	110.39
Turkey	46.69	53.30	52.83	52.53	53.77	51.09	48.33	55.76	62.55	62.68
Ukraine	98.14	106.24	104.09	95.15	100.69	107.81	105.52	103.72	99.12	90.17
Uruguay	51.70	53.25	55.06	49.72	49.09	45.33	41.31	39.76	39.99	41.03

Source: Calculated by author based on the data from World Development Indicators (World Bank).

Georgia, Iran, Mexico, Philippines, Poland, southern Africa, and Turkey are the countries with an increase in the ratio of trade to GDP in the same period.

The fact that those who have the ability to work at the current wage level cannot find a job is an indicator of unemployment. Unemployment is an important indicator of macroeconomic functioning. There are multiple factors that affect unemployment, but it is clear that a high level of unemployment is not desirable for economic stability.

Table 4.7 shows the unemployment rates in developing countries. In 2010, South Africa was the country with the highest unemployment rate of 24.68%. After South Africa, Georgia ranks second with a 20.2% unemployment rate and Armenia ranks third with 19.1%. The country with the lowest unemployment rate in 2010 was Thailand with 0.62%, Malaysia was second with 3.25%, and the Philippines was third with 3.61%.

In 2019, South Africa, where unemployment has increased by around 4%, is again the country with the highest unemployment rate (28.47%). The second country with the highest unemployment rate is Armenia with 18.81% and Turkey is the third country with an unemployment rate of 13.67%. Among the developing countries, Thailand has the lowest unemployment rate in 2019 with an unemployment rate of 0.72%. The Philippines is the second-lowest with an unemployment rate of 2.24%, while the Philippines and Malaysia are in third place with an unemployment rate of around 3%.

The countries with an increase in unemployment rates in the 2010–2019 period are Argentina, Brazil, Egypt, South Africa, Turkey, and Uruguay. Brazil was the country with the highest increase in unemployment in this period, with a 4.2% increase in unemployment. From 2010 to 2019, it is seen that South Africa is the second country with the highest increase in unemployment after Brazil.

Another one of the main macroeconomic indicators is poverty and income inequality. While income inequality is usually measured with indices such as the Gini coefficient, poverty is measured in the simplest form by the head number ratio and the poverty gap. The values of the Gini coefficient, which is an indicator of income inequality, are given in figures 4.7 and 4.8.

Figure 4.7 shows the 2016 Gini values of developing countries Argentina, Armenia, Brazil, China, Colombia, Croatia, Egypt, Georgia, India, Indonesia, Iran, and Kazakhstan. The Gini coefficient takes a value between 0 and 1, and a coefficient value close to 1 indicates higher inequality. While India was the country with the most unequal distribution of income with a Gini coefficient of 0.50, Kazakhstan was the country with the most equal distribution of income with a value of 0.26. When we consider figure 4.8, it is seen that Kazakhstan is the country with the least imbalance in income distribution among all the countries included in the study according to the Gini coefficient

TABLE 4.7
Unemployment, Total (% of Total Labor Force)

	2010	*2011*	*2012*	*2013*	*2014*	*2015*	*2016*	*2017*	*2018*	*2019*
Argentina	7.71	7.18	7.22	7.10	7.27	7.61	7.97	8.35	9.22	9.84
Armenia	19.01	18.44	17.30	16.18	17.50	18.26	17.62	17.71	18.97	18.81
Brazil	7.73	6.92	7.19	6.98	6.66	8.43	11.60	12.82	12.33	11.93
China	4.50	4.50	4.60	4.60	4.60	4.60	4.50	4.40	4.30	4.60
Colombia	10.98	10.11	9.74	9.05	8.57	8.30	8.69	8.87	9.11	9.96
Croatia	11.62	13.68	15.94	17.25	17.29	16.18	13.10	11.21	8.43	6.62
Egypt	8.76	11.85	12.60	13.15	13.11	13.05	12.41	11.74	9.82	9.73
Georgia	20.20	19.63	19.65	19.42	17.44	16.51	16.60	13.94	12.67	11.57
India	5.65	5.65	5.66	5.67	5.60	5.56	5.51	5.41	5.33	5.27
Indonesia	5.61	5.15	4.47	4.34	4.05	4.51	4.30	3.88	4.40	3.62
Iran	13.52	12.45	12.63	10.44	10.57	11.06	12.43	12.10	12.06	11.14
Kazakhstan	5.77	5.39	5.29	5.20	5.06	4.93	4.96	4.90	4.85	4.80
Kyrgyz Republic	8.64	8.53	8.43	8.33	8.05	7.56	7.21	6.89	6.79	6.72
Malaysia	3.25	3.05	3.04	3.11	2.88	3.10	3.44	3.41	3.30	3.31
Mexico	5.30	5.17	4.89	4.91	4.81	4.31	3.86	3.42	3.28	3.48
Philippines	3.61	3.59	3.50	3.50	3.60	3.07	2.69	2.55	2.34	2.24
Poland	9.64	9.63	10.09	10.33	8.99	7.50	6.16	4.89	3.85	3.28
Russia	7.37	6.54	5.44	5.46	5.16	5.57	5.56	5.21	4.85	4.60
South Africa	24.68	24.64	24.73	24.56	24.89	25.15	26.54	27.04	26.91	28.47
Thailand	0.62	0.66	0.58	0.21	0.58	0.60	0.69	0.83	0.77	0.72
Turkey	10.66	8.80	8.15	8.73	9.88	10.24	10.84	10.82	10.89	13.67
Ukraine	8.10	7.85	7.53	7.17	9.27	9.14	9.35	9.51	8.80	8.19
Uruguay	7.16	6.31	6.45	6.44	6.55	7.49	7.84	7.89	8.34	9.35

Source: Calculated by author based on the data from World Development Indicators (World Bank).

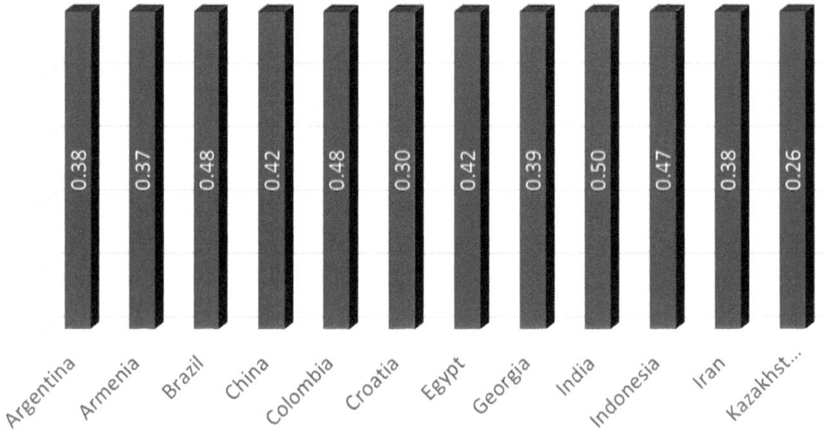

FIGURE 4.7
Gini_1 (2016). *Source*: Created by authors based on the Data from World Development Indicators (World Bank).

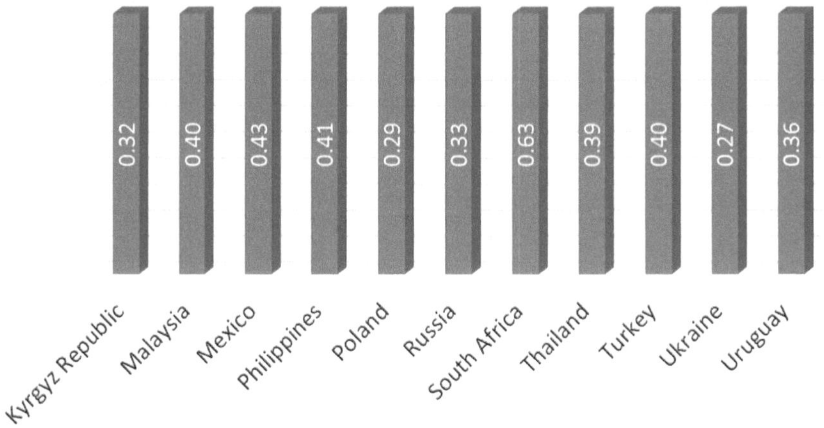

FIGURE 4.8
Gini_2 (2016). *Source*: Created by authors based on the Data from World Development Indicators (World Bank).

of 2016. Similarly, the fact that India is the country with the highest imbalance in income distribution among all developing countries is seen.

2016 Gini values for Kyrgyzstan, Malaysia, Mexico, Philippines, Poland, Russia, South Africa, Thailand, Turkey, Ukraine, and Uruguay are given in figure 4.8. A country with a Gini coefficient of over 0.50 is not seen in the chart. However, there are countries with Gini values below 0.30 such as Ukraine (0.27) and Uruguay (0.29). It is seen that the countries with the lowest income inequality after Kazakhstan are Ukraine and Uruguay third.

In table 4.8, headcount rates for developing countries are given for three different values as $1.90, $3.20, and $5.50 per day. The headcount ratio represents the percentage of the population living with an income of less than $1.90, $3.20, and $5.50 per day at 2011 prices.

In 2004, for the $1.90 per day limit, the poorest country was India, while the least poor country was Ukraine. When we look at the daily limit of $3.20, it is seen that India is the poorest country and Indonesia is the second poorest country. On the other hand, for the $3.20 limit, the developing country with the least poverty is Poland. For $5.50 per day, India and Indonesia are again the top three poorest countries. Poland is also the best among the developing countries, at the $5.50 border.

As seen in table 4.8 data are limited for 2019. Not all developing countries have headcount rates for 2019. South Africa, the Philippines, Malaysia, Iran, Croatia, and China are not included in the table because they do not have data for the period 2004–2019. As can be seen from the table, some of the developing countries excluding these countries, data for 2019 are limited. For $1.90, $3.20, and $5.50 per day, the country with the least poverty in 2019 is Ukraine. In 2019, Colombia is the poorest country for the $1.90 per day limit, while Indonesia is the poorest country for the $3.20 and $5.50 per day limits.

TABLE 4.8
Poverty Headcount Ratio (2011 PPP)

	$1.90 a day		*$3.20 a day*		*$5.50 a day*	
	2004	*2019*	*2004*	*2019*	*2004*	*2019*
Argentina	5.7	1.5	13.9	4.9	29.2	14.4
Armenia	5.5	1.1	29	9.8	68.1	44
Brazil	9.7	4.6	21.4	9.1	40.1	19.6
Colombia	11.2	4.9	26.9	12.7	51.4	29.4
Egypt	5.2	....	35.4	....	77.7	....
Georgia	9.9	3.8	27.8	14.9	58.8	42
India	39.9	..	76.2	....	92.9	..
Indonesia	21	2.9	59.8	20.5	87	52.8
Kazakhstan	1.8	....	14.3	..	48.6	....
Kyrgyz Republic	9.9	0.6	41.2	9.7	74	52.6
Mexico	6	....	15.8	....	37.4	....
Poland	2.1	....	4.5	....	12.7	....
Russia	1	....	5.6	....	21.8	....
Thailand	0.7	0.1	8.7	0.3	33.4	6.2
Turkey	2	0.4	9.7	2.2	27	10.2
Ukraine	0.5	0	4.8	0.2	26.7	2.5
Uruguay	0.8	0.1	5.8	0.5	19.6	3.2

Source: Created by authors based on the Data from World Development Indicators (World Bank).

Analysis of the Relationship between Income Inequality and Economic Growth in Developing Countries

The relationship between economic growth and income inequality for developing countries is analyzed within the framework of Kuznets's inverted-U hypothesis. Kuznets (1955) found that income inequality increases in the early stages of economic growth but decreases in later stages of growth. The validity of this hypothesis put forward in this part of the study has been tested.

Method and Model

In economic studies and analyses, it is argued that time series are problematic in practice due to data time size constraints. Due to the existence of such problems, cross-sectional diversity and heterogeneity and panel data analysis came to the fore. Panel data analysis, which takes into account both time and cross-section, allows the determination of behavioral differences of individuals. The use of panel data analysis solves the multicollinearity with the increase in the number of observations. The lack of retrospective datasets in many of the countries has also increased the orientation to panel data analysis. In terms of cross-section data, if the time series are of equal length, there is a balanced panel, while if the lengths of the time series are not equal, there is an unbalanced panel. Pooled panel datasets include cross-section data and time series simultaneously (Greene, 2003; Wooldridge, 2003; Gujarati, 2004; Hsiao, 2014).

The model established in the study:

$$\text{GINI} = \beta 0 + \beta 1 \ (\text{GDP1})\text{it} + \beta 2(\text{trade})\text{it} + \beta 3(\text{GDP2})\text{it}$$

$$+ \beta 4(\text{unemployment})\text{it} + \beta 5(\text{capital})\text{it} + +u\text{it}$$

i = 1,....15 (Developing Economies) t = 1,...14 (2004–2017).

The analysis is limited to this period and countries, as data from 2004 to 2017 are available for developing countries without interruption. Data were obtained from the WB (DB), SWIID (The Standardized World Income Inequality Database), and UNI-WIDER (United Nations University). Argentina, Brazil, China, Colombia, Croatia, Georgia, India, Indonesia, Malaysia, Mexico, Poland, Thailand, Turkey, Ukraine, Uruguay are countries, the data sets of which are available and included in the analysis. The variables in the model and their explanations are given in table 4.9.

Fixed-effect or random-effect models are used in panel data models, which are assumed to have unit or time effects on the data. Hausman test is used

TABLE 4.9
Variables and Data Descriptions

Type	*Code*	*Explanation*
Dependent Variable	GINI	Gini coefficients
Independent Variables	GDP1	GDP per capita (constant 2010 US$)
	Trade	Trade (% of GDP)
	GDP2	Square of GDP per capita (constant 2010 US$)
	Unemployment	Unemployment, total (% of total labor force)
	Capital	Gross fixed capital formation (% of GDP)

Source: Created by authors.

to determine the model to be used in the analysis. According to the result of the Hausman test, modeled fixed effects or random effects are preferred. The Hausman test, which is used to analyze the differences between the coefficients for each model, reveals the statistical differences. In addition, the existence of the variable variance problem is determined in the models established in panel data analysis with the Wald test. If there is a problem with varying variance, the estimation is made with the resistant error method (Hayes and Cai, 2007; Stock and Watson, 2008; Gujarati, 2004; Ahn and Moon, 2001; Hsiao, 2014).

According to the Hausman test result for the model to be used, it was decided that the fixed-effect models would give more consistent results (Prob > chi2 = 0.000). The Wald test in table 4.10 proves the existence of varying variance in the model. In order to overcome the changing variance problem, the analysis was made with the robust regression model, in which resistant errors were used.

Whether the models established for the analysis included autocorrelation was investigated with the GDW (Bhargava et al., 1982) and LBI (Baltagi and Wu, 1999) Tests, which are the improved versions of the Durbin-Watson Test. If autocorrelation and varying variance are detected in the model, the

TABLE 4.10
Wald chi2 and Durbin-Watson and Baltagi-WuTest

Wald chi2 Test	
chi2	Prob>chi2
1433.20	0.000
Ho: sigma(i)^2 = sigma^2 for all i	
Durbin-Watson And Baltagi-WuTest	
Durbin-Watson	Baltagi-Wu(LBI)
0.214	0.522
Basic threshold value "2"	

Source: Created by authors.

TABLE 4.11
Pesaran CD, Friedman, and Frees Tests

Pesaran CD Test	Friedman Test	Frees Test
1.202, Pr = 0.229	6.032, Pr = 0.965	4.646
Critical values from Frees's Q distribution		
alpha = 0.10 :0.1841	alpha = 0.05 : 0.2431	alpha = 0.01 : 0.3603

Source: Created by authors.

cluster standard errors method is used (Wooldridge, 2003; Williams, 2000; Arellano, 1987; Rogers, 1993).

The existence of a correlation between units in terms of error terms limits the effectiveness of cross-section data. The correlation between units can be determined by using Pesaran, Friedman, and Frees tests. If the existence of problems such as interunit correlation and varying variance is determined as a result of the tests, the Driscoll-Kraay (1998) method is used in the calculation of the model (Hoyos and Sarafidis, 2006; Driscoll and Kraay, 1995, 1998).

When we look at the results of the Durbin-Watson and Baltagi-Wu tests in table 4.10, it is seen that there is an autocorrelation problem in the established model. Autocorrelation was solved by reestimating the model with the cluster standard errors method.

Pesaran CD, Friedman, and Frees tests are used to determine the correlation between units. The test results in table 4.11 indicate the existence of a correlation between error terms. By reanalyzing the model with the Driscoll-Kraay method, the correlation problem between units was solved.

Findings

Table 4.12 shows the estimation results of the income inequality economic growth relationship for developing countries by three different methods. As a result of autocorrelation, varying variance, and correlation between units in the model, three different estimations were made: robust regression, clustered standard errors (cluster), and Driscoll-Kraay method. When we look at the results of all models, it is seen that they have similar results for Kuznets's inverted-U hypothesis, except for the control variables, and it is statistically significant.

The analysis results of the models show that developing countries are experiencing a process that supports Kuznets's inverted-U hypothesis. In this case, depending on the basic hypothesis, it was determined that income inequality increased in the first stage of economic development but decreased in later stages. This result is consistent with many empirical studies in the literature. Unemployment, which is included in the model as a control variable, is statistically significant according to the results of all three models. Other

TABLE 4.12
Model Estimations

	Robust	*Cluster*	*DK*
Variables	*Model 1*	*Model 2*	*Model 3*
ln_gdp1	0.052**	0.052**	0.052***
	[0.029]	[0.029]	[0.008]
ln_trade	0.055	0.055	0.055***
	[0.042]	[0.042]	[0.010]
ln_gdp2	−0.000***	−0.000***	−0.000***
	[0.000]	[0.000]	[0.000]
ln_unemplyment	0.040**	0.040**	0.040***
	[0.019]	[0.019]	[0.006]
ln_capital	0.062	0.062	0.062***
	[0.052]	[0.052]	[0.016]
Constant	−0.782***	−0.782***	−0.782***
	[0.173]	[0.173]	[0.059]
Observations	210	210	210
F	4.14	4.14	5.13
Prob > F	0.0012	0.0012	0.000
R-squared	0.454	0.454	
Number of countrycode	15	15	
rho	0.982	0.982	
sigma	0.0852	0.0852	
sigma_e	0.0115	0.0115	
r2_w	0.454	0.454	0.454
r2_between	0.00266	0.00266	
r2_overall	0.000315	0.000315	
Corr	−0.228	−0.228	
Lag			2

*** $p < 0.01$, ** $p < 0.05$, * $p < 0.1$
Source: Created by authors.

control variables, trade, and fixed capital ratio are statistically significant only in the analysis made with the Driscoll-Kraay method.

Conclusion and Evaluation

In this study, when some macroeconomic indicators such as per capita income, economic growth, and trade are taken into account, countries that differ from other countries and are classified as developing countries are examined. First, the conceptual framework of economic growth and income inequality, which is the main subject of the study, was explained. After the conceptual framework has been introduced, empirical studies on economic growth and income inequality were briefly presented.

Then, data per capita income, savings, inflation, health expenditures, labor force participation rate, population growth rate, trade rate, unemployment rate, and head number of almost all developing countries, with data provided by the WB, were presented in graphs or tables. After reflecting on the situation of developing countries regarding basic macroeconomic indicators, the application part of our study was started. In the application part, the validity of Kuznets's inverted-U hypothesis was investigated by panel data analysis for developing countries through the established model.

The findings of most of the empirical literature support Kuznets's inverted-U hypothesis in the relationship between income inequality and economic growth. However, as a result of some studies, Kuznets's hypothesis was either not supported or partially valid. Matyas et al. (1998), in their analysis for developed and developing countries, found that Kuznets's inverted-U hypothesis was not valid. Similarly, Anand and Kanbur (1993) concluded that Kuznets's inverted-U hypothesis is not valid in their study covering the 1953–1966 period. Clarke (1995), on the other hand, obtained results similar to Anand and Kanbur and stated that the size of the relationship formed within the framework of Kuznets's inverted-U hypothesis is limited. Deininger and Squire (1997) concluded that the result obtained from the analysis for a large group of countries is that Kuznets's inverted-U hypothesis is not valid for all countries. Malinen (2012) found that Kuznets's inverted-U hypothesis is valid for middle- and high-income countries but not for low-income countries. Desbordes and Verardi (2012) found that the relationship between economic growth and income inequality is in line with Kuznets's assumption, but the relationship is only one-way. Oczki et al. (2017) found that Kuznets's assumption is not fully valid in European Union countries, and the economic growth income inequality relationship is not inverted-U-shaped but U-shaped. A similar relationship, namely the U-shaped relationship between economic growth and income inequality, was determined by the analysis results for Turkey (Tokatlıoğlu and Atan, 2007; Ak and Altıntaş, 2016).

The empirical findings of our study, which examines the relationship between economic growth and income inequality with current data for developing countries, show that Kuznets's inverted-U hypothesis is valid. In developing countries, it was found that while income inequality increased in the first periods of the economic growth predicted in the hypothesis, inequality decreased in the following growth periods. While unemployment, one of the control variables in the study, is statistically significant for all three models, fixed capital and trade variables are statistically significant only according to the result of the third model. According to the analysis results, the increase in unemployment has an increasing effect on income inequality. In other words, as a result of an increase in unemployment, there is also an increase in income inequality.

Income inequality emerges quickly when the income is not distributed unequally to the individuals living in the society, but it takes a long time to resolve. Income inequality is not only an economic result but also affects the social and cultural areas of the society. If the individuals in the society cannot earn equal income, they will not be able to spend at the same rate and will not be able to access the same goods or services. While the high-income group tends to consume luxury and basic consumer goods, the groups that receive lesser income will make an effort for compulsory subsistence or living.

As a result, although income inequality has emerged in different ways and different dimensions in all societies, its effects are similar. Of course, the unique circumstances of countries are one of the main reasons for this difference. However, we are faced with the fact that the solution of the problem will reduce the relative living standards differences between individuals and will also be felt in all areas of social life.

References

Ahn, Seung, Chan; Moon, Hyungsik, Roger. 2001. "Large-N and Large-T Properties of Panel Data Estimators and the Hausman Test." *Centre for Research in Economic Development and International Trade, University of Nottingham CREDIT Research Paper, 02-28.*

Ak, Mehmet, Zeki; Altıntaş, Nurullah. 2016. "The Relationship Between Income Inequality and Economic Growth in Turkey in the Context of Kuznets' Inverted U Curve: 1986–2012." *Journal of Finance Studies*, 2(3), 93–102.

Akalin, Güray; Özbek, Rabia, İnci; Çiftçi, İsmail. 2018. "The Nexus Between Income Distribution and Economıc Growth in Turkey: An ARDL Bounds Testing Approach." *Journal of Kastamonu University Faculty of Economics and Administrative Sciences*, 20(4), 59–76.

Akıncı, Gönül, Yüce; Akıncı, Merter. 2016. "On the Mechanics of Economic Growth, Financial Development and Income Inequality in the Context of Inverted-U Hypothesis." *Financial, Political and Economic Comments*, 53(622), 61.

Anand, Sudhir; Kanbur, S. R. 1993. "The Kuznets Process and the Inequality-Development Relationship." *Journal of Development Economics*, 40(1), 25–52.

Arellano, Manuel. 1987. "Computing Robust Standard Errors for Within-Groups Estimators." *Oxford Bulletin of Economics and Statistics*, 49(4), 431–434.

Atkinson, Anthony, B.; Bourguignon, François. 2014. *Handbook of Income Distribution*. Vol. 2. Elsevier.

Baltagi, Badi, H.; Ping, X. Wu. 1999. "Unequally Spaced Panel Data Regressions With AR (1) Disturbances." *Econometric Theory*, 15, 814–823.

Barro, Rovert, J. 2000. "Inequality and Growth in a Panel of Countries." *Journal of Economic Growth*, 5(1), 5–32.

Bhargava, Alok; Franzini, Luisa; Narendranathan, Wiji. 1982. "Serial Correlation and the Fixed Effects Model." *The Review of Economic Studies*, 49(4), 533–549.

Bleaney, Michael; Nishiyama, Akira. 2002. "Economic Growth and Income Inequality." *No. 02/28. CREDIT Research Paper.*

Brian, Keeley. 2015. *OECD Insights Income Inequality the Gap Between Rich and Poor: The Gap Between Rich and Poor.* Paris: OECD Publishing.

Chen, Been, Lenon. 2003. "An Inverted-U Relationship Between Inequality and Long-Run Growth." *Economics Letters*, 78(2), 205–212.

Clarke, George, R. G.1995. "More Evidence on Income Distribution and Growth." *Journal of Development Economics*, 47(2), 403–427.

DataHelpdeskWorldBank.Org. https://databank.worldbank.org/source/world-development-indicators# (Retrieved, 03.05.2021).

DataHelpdesk.WorldBank.Org. https://datahelpdesk.worldbank.org/knowledgebase/articles/906519 -world-bank-country-and-lending-groups (Retrieved, 03.05.2021).

De Hoyos, Rafael, E.; Sarafidis, Vasilis. 2006. "Testing for Crosssectional Dependence in Panel Data Models." *The Stata Journal*, 6(4), 482–496.

Deininger, Klaus; Squire, Lyn. 1997. "Economic Growth and Income Inequality: Reexamining The Links." *Finance & Development, International Monetary Fund*, 34(1), 38–41.

Desbordes, Rodolphe; Verardi, Vincenzo. 2012. "Refitting the Kuznets Curve." *Economics Letters*, 116(2), 258–261.

Deutsch, Joseph; Silber, Jacques. 2004. "Measuring the Impact of Various Income Sources on the Link Between Inequality and Development: Implications for the Kuznets Curve." *Review of Development Economics*, 8(1), 110–127.

Driscoll, John, Christopher; Kraay, Aart. 1995. "*Spatial Correlations in Panel Data.*" The World Bank Policy Research Department. Policy Research Working Paper, No: 1553.

Driscoll, John, Christopher; Kraay, Aart. 1998. "Consistent Covariance Matrix Estimation With Spatially Dependent Data." *Review of Economics and Statistics*, 80, 549–560.

Gallet, Craig, A.; Gallet, Rachel, M. 2004. "US Growth and Income Inequality: Evidence of Racial Differences." *The Social Science Journal*, 41(1), 43–51.

Greene, William, H. 2003. *Econometric Analysis.* India: Pearson Education.

Gujarati, Damodar, N. 2004. *Basic Econometrics.* 4th edn. New York: The Mcgraw-Hill Companies.

Haughton, Jonathan; Khandker, Shahidur, R. 2009. *Handbook on Poverty and Inequality.* USA: World Bank Publications.

Hayes, Andrew, F.; Li, Cai. 2007. "Using Heteroskedasticityconsistent Standard Error Estimators in OLS Regression: An Introduction and Software Implementation." *Behavior Research Methods*, 3(4), 709–722.

Hsiao, Cheng. 2014. *Analysis of Panel Data.* No. 54. Cambridge: Cambridge University Press.

Huang Ho-Chuan River. 2004. "A Flexible Nonlinear Inference to the Kuznets Hypothesis." *Economics Letters*, 84(2), 289–296.

Jalil, Abdul. 2012. "Modeling Income Inequality and Openness in the Framework of Kuznets Curve: New Evidence from China." *Economic Modelling*, 29(2), 309–315.

Khasru, Syed, Munir; Jalil, Mohammad, Muaz. 2004. "Revisiting Kuznets Hypothesis: An Analysis With Time Series and Panel Data." *The Bangladesh Development Studies*, 30, 89–112.

Kuştepeli, Yeşim. 2006. "Income Inequality, Growth, and the Enlargement of the European Union." *Emerging Markets Finance and Trade*, 42(6), 77–88.

Kuznets, Simon. 1946. *National Product Since 1869*. New York: National Bureau of Economic Research.

Kuznets, Simon. 1955. "Economic Growth and Income Inequality." *The American Economic Review*, 45, 1–28.

List, John A.; Gallet, Craig, A. 1999. "The Kuznets Curve: What Happens After the Inverted-U?" *Review of Development Economics*, 3(2), 200–206.

Malinen, Tuomas. 2012. "Estimating the Long-Run Relationship Between Income Inequality and Economic Development." *Empirical Economics*, 42(1), 209–233.

Matyas, Laszlo; Konya, Laszlo; Macquarie, Lachlan. 1998. "The Kuznets U-Curve Hypothesis: Some Panel Data Evidence." *Applied Economics Letters*, 5(11), 693–697.

Mckay, Andrew. 2002. *Defining and Measuring Inequality*. Briefing Paper No (1). Washington: The World Bank.

Mollick, André, Varella. 2012. "Income Inequality in The US: The Kuznets Hypothesis Revisited." *Economic Systems*, 36(1), 127–144.

Nel, Philip. 2003. "Income Inequality, Economic Growth and Political Instability in Sub-Saharan Africa." *The Journal of Modern African Studies*, 41(4), 611–639.

Oczki, Jarosław; Muszynska, Joanna; Wedrowska, Ewa. 2017. "Kuznets Hypothesis of Income Inequality: Empirical Evidence From EU." *Nicolaus Copernicus University Repository RUM@K*, 4909, 643–651.

Odekon, Mehmet. 2006. *Encyclopedia of World Poverty*. Vol. 1. California: Sage Publication.

Paukert, Felix. 1973. "Income Distribution at Different Levels of Development: A Survey of Evidence." *International Labor Review*, 108, 97–125.

Ram, Rati. 1989. "Level of Development and Income Inequality: An Extension of Kuznets-Hypothesis to the World Economy." *Kyklos*, 42(1), 73–88.

Ram, Rati. 1997. "Level of Economic Development and Income Inequality: Evidence From the Postwar Developed World." *Southern Economic Journal*, 64, 576–583.

Robinson, Sherman. 1976. "A Note on the U Hypothesis Relating Income Inequality and Economic Development." *American Economic Review*, 66, 437–440.

Rogers, William, H. 1993. "Regression Standard Errors in Clustered Samples." *Stata Technical Bulletin*, 13(3), 19–23.

Rubin, Amir; Segal, Dan. 2015. "The Effects of Economic Growth on Income Inequality in the US." *Journal of Macroeconomics*, 45, 258–273.

Rycroft, Robert, S. 2014. *The Economics of Inequality, Discrimination, Poverty, and Mobility*. New York: Routledge.

Samy, Yiagadeesen. 2014. "Globalization, Income Inequality and Deindustrialization: The Case of South Korea." *Korea Economic Institute of America, (KEI) Academic Paper Series, 1–17.*

Sen, Amartya, Kumar. 1997. *On Economic Inequality*. New York: Oxford University Press Catalogue.

Şengür, Mehmet. 2020. "The Relationships Between Income Inequality and Economic Growth: Panel Data Analysis on Transition Economies." *Eskişehir Osmangazi University Journal of Economics and Administrative Sciences*, 15(1), 331–346.

Shahbaz, Muhammad. 2010. "Income Inequality-Economic Growth and Non-Linearity: A Case of Pakistan." *International Journal of Social Economics*, 37(8), 613–636.

Solt, Frederick. 2020. "Measuring Income Inequality Across Countries and Over Time: The Standardized World Income Inequality Database." *Social Science Quarterly*. SWIID Version 9.1.

Stock, James, H.; Watson, Mark, W. 2008. "Heteroskedasticity-Robust Standard Errors for Fixed Effects Panel Data Regression." *Econometrica*, 76 (1), 155–174.

Thornton, John. 2001. "The Kuznets Inverted-U Hypothesis: Panel Data Evidence From 96 Countries." *Applied Economics Letters*, 8(1), 15–16.

Tokatlıoğlu, İbrahim; Atan, Murat. 2007. "Inter-Regional Differences in Terms of Development and Income Inequality in Turkey: Is Kuznets Inverse-U Curve Valid?" *Ekonomik Yaklasim*, 18(65), 25–58.

Topuz, Seher, Gülşah; Dağdemir, Özcan. 2016. "The Relationship Between Economic Growth and Income Inequality: The Validity of Kuznets Inverted-U Hypothesis." *Eskişehir Osmangazi University Journal of Economics and Administrative Sciences*, 11(3), 115–130.

Williams, Rick, L. 2000. "A Note on Robust Variance Estimation for Cluster-Correlated Data." *Biometrics*, 56, 645–646.

Wooldridge, Jeffrey, M. 2003. "Cluster-Sample Methods in Applied Econometrics." *American Economic Review*, 93(2), 133–138.

Zang, Hyoungsoo. 1998. "The Stability of the Kuznets Curve: Some Further Evidence." *Applied Economics Letters*, 5(3), 131–133.

5

The Relationship between the Exchange Rate, Inflation, and Unemployment in Turkey, 2014–2021

Osman Bahadır SİNAN

Introduction[1]

The aim of this study is to examine the relationship between inflation rate, real effective exchange rate, and unemployment rate for Turkey, using the ARDL test for the period January 2014 to September 2021. The work plan consists of four parts. First of all, the interaction between real effective exchange rate unemployment rate and inflation rates is examined and information about the interaction is given. In the second part, the literature review on the subject is summarized. In the third part, econometric analysis is done, and in the last part, the results and evaluations are included.

After the neoliberal policies were implemented after 1980, the economy was opened to foreign markets, and with this realization, exchange rate convertibility was started and the free exchange rate regime was started to be implemented. Therefore, since the growth model turned into export-based growth, there were deteriorations in income distribution, and unemployment rates increased due to the increase in population. The impact of the worldwide COVID-19 crisis at the end of 2019, as well as the expansionary monetary policies implemented all over the world, negatively affected the inflation rate and unemployment rate.

Relationship between the Reel Effective Exchange Rate, Inflation, and Unemployment Rate

The most well-known problem posed by inflation is the erosion of purchasing power. As inflation occurs and commonly purchased household items become more expensive, a single currency loses value as it buys fewer goods and services. This affects the cost of living for individuals who may purchase fewer items later on. Inflation also creates uncertainty, and savings are adversely affected by this uncertainty. Inflation in Turkey reached 36.8 at the end of 2021. Some of this inflation is demand-driven and is fed by sources such as money supply growth and population growth. Again, due to the increase in the exchange rate, there is also an increase in input prices, and there is also inflation due to the increase in cost. In recent years, it has been observed that there has been an increase in inflation in our country depending on the exchange rate.

After the neoliberal policies were implemented after 1980, the economy was opened to foreign markets, and with this realization, the exchange rate was converted into convertibility and the free exchange rate regime began to be implemented. Therefore, since the growth model has turned into export-led growth, exchange rate practices have gained great importance for Turkey and developing countries. With the effect of the crises experienced in the 2000s, the free exchange rate regime, in which the interventions of the CBRT were limited, was adopted. Similarly, with the 2000s, a completely export-based growth model began to emerge.

With the effect of the applied free exchange rate policy, the foreign trade volume has increased continuously, and the increasing foreign trade volume has created interim financial import dependency (Hepaktan, 2008:9). It is seen that the exchange rate has an effect on inflation in Turkey. In the export-led growth model, imports of intermediate goods and uncertainty about inflation create cost inflation by increasing prices, and in this case, it directly affects inflation. Again, there are deteriorations in income distribution during inflation periods, and middle-income and lower-income groups are affected by this situation. Again, increasing population and external migration increase the unemployment rate, and this increase negatively affects income distribution. Increasing unemployment has the same effect on inflation due to idle capacity and other reasons. Again, since the increase in inflation will increase the cost of the companies, the companies will lay off workers by reducing their labor costs as the first cost reduction. In this case, it is seen that inflation will directly affect unemployment in the same direction. Again, due to the increasing uncertainty in inflation periods, it is seen that enterprises avoid making new investments, and this situation negatively affects the recruitment of new labor force and has negative effects on unemployment. Since it is not possible for the unemployed individuals to participate in the production process, they will become impoverished and the income distribution in the country will be adversely affected.

İn order to improve the income distribution, it is necessary to adopt policies that increase employment and develop social policies for those with low-income distribution. In particular, the development of globalization and the effect of external migration also negatively affect the unemployment rate of the country's population. Again, hot money inflows and outflows that emerged with globalization cause fluctuations in the exchange rate, causing fluctuations and increases in inflation.

Again, in the crises experienced due to capital movements, as a result of the policies implemented due to IMF agreements in the past, the wages of the wage earners were suppressed and the income distribution was negatively affected (Şenkal, 2005). Inflation also seems to accelerate this deterioration in this process. In the current period, fluctuations in exchange rates due to the false estimation perception in the official inflation forecast and the interest policy applied have negative effects on inflation. Again, the perception of the society that wage increases are made according to official inflation rates and that the actual inflation is at higher levels also indicates that the deterioration in income distribution will increase in the coming periods.

Literature Review

The summary of studies on the relationship between exchange rate, unemployment, and inflation in the literature is as follows.

Data—Econometric Methods and Findings

In this analysis, in which the relationship between inflation rate (İNF), real effective exchange rate (EFRATE), and unemployment rate (UNEMP) is investigated, monthly data for the period January 2011 to September 2021 are used. The data were obtained from the Central Bank of the Republic of Turkey Electronic Data Distribution System (EVDS).

The econometric model made is shown in the following figure:

İNF= B0+B1UNEMP+B2EFRATE+ut
EFRATE: Reel Effective Exchange Rates
UNEMP: Unemployment Rates
INF: İnflation Rates

In order to analyze the relationships between the variables, it is first necessary to investigate whether the series is stationary. The stationarity of the time series was investigated with the help of the extended Dickey Fuller Test (ADF), the Philips-Perron (1988) unit root test, and the KPSS test developed by Kwiatkowski, Philips, Schmidt, and Shin (1992). Table 5.1 shows the test results for the INF data.

Table 5.2 shows the ADF, PP, and KPSS test results of the inflation data. According to the table, ADF in the level value according to the İNF series KPSS test results is not stationary when compared to the critical values of the 1%, 5%, and 10% significance levels according to the PP test results. When first-order differences are taken, INF series ADF becomes stationary when compared with critical values at 1%, 5%, and 10% significance levels according to the PP test results.

Table 5.3 shows the ADF, PP, and KPSS test results of the UNEMP data. According to the table, the level value according to the results of the UNEMP series ADF and KPSS tests is not stationary when compared to the critical values of the 1%, 5%, and 10% significance levels according to the PP test results. When first-order differences are taken, according to all test results, the significance levels of 1%, 5%, and 10% become stationary when compared with the critical values.

Table 5.4 shows the ADF, PP, and KPSS test results of the EFRATE data. According to the table, the level value according to the results of the EFRATE series ADF and PP is not stationary when compared with the critical values of the 1%, 5%, and 10% significance levels according to the KPSS test results. When first-order differences are taken, according to all test results, the significance levels of 1%, 5%, and 10% become stationary when compared with the critical values.

Estimating the ARDL Test Model

Pesaran (2001) found that the ARDL test is frequently used to determine the relationship between nonstationary series at the same degree. ARDL test was used in the analysis:

$$\dot{I}NF = B0 + B1UNEMP + B2EFRATE + u \quad (1)$$

TABLE 5.1
Literature Review

Author	*Country*	*Period*	*Variables*	*Method*	*Results*
Mohanty, Klau (2001)	13 Country	1995.2–2000.4	İnflation, import prices, exchange rates	VAR, Granger Causality	Exchange rate and inflation relationship is positive and strong.
Uysal, Erdoğan (2003)	Turkey	1980–2002	İnflation, unemployment rates	Regressive analysis Granger Causality	There is a negative relationship between inflation and unemployment rate.
Bilgin (2004)	Turkey	1990–2004	Unemployment, exchange rate, inflation	Regressive analysis	There is a positive and strong relationship between the Real Exchange Rate and unemployment.
Saatçioğlu (2005)	Turkey	1998.1–2005.5	Exchange rate, domestic loans, bond interest rates, wages, inflation	VAR, Johansen cointegration	There is a long-run relationship between exchange rate and inflation.
Girginer, Yenilmez (2005)	Turkey	1982–2002	Inflation, unemployment, exchange rate oil price, wages, budget deficit	Ridge Regressive analysis	Exchange rate affects inflation the most.
Gül, Ekinci (2006)	Turkey	1984–2003	Inflation, exchange rate	Johansen Cointegration, Granger Causality	There is a long-term relationship. There is a causal relationship from exchange rate to inflation.
Karagöz, Ergün (2010),	Turkey	1987–2010	Inflation, real exchange rate, production level, money supply, forward interest rates	ARDL	The real exchange rate has a significant impact on inflation.
Djivre, Ribon (2012)	Israel	1990–1999	Inflation, exchange rate, unemployment	SVAR	Tighter monetary policy lowers inflation and increases unemployment.
Selim , Güven (2014)	Turkey	1990–2012	Inflation, exchange rate, unemployment	VAR, Johansen cointegration, Granger causality	Real effective exchange rate affects CPI.

(continued)

TABLE 5.1
(Continued)

Author	*Country*	*Period*	*Variables*	*Method*	*Results*
Günaydın , Çetin (2015)	Turkey	1988–2013	Inflation, Youth Unemployment exchange rate, trade openness, real income, foreign direct investment	ARDL, Granger Causality	There is a causal relationship from inflation to youth unemployment.
İslam, Ghani, Manickam (2017)	Malaysia	1980–2014	Inflation, exchange rate, unemployment, money supply	Regressive analysis	There is a negative relationship between inflation and exchange rate and between inflation and unemployment rate.
Korkmaz (2017)	Turkey	1998–2015	Inflation, exchange rate, unemployment, GDP, money supply, interest rate	Correlation Matrix	Inflation rates are affected by the real exchange rate in the short run.
Hossain, Mitra(2017)	USA	1978–2014	Inflation, exchange rate, unemployment, trade openness, money supply, interest rate, economic growth	Johansen, Engle Granger, Granger causality	The Philips curve hypothesis is not valid, and the exchange rate and unemployment have not a statistically significant effect on inflation.
Akçan (2018)	Turkey	2000.1–2015.3	Inflation, exchange rate, unemployment, export, import	İmpact response, Variance analysis	The best exchange rate explains the unemployment rate. In addition, there is a positive relationship between unemployment rate and inflation.
Kaygısız (2018)	Turkey	2002.1–20164	Inflation, exchange rate, oil price, industrial production, index	VAR analysis	Exchange rate affects inflation at the same rate in the short and long run.

Günay, Balkaya (2019)	Turkey	2005.1–2016.3	Inflation, exchange rate, unemployment labor cost, income level	ARDL	There is a positive relationship between real effective exchange rate and labor cost and unemployment.
Geerof (2020)	USA, United Kingdom, OECD Countries	1780–2016	Inflation, exchange rate, unemployment	Regressive analysis	The negative relationship between inflation and unemployment, which is stated in the Philips curve, is valid in the fixed exchange rate system, and there is a relationship between inflation and the real exchange rate, which measures competitiveness, in flexible exchange rate systems.
Makdum (2021)	Turkey	2005.1–2019.10	Inflation, exchange rate, unemployment, export, import	ARDL	There is a cointegration relationship. While there is a positive relationship between exchange rate and inflation in the long run, there is a negative relationship between exchange rate and unemployment.

Source: Created by the authors.

TABLE 5.2
(INF) ADF-PP-KPSS Test Results

Variable	*Level Values*			*(−1) Level Values*		
(SIC)	*ADF*	*PP*	*KPSS*	*ADF*	*PP*	*KPSS*
t statistics	0,02777*	0,020613	0.309907***(4)(LM-stat	−5.610261	−7.026109*	0.044940***(4)(LM-stat
Probability	0,993**	0.996**		0.0001	0.0000**	
Critic Values						
1%	−4.0657002	−4.0657002	0.21600	−4.0657002	−4.0657002	0.21600
5%	−3.461.686	−3.461.686	0.146000	−3.461.686	−3.461.686	0.146000
10%	−3.157.121	−3.157.121	0.119000	−3.157.121	−3.157.121	0.119000

H0: The variable CA contains a unit root.
* Appropriate delay lengths. Schwartz Information Criterion in ADF test, Newey-West bandwidth using Barlett kernel in PP and KPSS tests.
** Since the probability value is less than 0.05, the H0 hypothesis is rejected, the series is stationary.
*** Since the calculated LM statistical value is less than the critical value at the 1% level, the H0 hypothesis is rejected, the series is stationary.
Source: Created by the authors.

TABLE 5.3
UNEMP Variable ADF-PP-KPSS Test Results

Variable	*Level Values*			*(−1) Level Values*
(SIC)	*ADF*	*PP*	*KPSS*	*PP*
t Statictics	−3.924113*	−3.158.443	0.075177***(4)(LM-stat	−7.723422*
Probality	0.0148**	0.0994**		0.0000**
Critical Values				
1%	−4.0657002	−4.0657002	0.216000	−4.0657002
5%	−3.461.686	−3.461.686	0.146000	−3.461.686
10%	−3.157.121	−3.157.121	0.119000	−3.157.121

Source: Created by the authors.

TABLE 5.4
EFRATE Variables ADF-PP-KPSS Test Results

Variable	*Level Values*			*(−1) Level Values*
(SIC)	*ADF*	*PP*	*KPSS*	*PP*
t Statistics	−4,348597*	−3.580.321	0.123175***(4)(LM-stat	0.6576
Probality	0.0042**	0.0371**		
Critical Values				
1%	−4.0657002	−4.0657002	0.216000	−4.0657002
5%	−3.461.686	−3.461.686	0.146000	−3.461.686
10%	−3.157.121	−3.157.121	0.119000	−3.157.121

Source: Created by the authors.

$$\Delta \dot{\text{I}}\text{NFt} = c0 + \sum c1i\, m\, i = 1\Delta \dot{\text{I}}\text{NFt} - \text{i} + \sum c2i\Delta\, n\, i = 0\,\text{UNEMP}t - i$$
$$+ + \sum c3i\Delta\, n\, i = 0\ \text{EFRATE}\ t - i + \delta\ \dot{\text{I}}\text{NF}t - 1 + \delta 2\text{UNEMP}t - 1 \quad (2)$$
$$+ \delta 2\ \text{EFRATE}\ t - 1 + \varepsilon$$

In order to make the econometric estimation, equation (1) is first estimated and then a long-term relationship is investigated. The Wald test helps in this regard. The following hypotheses are established according to the Wald test:

$$\text{H0} : \delta 1 = \delta 2 = 0, \text{H1} : \delta 1 \neq \delta 2 \neq 0 \quad (3)$$

The F value found as a result of the estimation is compared with the values obtained according to the analysis results developed by Pesaran and Smith (2001).

In the model, long-term coefficients are estimated after the cointegration status is determined. In making this estimation, the ARDL (m,n) model specified in equation (4) should be used:

$$\dot{\text{I}}\text{NF}t = c0 + \sum m\, i = 1c1i\dot{\text{I}}\text{NF}\,t - i + \sum c2i\text{UNEMP} - i$$
$$+ + \sum c3i\text{EFRATE}t - i + \varepsilon\, t \quad (4)$$

After the values are determined with the help of ARDL (m,n) model, there is a need to test the suitability of the model by performing descriptive tests of the model. An error correction model based on ARDL should be established, and it should be investigated whether the error model works. This is done with the help of equation (5):

$$\Delta \dot{\text{I}}\text{NF}t = c0 + c1ECMt - 1 + \sum c2\text{i}\, m\, i = 1\Delta \dot{\text{I}}\text{NF}t - i$$
$$+ \sum c3i\Delta\text{UNEMP}t - i + i + \sum c4i\Delta\text{EFRATE}t - i + \varepsilon\, t$$

In this context, the ARDL test steps are followed for the following equation and the test results are given here. (5)

$$\dot{\text{I}}\text{NF} = \text{B0} + \text{B1UNEMP} + \text{B2EFRATE} + \text{u} \quad (5)$$

In the ARDL test, the appropriate lag length was determined as 4 by the Eviews 10 program, and the ARDL (4,4,2,3) model was selected as the most

TABLE 5.5
Boundary Test Results

k (Number of Independent variables)	*F Statistics*	
1	6.446711*	
	Lower Limit	Upper Limit
%5	2.79	3.67

*% 5 refers to the levels of significance
Source: Created by the authors.

suitable model by using test values such as AIC, SIC, and HQ. In order for the CUSUM SQ test to be significant, a dummy variable was added to the model.

Following the abovementioned steps, the F test was performed to determine the cointegration relationship. The calculated F statistics values are greater than the upper bound data at the 5% significance level. Therefore, there is cointegration between the series. Table 5.5 shows the analysis of the relevant limit test.

After the results of the bounds test, the long- and short-term coefficients of the variables should be estimated. The short- and long-term coefficient estimates for the ARDL (9,9,9,9) model using a maximum of 9 lags and AIC are given in table 5.6. Since the CUSUM 2 graphic (between 2017.2-2018.9) does not meet the necessary conditions in the model, a dummy variable has been added.

Descriptive tests were carried out to demonstrate that the selected ARDL (9,9,9,9) model is suitable and stable. According to the test results, it is seen that there is no autocorrelation in the ARDL (9,9,9,9) model, there is no changing variance problem, and the error terms are normally distributed.

Among the variables, the long-term coefficients of the ARDL (9,9,9,9) model are shown in table 5.7.

As seen in table 5.7, the test values of the long-term coefficients of the ARDL (9,9,9,9) model are also significant. The short-run coefficients were estimated by establishing an error correction model derived from the ARDL (9,9,9,9) model.

ERROR (−1) is the error correction term. If the coefficient of this term takes a value between 0 and −1 and the probability value is significant, the error correction model will work.

According to the results in table 5.8, the error term is negative and between 0 and −1. Thus, 2.9% of the short-term deviations are corrected in the next period, and it is seen that the long-term balance is reached quickly.

The CUSUM and CUSUMSQ graphs made to ensure the stability of the long-term coefficients of ARDL (9,9,9,9) are also shown in figures 5.1 and 5.2. According to the graph, it is seen that the stability condition is met and there is no structural break.

TABLE 5.6
ARDL (9,9,9,9) Model Test Results

Variables	*Coefficient*	*Std. Error*	*t-values*	*Probability*
C	93.35082	22.79374	4.095458	0.0002
INF (−1)*	−0.029803	0.023420	−1.272575	0.2099
EFRATE (−1)	−0.588416	0.149050	−3.947763	0.0003
UNEMP (−1)	−2.296866	0.547743	−4.193325	0.0001
KUKLA (−1)	−3.437999	1.261883	−2.724500	0.0092
D (İNF −1)	0.305973	0.146364	2.090485	0.0424
D (İNF −2)	−0.400414	0.144550	−2.770069	0.0082
D (İNF −3)	0.409453	0.153900	2.660516	0.0108
D (İNF −4)	−0.549858	0.157548	−3.490098	0.0011
D (İNF −5)	0.277987	0.153701	1.808616	0.0773
D (İNF −6)	−0.321431	0.138796	−2.315854	0.0253
D (İNF −7)	0.055354	0.135860	0.407435	0.6857
D (İNF −8)	−0.198822	0.123166	−1.614261	0.1136
D (EFRATE)	−0.346980	0.131928	−2.630080	0.0117
D (EFRATE −1)	−0.024620	0.181819	−0.135407	0.8929
D (EFRATE −2)	0.253155	0.172455	1.467950	0.1492
D (EFRATE −3)	0.425586	0.179870	2.366069	0.0224
D (EFRATE −4)	0.196338	0.165531	1.186111	0.2419
D (EFRATE −5)	0.135239	0.162028	0.834661	0.4084
D (EFRATE −6)	0.379239	0.154693	2.451563	0.0183
D (EFRATE −7)	−0.133323	0.153550	−0.868272	0.3900
D (EFRATE −8)	0.276166	0.151148	1.827128	0.0745
D (UNEMP)	0.142327	0.519945	0.273734	0.7856
D (UNEMP −1)	2.127693	0.646789	3.289625	0.0020
D (UNEMP −2)	1.659719	0.636695	2.606772	0.0124
D (UNEMP −3)	1.820953	0.677651	2.687154	0.0101
D (UNEMP −4)	2.369290	0.674034	3.515090	0.0010
D (UNEMP −5)	1.022793	0.695586	1.470406	0.1486
D (UNEMP −6)	1.061765	0.611368	1.736705	0.0894
D (UNEMP −7)	0.550516	0.573415	0.960066	0.3423
D (UNEMP −8)	1.023897	0.591108	1.732167	0.0902
D (DUMMY)	−0.356535	1.928143	−0.184911	0.8541
D (DUMMY −1)	7.205637	2.328720	3.094248	0.0034
D (DUMMY −2)	7.452765	2.376557	3.135950	0.0031
D (DUMMY −3)	4.535449	2.417595	1.876016	0.0673
D (DUMMY −4)	4.234854	2.403670	1.761828	0.0850
D (DUMMY −5)	4.788096	2.335963	2.049732	0.0464
D (DUMMY −6)	2.953522	2.226999	1.326234	0.1916
D (DUMMY −7)	4.798815	2.334264	2.055815	0.0458
D (DUMMY −8)	7.073310	2.100032	3.368192	0.0016
Breusch-Godfrey LM Test		0,726459		0,4919
Jarque-Bera		1,893818		0,387918
Ramsey Reset Test		0.439787		0.5108
Breuch Pagan		0.771686		0.7935
Harvey		0.79960		0.7595
ARCH		0.221803		0.6389

Source: Created by the authors.

TABLE 5.7
ARDL (9,9,9,9) for Estimation of Long-Run Coefficients

Variables	*Coeffecient*	*Standart Error*	*t-statistics*	*P-value*
UNEMP	−77.06715	64.85276	−1.188340	0.2411
REEL_EFRATE	−19.74322	11.57101	−1.706266	0.0950
DUMMY	−115.3558	68.65408	−1.680247	0.1000

EC = TP_FG_J0—(−19.7432*TPREELEFRATE −77.0672*TP_UNEMP −115.3558*DUMMY + 3132.2168)

Source: Created by the authors.

TABLE 5.8
ARDL (9,9,9,9) Error Correction

Variables	*Coeffecient*	*Std. error*	*t-values*	*Probability*
D (İNF −1)	0.305973	0.125416	2.439653	0.0188
D (İNF −2)	−0.400414	0.134858	−2.969143	0.0048
D (İNF −3)	0.409453	0.137113	2.986236	0.0046
D (İNF −4)	−0.549858	0.147310	−3.732649	0.0005
D (İNF−5)	0.277987	0.141380	1.966241	0.0556
D (İNF−6)	−0.321431	0.130440	−2.464202	0.0177
D (İNF−7)	0.055354	0.127077	0.435596	0.6653
D (İNF−8)	−0.198822	0.110873	−1.793248	0.0798
D (EFRATE)	−0.346980	0.110024	−3.153688	0.0029
D (EFRATE −1)	−0.024620	0.151468	−0.162540	0.8716
D (EFRATE −2)	0.253155	0.149675	1.691362	0.0978
D (EFRATE −3)	0.425586	0.150592	2.826085	0.0071
D (EFRATE −4)	0.196338	0.150416	1.305304	0.1986
D (EFRATE −5)	0.135239	0.145047	0.932375	0.3562
D (EFRATE −6)	0.379239	0.137709	2.753915	0.0085
D (EFRATE −7)	−0.133323	0.144552	−0.922319	0.3614
D (EFRATE −8)	0.276166	0.129967	2.124899	0.0392
D (UNEMP)	0.142327	0.476806	0.298500	0.7667
D (UNEMP −1)	2.127693	0.530169	4.013232	0.0002
D (UNEMP −2)	1.659719	0.543157	3.055686	0.0038
D (UNEMP −3)	1.820953	0.556725	3.270830	0.0021
D (UNEMP −4)	2.369290	0.591154	4.007905	0.0002
D (UNEMP −5)	1.022793	0.620798	1.647545	0.1066
D (UNEMP −6)	1.061765	0.553032	1.919897	0.0614
D (UNEMP −7)	0.550516	0.544720	1.010642	0.3177
D (UNEMP −8)	1.023897	0.515741	1.985291	0.0534
D (DUMMY)	−0.356535	1.749126	−0.203836	0.8394
D (DUMMY −1)	7.205637	1.989050	3.622652	0.0008
D (DUMMY −2)	7.452765	2.015106	3.698448	0.0006
D (DUMMY −3)	4.535449	2.115271	2.144145	0.0376
D (DUMMY −4)	4.234854	2.192175	1.931805	0.0598
D (DUMMY −5)	4.788096	2.148495	2.228582	0.0310
D (DUMMY −6)	2.953522	2.051362	1.439785	0.1570
D (DUMMY −7)	4.798815	2.045052	2.346549	0.0235
D (DUMMY−8)	7.073310	1.926443	3.671695	0.0006
ERROR (−1)	−0.029803	0.005026	−5.929914	0.0000

Source: Created by the authors.

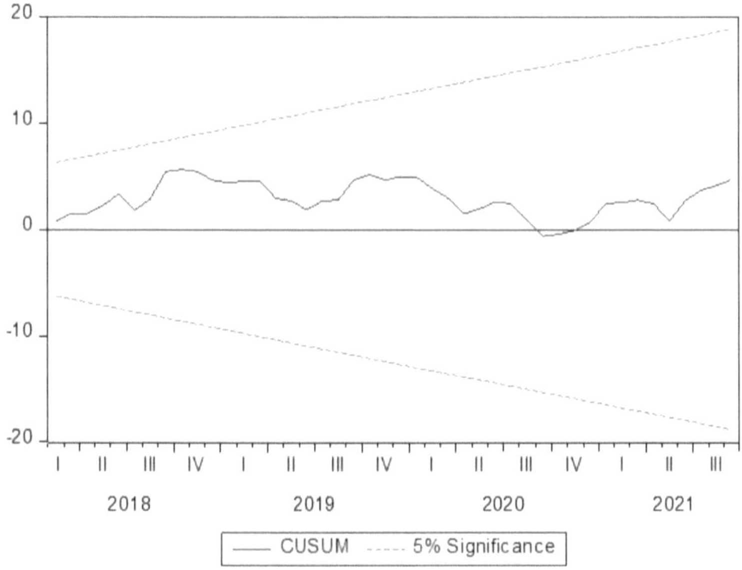

FIGURE 5.1
CUSUM Chart. *Source*: Created by the authors.

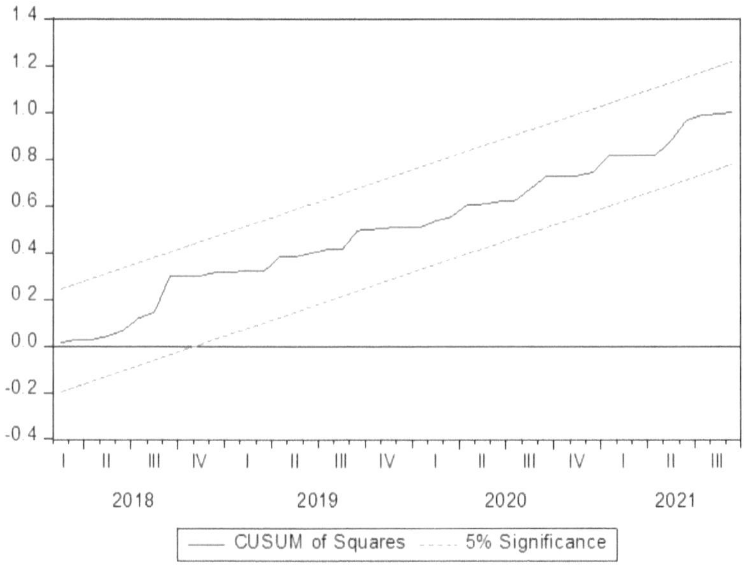

FIGURE 5.2
CUSUM SQ Chart. *Source*: Created by the authors.

Conclusion

In the study, the relationship between inflation rate, real effective exchange rate, and unemployment rate for Turkey was examined using the ARDL test for the period January 2014 to September 2021. According to the test results, it has been determined that there is a relationship between the variables in the short and long term.

Short- and long-term coefficient estimates calculated for the maximum 9 delay ARDL (9,9,9,9) model were made. Since the CUSUM 2 graph (between February 2017and September 2018) did not meet the necessary conditions in the model, a dummy variable was added. It has been determined that the selected ARDL (9,9,9,9) model is suitable and stable. According to the derived error correction model, it was concluded that the error correction model works, with the error term "coefficient" being negative and between 0 and −1.

With the effect of the applied free exchange rate policy, the foreign trade volume has increased continuously, and the increasing foreign trade volume has created interim financial import dependency. It is seen that the exchange rate has an effect on inflation in our country. In the export-led growth model, imports of intermediate goods are needed and inflation uncertainty creates cost inflation by increasing prices. Inflation has a non-linear effect on income distribution: high inflation significantly increases income inequality; However, lowering the inflation rate does not lead to a direct improvement in income distribution. Again, increasing population and foreign migration increase the unemployment rate throughout the country, and this increase negatively affects income distribution due to low labor wages and unregistered employment. Increasing unemployment has the same effect on inflation due to idle capacity and other reasons. Again, since the increase in inflation will increase the cost of the companies, the companies will lay off workers by reducing their labor costs as the first cost reduction. In this case, it is seen that inflation will directly affect unemployment in the same direction.

Note

1. This chapter should not be reported as representing the views of the Capital Markets Board of Turkey. The views expressed herein are those of the author and do not necessarily represent those of the Capital Markets Board of Turkey.

References

Akçan, A. T. (2018). "Makroekonomik Değişkenlerin İşsizlik İle İlişkisi: Türkiye Örneği." *Yönetim Bilimleri Dergisi*, 16(31), 263–285.

Bilgin, M. H. (2004). "Döviz kuru işsizlik ilişkisi: Türkiye üzerine bir inceleme." *Kocaeli Üniversitesi Sosyal Bilimler Enstitüsü Dergisi*, 8(2), 80–94.

Djivre, J., and Ribon, S. (2003). "Inflation, Unemployment, the Exchange Rate, and Monetary Policy in Israel, 1990–99: A SVAR Approach." *Israel Economic Review*, 1(2). Available at SSRN: https://ssrn.com/abstract=2171835.

Geerof, F. (2020). "The Phillips Curve: a Relation between Real Exchange Rate Growth and Unemployment." SED 2018 Mexico Meetings.

Girginer, N., and Yenilmez, F. (2005). "Türkiye'de Enflasyonun Ekonometrik Olarak İncelenmesi (1982-2002)." *Eskişehir Osmangazi Üniversitesi Sosyal Bilimler Dergisi*, 6(1), 101.

Gül, E., and Ekinci, A. (2006). "Türkiye'de Enflasyon ve Döviz Kuru Arasındaki Nedensellik İlişkisi:1984-2003." *Anadolu Üniversitesi Sosyal Bilimler Dergisi*, 6(1), 91–106.

Günay, A., and Balkaya, E. (2019) "Gelir, Fiyat, Reel Efektif Döviz Kuru Ve İşgücü Maliyetlerinin İşsizlik Oranı Üzerindeki Etkileri: Türkiye İçin Bir Ardl Yaklaşımı." *Hak iş Uluslarararası Emek ve Toplum*, Cilt 8, Yıl 8, Sayı, 21, 80–105.

Günaydın, D., and Çetin, M. (2015). "Genç İşsizliğin Temel Makroekonomik Belirleyicileri: Ampirik Bir Analiz." *Pamukkale Üniversitesi Sosyal Bilimler Enstitüsü Dergisi, Sayı*, 22, S:17–31.

Hepaktan, E.; Çınar, S., and Dündar, Ö. (2011). "Türkiye' de Uygulanan Döviz Kuru Sistemlerinin Dış Ticaret İle İlişkisi." *Akademik Araştırmalar ve Çalışmalar Dergisi*, Cilt 3, Sayı 5, ss: 62–82.

Hossain, S., and Mitra, R., (2017). "The Determinants of Price Inflation in the United States: A Multivariate Dynamic Cointegration and Causal Analysis." *The Journal of Developing Areas*, 51(1), 153–175.

Islam,R., A.,G., Bashawir,A., Mahyudin, E., and Manickam, N. (2017). "Determinants of Factors that Affecting İnflation in Malaysia." *International Journal of Economics and Financial Issues*, 7(2), 355–364.

Johansen, S.(1988). "Statistical Analysis of Cointegration Vectors." *Journal of Economic Dynamics and Control*, 12(2–3), 231–254.

Karagöz, K., and Ergün, S. (2010). "Türkiye'de Ekonomik İstikrarsızlığın Kaynakları: Ekonometrik Bir Değerlendirme." *Süleyman Demirel Üniversitesi İktisadi ve İdari Bilimler Fakülte Dergisi*, C:15, S.2, 169-18.

Kaygısız, A.D. (2018). "Döviz Kuru Dalgalanmalarının Enflasyon Üzerindeki Geçiş Etkisi: Türkiye Örneği." *İnternational Review of Economics and Management*, 6(2), 117–137.

Korkmaz, Ö. (2017). "Enflasyon Oranını Etkileyen Faktörlerin Belirlenmesi: Türkiye Üzerine Bir Uygulama." *Dokuz Eylül Üniversitesi İktisadi ve İdari Bilimler Fakültesi Dergisi* Online Cilt:32, Sayı:2, Yıl:2017, ss. 109.

Makdum, M.A. (2021). "Makroekonomik Göstergeler İle Döviz Kuru Arasındaki İlişkinin Analizi: (2005:01-2019:10) Türkiye Uygulaması." *İşletme Araştırmaları Dergisi Cilt 13 Sayı1.*

Mohanty, M.S., and Klau, M. (2001). "What Determines İnflation in Emerging Market Economies?," BIS Papers chapters, in: Bank for International Settlements (ed.), *Modelling Aspects of the İnflation Process and the Monetary Transmission Mechanism in Emerging Market Countries*, volume 8, pp. 1–38. Bank for International Settlements.

Saatçioğlu, C. (2005), "Türkiye Ekonomisindeki Enflasyonist Sürecin İncelenmesine Yönelik Bir Uygulama." *ODTÜ Gelişim Dergisi*, 32(Haziran), 155–184.
Selim S., and Güven, E.,T.,A. (2014). "Türkiye'de Enflasyon, Döviz Kuru Ve İşsizlik Arasındaki İlişkinin Ekonometrik Analizi." *Ekonomik ve Sosyal Araştırmalar Dergisi*, Cilt 10, Yıl 10, Sayı 1, 2014, ss. 127–146.
Şenkal, A. (2005). *Küreselleşme Sürecinde Sosyal Politika*. İstanbul: Alfa Yayınları.
Sevüktekin, M., and Nargeleçekenler, M. (2007). *konometrik Zaman Serileri Analizi*. Ankara: Nobel Yayınları.
Seyidoğlu, H. (1991). *Uluslararası İktisat*. İstanbul: Güzem Yayınları.
Türkiye Cumhuriyet Merkez Bankası (TCMB). Genel İstatistikler http://evds.tcmb.gov.tr/ (Erişim Tarihi: November 18, 2017).
Uysal, D., and Erdoğan, S. (2003). "Enflasyon İle İşsizlik Oranı Arasındaki İlişki Ve Türkiye Örneği (1980-2002)." *SÜ İİBF Sosyal ve Ekonomik Araştırmalar Dergisi*, Sayı 35.

6

The Effect of Women Discrimination on Pay Fairness, Work Well-Being, and Turnover Intentions

A Study in Turkey

İlksun Didem ÜLBEĞİ and Esengül İPLİK

Introduction

Despite the legal regulations related to employment discrimination based on race, color, religion, gender, or national origin in many countries, discrimination in the workplace is a matter that has existed for many years and continues to affect many people (Elmes 2021, 1). Discrimination in the workplace, which occurs as a behavioral manifestation of biased cognitions (stereotypes) and attitudes (prejudice) held toward someone based on the social group they belong to, is defined as making employment decisions such as selection, evaluation, promotion, and award distribution based on a person's characteristics such as age, appearance, gender, and race rather than their productivity, performance, or qualifications (Khan and Rainaye 2018, 62). The "Discrimination (Employment and Occupation) Convention" of the United Nations International Labor Organization defines discrimination in the workplace as any distinction, exclusion, or preference made based on the individual's race, color, sex, religion, political opinion, national extraction, or social origin that has the effect of nullifying or impairing equality of opportunity or treatment in employment or occupation (Cheung et al. 2016, 4). Discrimination, when considered in a sociological perspective, is expressed as negative attitudes and behaviors resulting from prejudices against someone, a group, or the members of a group (Erikli 2020, 42) and can reduce the growth potential and competitiveness of organizations and countries by causing both financial losses and a decrease in innovation. Therefore, preventing discrimination in organizations all over the world is not only a moral but also an economic obligation (Triana et al. 2018, 2420).

When evaluating whether they experience discrimination or not, people use social comparisons that provide information about what types of outcomes and/or treatments, such as salary increases and promotions, are possible to achieve (Foley et al. 2005, 423). In this respect, one of the factors that can affect one's perception of discrimination is that person's personal experiences or the experiences of other people with whom they identify themselves. Therefore, the perception of discrimination in the workplace can be explained by social identity theory. Although originally developed to understand intergroup conflict, the scope of social identity theory expanded to posit that there are three mental processes for social identity: social categorization, social identification, and social comparison (Tajfel and Turner 1979). Accordingly, social categorization refers to the division of individuals into categories (such as age and gender) based on the characteristics, which they perceive that they have, to better understand and define the social environment, while social identification includes one's adoption of the identity of the group to which he or she belongs (Elmes 2021, 25).

And the social comparison which is the third mental process to create social identity and involves intergroup comparison refers to one's comparison of one's group (female, young) with another group (male, old). According to social identity theory, people are inclined to favor their group but despise the other group in this social comparison (Demirtaş 2003, 130; Elmes 2021, 26). Different groups are called in-groups (to which the individual belongs) and out-groups (other groups) and provide individuals with a sense of belonging and self-worth (Vang et al. 2019, 1916). Individuals who perceive that they are treated unfairly or differently by out-groups due to their certain characteristics such as age and gender experience feelings of inadequacy and personal conflict. Therefore, perceived discrimination represents the individual's perception of selective and differential treatment due to group membership (Sanchez and Brock 1996, 705).

While employees may be discriminated against in the workplace based on a variety of factors including age and gender (Elmes 2021, 1), the gender factor, with the increasing number of women in the labor market in recent years, has started to come to the fore more and more in discrimination in the workplace. The sustainable development of countries depends on ensuring gender equality in all areas of life, from family life, education life, social life to business life. For this purpose, it is tried to ensure that women, who are a very important component in the socioeconomic development of nations, are equipped with equal conditions with men in access to opportunities in business life, both by the laws of the countries and by international conventions. Nevertheless, gender inequality is one of the most important issues in both rich and poor countries. A recent report by the United Nations (2019) stated that an average of 18% of married women and girls aged 15–49 had experienced physical and/or sexual violence in the previous 12 months and that this rate was higher in underdeveloped countries than in developing and developed countries (Dang and Viet Nguyen 2021, 1). The best solution to this issue is to empower women financially and provide them with employment opportunities. In this regard, creating employment opportunities for women in different sectors such as health and services in a steadily growing and increasingly diversified economy has made it possible to achieve progress in gender equality in working life. On the other hand, the economic crisis due to the COVID-19 outbreak and the negative effects of rapid digitalization on sectors where women are mostly employed has led to a halt in progress toward gender equality in many economies and sectors. According to the World Economic Forum's "Global Gender Gap Index 2021" examining four overall areas of inequality (economic participation and opportunity, educational attainment, health and survival, and political empowerment) between men and women in 156 countries, one of the two areas with the biggest gender gap is "Economic Participation and Opportunity." According to the indices included in the report, 58% of this gap has been closed so far, but it is estimated that it will take another 267.6 years, under today's conditions, to fully close the gap (World Economic Forum 2021, 5).

Gender discrimination, which is considered to be an obstacle to sustainable development goals and an important ongoing global problem by the United Nations (UN) and other global organizations (Triana et al. 2018, 2420), arises when decisions regarding employees are based on gender rather than employees' qualifications or job performance (Gutek et al. 1996, 791). Because existing gender stereotypes force male employees to adhere to traditional masculine images and take responsibility for physically demanding jobs, not only women but also men can be subject to gender discrimination in the workplace. However, findings reported from various studies reveal that women are more likely to be discriminated against than men in organizations (Qu et al. 2020, 81).

Gender discrimination, based on a person's perception of being denied equal treatment in the workplace because of their gender, generally stems from cultural attitudes toward gender roles (Bobbitt-Zeher 2011, 765). Traditionally, what both genders should or should not do is determined by society and culture, and this, consciously or unconsciously, leads to gender stereotypes (Munda 2015, 111). Gender roles that arise due to these gender stereotypes lead to occupational gender segregation. While male-dominated jobs are traditionally perceived to require masculine characteristics, female-dominated jobs employ women more as they require feminine characteristics. Accordingly, while nursing is considered to be a female profession, engineering is mostly identified with men (Cejka and Eagly 1999, 413–414). It is thought that successful performance in these jobs, which are classified to be feminine or masculine jobs, requires gender-specific characteristics, skills, and qualities (Munda 2015, 111). Gender stereotypes in the workplace can lead to discrimination when the characteristics of the gender are not compatible with the characteristics assumed to be necessary for success in most jobs and occupations (Bobbitt-Zeher 2011, 766).

While cultural beliefs are considered to be the primary cause of gender discrimination, organizational structures, policies, and practices are also considered to be the secondary factors that can lead to discrimination. Building on gender stereotypes that affect male and female workers differently, such policies and procedures as institutionalized elements of organizational structure are legitimatized and seem gender-neutral, but only formalize men's privilege in the workplace (Bobbitt-Zeher 2011, 767). In this sense, human resources (HR) practices embedded in organizations play a critical role in shaping the scope of discrimination by causing unfair or biased treatment of employees in the recruitment process and affecting access to opportunities and valuable rewards within the organization. Determination of objective or formalized criteria leading to the elimination of bias and subjectivity in HR practices in organizations can enable taking decisions based on objective criteria and thus reducing the impact of irrelevant criteria such as race and gender in employment decisions (Gelfand et al. 2007, 17).

The most common forms of discrimination faced by women in organizations are the pay gap and the "glass ceiling" which refers to the unseen barrier that prevents women from being promoted to top jobs in management (Gauci et al. 2021, 2; Gelfand et al. 2007, 8). The glass ceiling is a popular metaphor coined to refer to the unseen barriers that prevent many women, regardless of their qualifications or achievements, from advancing past a certain point in their jobs and reaching higher-level positions, particularly managerial positions (Ramesh and Srivastava 2016, 1; Martínez-Fierro and Lechuga Sancho 2021, 8011). Organizational and individual prejudices negatively affect female employees' job performance despite their talents, experiences, successes, and skills, preventing their progress and advancement (Yörük Karakılıç 2019, 218).

Wage, one of the most important components of the organizational commitment of employees (Deconinck and Bachmann 2007, 135), is one of the most discussed issues in the context of existing gender inequality in the workplace. Although the Equal Remuneration Convention, 1951 (No.

100), one of the main conventions of the International Labor Organization, aimed at equal remuneration for men and women, women continue to earn less than men in many countries (Cheung et al. 2016, 13). According to the "Women in Work Index (2021)," which is compiled every year and covers the data from OECD countries, the average gender pay gap in OECD countries is 15%, and this gap is predicted to be closed on an average of 112 years (Women in Work Index 2021). The gender pay gap is explained with two different approaches. One of them is the human capital model developed by Mincer and Polachek (1974), attributing pay inequality to the lack of education and experience in women. According to this model, women, due to their traditional gender roles, spend more time raising their children and taking care of their families, and therefore, they have less work experience than men, which is one of the factors that leads to the gender pay gap. Accordingly, more limited investment in human capital is a factor that explains why women earn less than men (Constantopoulos 2021, 10; Kümbül Güler and Kiren Gürler 2016, 54).

The second approach to the gender pay gap emphasizes the discrimination in the labor market resulting from discriminatory behaviors toward women's labor. Accordingly, scientists, economists, and politicians argue that one of the most important factors contributing to the gender pay gap is discrimination (Constantopoulos 2021, 8; Kümbül Güler and Kiren Gürler 2016, 54). The link between the pay gap and gender inequality has been highlighted by Stockdale and Nadler (2012) in their discussion of occupational gender inequality. Similarly, Huffman (2012), Olson (2012), and Tharenou (2012) seem to agree that the pay gap is a reflection of gender discrimination.

The gender pay gap arising from discrimination in the workplace may stem from various reasons (Petersen and Morgan 1995, 329). The first of these reasons is that women tend to work in professions and organizations that differ in terms of wages. In this process, which is defined as "distribution discrimination," discrimination begins in the recruitment process and continues during the promotion process. Second, despite the same skill requirements and other pay-related factors, female-dominated professions may offer lower wages than male-dominated ones. This wage discrimination is called "value discrimination." Lastly, in some workplaces, female employees receive lower wages than their male counterparts even though they do the same job. This discrimination is defined as the "gender pay gap arising from work" (Sayar Özkan and Özkan 2010, 95–96; Petersen and Morgan 1995, 329–330). In wage discrimination resulting from distribution and work, discrimination is directed at specific individuals, while value discrimination refers to discrimination against the professions dominated mainly by females.

H_1: Perceived gender discrimination has a negative effect on pay justice.

The chronic and often ambiguous nature of discrimination makes it a source of stress that is difficult to deal with, and victims may, as a result, experience a range of psychological and physical ailments, including psychological disorders such as stress (Channar et al. 2011), depression (Foster 2000; Klonoff et al. 2000), anxiety (Foster 2000; Landrine et al. 1995), and post-traumatic mood disorder and physical ailments such as heart disease (Krieger and Sidney 1996; Foster and Tsarfati 2006). In addition, while many theoretical approaches posit that women's sense of worthlessness due to discrimination negatively affects their self-esteem (Cooley 1956; Tajfel and Turner 1986), previous empirical studies (Perry et al. 2013; Kobrynowicz and Branscombe 1997) support the claim that such exclusion harms psychological well-being (Schmitt et al. 2002, 199).

Employee well-being, which is critical to the survival and development of organizations across the world and has emerged as an important research topic in organizational behavior and related fields, is a concept of which meaning is known by everyone but no one can define precisely (Zheng et al. 2015, 621). Current research on well-being has been derived from two general perspectives. The first is the hedonic approach which focuses on happiness and defines well-being in terms of pleasure attainment and pain avoidance, while the second is the eudaimonic approach which focuses on self-realization and describes well-being in terms of the extent to which a person is fully functioning (Ryan and Deci 2001, 141).

Well-being is tried to be explained with an approach that combines psychological well-being and subjective well-being, which are two different but related concepts. Psychological well-being is a comprehensive concept that is based on the existential challenges of life and encompasses the emotional aspects of an individual's daily life (Warr 1978, 111), whereas subjective well-being refers to one's overall evaluation of their life (Diener 1984, 543). Subjectivity, that is, the assessment of well-being based on one's standards, is the most important feature of subjective well-being which has two basic elements: life satisfaction or the perception of one's quality of life and emotional experience including positive and negative emotions (Zheng et al. 2015, 623). Well-being can cover the whole of life or be measured concerning one's job. Accordingly, concepts such as job satisfaction, workplace tension, and workplace depression are related to workplace well-being (Siu et al. 2005, 276).

Many factors influence workplace well-being, which is a key factor in determining an organization's long-term effectiveness. People derive a great part of their identities and most of their core values from the groups they belong to. In this direction, social groups, which are an important source of individual and collective self-esteem for people (Tajfel and Turner 1979), provide their members with a sense of identity, belonging, and self-worth, and group members' self-esteem develops depending on the status of the social groups. Members feel good about their group when they think that their group is evaluated more positively or that members of the other group are perceived as negative. Accordingly, while the perception of the high-status group has positive effects on the members' self-esteem, the decrease in the status of the group may have negative effects on the members' self-esteem (Branscombe and Wann 1994, 642–644; Cooper et al. 2017, 846). For this reason, members of humiliated social groups may experience a decrease in their well-being, considering the strong relationship between self-esteem and well-being (Vang et al. 2019, 1916). Schmitt and Branscombe (2002) also argue that perceived discrimination in the organization harms the psychological well-being of disadvantaged group members because the person realizes that the group to which they belong is not accepted by the majority and that their group has limited life opportunities compared to other groups (Schmitt et al. 2002, 198).

HRM policies and practices (recruitment, firing, promotion, remuneration, etc.) that harm employees' organizational justice perceptions are one of the important factors affecting workplace well-being. Accordingly, perceiving that the organization adopts ethical principles such as honesty, equality, transparency, and respect in HRM policies and practices increases employees' workplace well-being (Oliveira et al. 2020, 17). When an employee perceives that the ratio of their output to input differs from the ratio of other coworkers, pay inequality occurs, which leads to job dissatisfaction and distress (Fields et al. 2000), as well as less workplace well-being and less respect for one's job (Khoreva and Tenhiälä 2015, 791).

H_2: Perceived gender discrimination has a negative effect on workplace well-being.
H_3: Perceived pay justice has a positive effect on workplace well-being.

Gender discrimination has serious consequences not only for employees but also for the workplace as a whole. When employees perceive that their gender limits their career advancement, they may engage in deviant behaviors, especially as a form of protest or revenge against the entire organization or certain employees (Qu et al. 2020, 78). The perception of inequality and gender discrimination in an organization causes employees to be less satisfied with their jobs, which, in turn, leads to a decrease in their motivation and job performance. Employees working with less energy cause results such as a decrease in the efficiency of the organization (Ganji and Joshi 2020, 1978). Pay inequality (Khoreva and Tenhiälä 2015) and gender discrimination can lead to consequences such as high employee turnover rates, and organizations may lose many of their qualified employees because of this (Ganji and Joshi 2020, 1977).

The prerequisite for leaving a job or organization is the turnover intention, which can also be called the intention to quit. The turnover intention, which is a critical HR issue that affects productivity, product and service quality, and profitability in all sectors of the economy, refers to the possibility of an employee leaving their current job. From a theoretical point of view, the attitude theory (Fishbein and Ajzen 1975), which highlights the importance of intention in predicting behaviors, argues that the best indicator of a behavior is the intention to perform that behavior. In line with this theory, one of the most important antecedents of employee turnover is the intention to quit the job (Hellman 1997, 677). Similarly, studies on workforce turnover (Michaels and Spector 1982; Griffeth et al. 2000) have also reported that the intention to quit an organization is one of the important determinants of actual workforce turnover. The turnover intention, which refers to conscious and deliberate willfulness to leave the organization, has been described as the last step in a sequence of withdrawal cognitions, which also includes thinking of quitting and intent to search for an alternative job (Tett and Meyer 1993, 262).

Taking measures to reduce the rate of employee turnover by organizations is important in terms of maximizing the return on investment made in employees in both the recruitment process and during their tenure in the organization. For this, the reasons that increase the turnover intention should be well known by the managers of the organization. Most of the traditional models on employee turnover have focused on employees' attitudes toward their jobs and organizations as the antecedents of the quitting process. Most of these models argue that employees begin to consider quitting their job because of low job satisfaction and low organizational commitment. When individuals feel that they are treated differently or unfairly because of their group membership, they often feel alienated and angry, which, in turn, can result in negative workplace behaviors (Özer and Günlük 2010, 1500). Accordingly, employees who perceive that they are treated differently or unfairly in issues such as compensation, wages, promotions, and disciplinary penalties due to their group membership have less job satisfaction, well-being, and organizational commitment, and as a result, the intention to quit the job increases (Buttner and Lowe 2017; Khoreva and Tenhiälä 2015; Miceli et al. 1991; Özer and Günlük 2010; Triana et al. 2018).

H_4: Perceived gender discrimination has a positive effect on turnover intention.
H_5: Perceived pay fairness has a negative effect on turnover intention.
H_6: Workplace well-being has a negative effect on turnover intention.

This study aims to investigate the direct effect of the perception of gender discrimination against female employees on employees' turnover intentions, as well as its indirect effects along with the perception of pay fairness and workplace well-being. Previous studies in the literature have revealed direct relationships among these variables. The direct relationships between the said variables indicate that the perception of pay fairness and workplace well-being may also have indirect effects on the relationship between the perception of discrimination and turnover intention.

> H_7: Perceived pay fairness has a mediating role in the effect of perceived gender discrimination on turnover intention.
> H_8: Workplace well-being has a mediating role in the effect of perceived gender discrimination on turnover intention.
> H_9: Perceived pay fairness and workplace well-being have serial mediating effects on the effect of perceived gender discrimination on turnover intention.

Method

This study utilized a sample of 197 female private-sector employees from Adana, Turkey. Data analysis was conducted for revealing Cronbach's alpha coefficients, factor structure of the model, correlations between variables, and hypothesis test results.

Participants and Procedure

According to the results, 57.9% of the participants were married and 42.6% were single. The respondents' mean age was 29.2 years, and their tenure was 6.2 years. Findings showed that 1.5% were primary school graduates, 41.6% were high school graduates, 52.8% were university graduates, and 4.1% had master's degrees.

Instruments

Perceived discrimination was measured with the scale developed by Foley et al. (2005). This scale has one dimension with four items. Perceived pay fairness was measured with a scale created by Buttner and Lowe (2017). Perceived pay fairness scale comprised of one dimension and three items. Intentions of turnover were measured with a scale developed by Camman et al. (1979). This scale has one dimension and three items. Workplace well-being was measured with a scale developed by Zheng et al. (2015). Workplace well-being is a dimension of a scale measuring employee well-being. This dimension has six items. All scales were measured on a five-point Likert-type scale.

Results

Exploratory Factor Analysis and Reliability Results

Exploratory factor analysis was conducted to establish the factor structure of the model. Principal component analysis method and varimax rotation were used for extraction and rotation of the factors. According to the results four dimensions in the model emerged. (KMO = 0.91, $\chi 2$ = 1796.14; df = 120, p < 0,000). Factor loadings were between 0.63 and 0.85 (see table 6.1). Total explained variance was 72.05% (see table 6.1).

Internal consistency coefficient Cronbach Alpha was used to assess the reliability of the scales (see table 6.2). According to the results, Cronbach's alpha coefficient for discrimination was 0.73, for pay fairness 0.85, for work well-being 0.93, and for turnover intentions 0.86.

The correlations between variables were statistically significant (see table 6.2). Discrimination was correlated negatively with pay fairness and work

TABLE 6.1.
Factor Loadings of the Model

Items	*Discrimination*	*Pay Fairness*	*Work Well-Being*	*Turnover Intentions*
Discrimination				
D1	0.76			
D2	0.76			
D3	0.63			
D4	0.68			
Pay Fairness				
P1		0.84		
P2		0.83		
P3		0.77		
Work Well-Being				
W1			0.82	
W2			0.80	
W3			0.82	
W4			0.81	
W5			0.78	
W6			0.81	
Turnover Intentions				
T1				0.85
T2				0.81
T3				0.75
% Variance explained	13.96	15.23	27.30	15.56

KMO = 0.91, Bartlett's Test of Sphericity, χ^2 = 1796.14; df = 120; p < 0,000, % Variance explained = 72.05
Principal component analysis, Varimax rotation, 5 iterations
Source: Created by the authors.

TABLE 6.2
Means, Standard Deviations, Cronbach's Alphas, and Correlations

Variables	*Mean*	*SD*	*Discrimination*	*Pay Fairness*	*Work Well-Being*	*Turnover Intentions*
Discrimination	3.48	0.83	0.73			
Pay Fairness	2.71	0.88	−0.33**	0.85		
Work Well-Being	2.59	0.84	−0.45**	0.49**	0.93	
Turnover Intentions	3.62	0.89	0.36**	−0.50**	−0.52**	0.86

** $p < 0{,}01$
Source: Created by the authors.

well-being, while positively with turnover intentions. Additionally, pay fairness was correlated positively with work well-being and negatively with turnover intentions. Moreover, work well-being was correlated negatively with turnover intentions (see table 6.2).

Model Test Results

Maximum likelihood and bootstrap method were used to test the model, revealing the direct, indirect, and total effects with unstandardized coefficients. The goodness of fit values showed an excellent model fit ($\chi2 = 106.29$, df = 98, $\chi2$/df = 1.09, p = 0.27, CFI = 0.99, TLI = 0.99, RMSEA = 0.021, SRMR = 0.047) (see table 6.3). Standardized path coefficients can be seen in figure 6.1 and unstandardized direct effects can be seen in table 6.4. According to the model, discrimination had a negative effect on pay fairness and work well-being, and a positive effect on turnover intentions. Moreover, pay fairness had a positive effect on work well-being and a negative effect on turnover intentions. Additionally, work well-being had a negative effect on turnover intentions according to the test results.

Bootstrapping with 5,000 resampling, 95% symmetric confidence interval, and a 95% confidence interval corrected for bias were used to test the serial mediation in the study. According to the results, pay fairness has a mediating role in the relationship between discrimination and turnover intentions (estimate = 0.240 (0.104), 95%CI = [0.270–0.878], BC95%CI = [0.270–0.878]). Moreover, work well-being mediates the relationship between discrimination

TABLE 6.3
Model Fit Results

	χ2	*df*	*χ2 / df*	*p-value*	*CFI*	*TLI*	*RMSEA*	*SRMR*
Model fit	106.29	98	1.09	0.27	0.99	0.99	0.021	0.047

χ^2 = Chi-Square, df = Degrees of Freedom, CFI = Comparative Fit Index, TLI = Tucker-Lewis Index, RMSEA = Root Mean Square Error of Approximation, SRMR = Standardized Root Mean Square Residual
Source: Created by the authors.

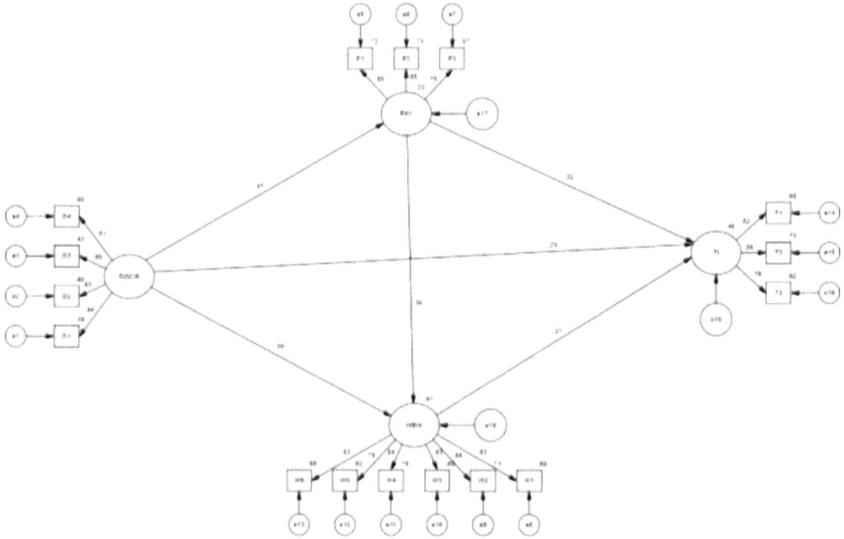

FIGURE 6.1
Model Results. *Source*: Created by the authors.

TABLE 6.4
Path Coefficients in the Model

	Path Coefficients		
	Turnover Intentions	*Pay Fairness*	*Workplace Well-Being*
Discrimination	0.357** (0.204)	−0.773** (0.271)	−0.608** (0.196)
Pay Fairness	−0.311** (0.087)		0.340** (0.081)
Workplace Well-Being	−0.274** (0.090)		

Standard Errors in Parentheses, *p < 0.05, **p < 0.01.
Source: Created by the authors.

TABLE 6.5
Indirect Effects in the Model

	Indirect Effects		
	Estimate	*Symmetric 95%CI*	*Bootstrap 95%CI*
Total	0.479 ** (0.158)	0.270–0.878	0.270–0.878
D→PF→TI	0.240 ** (0.104)	0.097–0.499	0.101–0.512
D→WWB→TI	0.166 ** (0.075)	0.056–0.347	0.061–0.357
D→PF→WWB→TI	0.072 ** (0.040)	0.020–0.175	0.022–0.184

Total Effect (D→TI) = 0.836** (0.284), Standard Errors in Parentheses, *p < 0.05, **p < 0.01.
Source: Created by the authors.

and turnover intentions (estimate = 0.166 (0.075), 95%CI = [0.056–0.347], BC95%CI = [0.061–0.357]). In addition to these findings, pay fairness and work well-being mediate the relationship between discrimination and turnover intentions (estimate = 0.072 (0.040), 95%CI = [0.020–0.175], BC95%CI = [0.022–0.184]) (see table 6.5).

Discussion

Despite the comprehensive laws, policies, and international commitments that are in effect in many countries (Gauci et al. 2021, 2), women continue to be discriminated against in organizational processes such as recruitment, compensation, and performance appraisal (Gelfand et al. 2007, 17). Increasing automation and digitization after the COVID-19 pandemic has accelerated the labour market disruption and has further deepened the gender discrimination (World Economic Forum 2021, 6). Gender discrimination, which is both a social and an economic issue, can have negative consequences both for the physical and mental health of discriminated employees and for the entire organization. In this context, aiming to investigate the relationships between perceived discrimination against women and employees' perception of pay fairness, workplace well-being, and turnover intention, this study was carried out with 197 female employees working in the private sector in Adana.

According to the findings of the analysis, the perception that there is gender discrimination against women in the workplace negatively affects employees' perceptions of pay fairness. In addition, it has been determined that the perception of gender discrimination negatively affects workplace well-being and increases turnover intention. The findings reveal that in women who perceive that they are exposed to gender-based discrimination in the workplace, the perceptions of pay fairness increase, their workplace well-being decreases, and they start considering leaving the organization. The findings of previous studies on gender discrimination (Constantopoulos 2021; Huffman 2012; Khoreva and Tenhiälä 2016; Kümbül Güler and Kiren Gürler 2016; Olson 2012; Özer and Günlük 2010; Perry et al. 2021; Stockdale and Nadler 2012; Tharenou 2012; Vang et al. 2018) are also consistent with the results of this study.

Another result obtained in the study is that if employees think that there is no pay inequality in the organization, their workplace well-being will increase and their intention to leave the organization will decrease. The results of previous studies (Buttner and Lowe 2017; Khoreva and Tenhiälä 2016; Miceli et al. 1991; Oliveira 2020) also support these results. On the other hand, the indirect relationships examined in addition to the direct relationships in the study suggest that perceived pay justice and workplace well-being have mediating effects, both separately and together, on the relationship between the perception of gender discrimination in the workplace and turnover intention.

In this context, women's perceptions of gender-based discrimination and the pay gap may have negative consequences for both employees and the organization. For this reason, finding ways to eliminate these negative perceptions is important to create a healthy working environment in the organization. To achieve this, organizations must first implement HR practices within the framework of objective and formalized criteria so that processes such as selection, promotion, remuneration, relocation, and performance appraisal can be carried out fairly. Distributing organizational rewards (such as wage increases and promotions) based on consistent and valid moral and ethical standards will eliminate women's perceptions of discrimination and inequality. Thus, organizations will be able to attract more qualified female employees to the organization, get more efficiency from qualified employees, and ensure that these employees do not quit the organization.

As in every study, this study has also some limitations. The study was carried out in only one city and used surveys to collect data. Future studies may expand the scope by collecting data from samples from different cities, allowing more comprehensive evaluations, and may use qualitative techniques to collect data to reduce the risk of response bias in surveys. Among the types of discrimination, only gender-based discrimination was examined in the study. Examining different types of discrimination together in future studies can make it possible to compare different reactions to discrimination by disadvantaged groups. Despite all these limitations, this study is expected to contribute to the relevant literature by revealing the direct and indirect relationships between women's perceived gender-based discrimination, perceived pay fairness, workplace well-being, and turnover intention. The study is also expected to contribute to the practice by raising awareness about the importance of the perception of discrimination and inequality for organizations and by drawing attention to what organizations can do to prevent possible problems.

References

Áurea F. Oliveira, Sinésio Gomide Júnior, and Bânia V. Poli. "Antecedents of Well-Being at Work: Trust and People Management Policies." *RAM. Revista de Administração Mackenzie* 21, no. 1 (2020): 1–26. doi:10.1590/1678-6971/eramd200105.

AcademicJournals.Org. https://academicjournals.org/journal/AJBM/article-full-text-pdf/BC6E8F526303.

Azra Khan and Riyaz Ahmad Rainaye. "Relationship between Women Discrimination in HRM Practices and Organisational Commitment: A Review." *International Journal of Advance and Innovative Research* 5, no. 4 (2018): 62–66.

Barbara A. Gutek, Aaron Groff Cohen, and Anne Tsui. "Reactions to Perceived Sex Discrimination." *Human Relations* 49, no. 6 (1996): 791–813. doi:10.1177/001872679604900604.

Brea L. Perry, Kathi L. Harp, and Carrie B. Oser. "Racial and Gender Discrimination in the Stress Process: Implications for African American Women's Health and Well-Being." *Sociological Perspectives* 56, no. 1 (2013): 25–48. doi:10.1525/sop.2012.56.1.25.

Burcu Kümbül Güler and Özlem Kiren Gürler. Türkiye'de kadın işgücünün ücret düzeyini belirleyen faktörler ve ücrette ayrımcılık. *KARATAHTA İş Yazıları Dergisi* 4 (2016): 51–66. https://www.dergikaratahta.com/files/4/3.pdf.

Chan M. Hellman. "Job Satisfaction and İntent to Leave." *The Journal of Social Psychology* 137, no. 6 (1997): 677–89. doi:10.1080/00224549709595491.

Charles E. Michaels and Paul E. Spector. "Causes of Employee Turnover: A Test of the Mobley, Griffeth, Hand, and Meglino Model." *Journal of Applied Psychology* 67, no. 1 (1982): 53–59. doi:10.1037/0021-9010.67.1.53.

Constantopoulos Chris. "Pay inequality and gender pay gap." Master's Thesis, The City University of New York, 2021.

Cortlandt Cammann, Mark Fichman, Douglas Jenkins, and John Klesh. "The Michigan Organizational Assessment Questionnaire." Unpublished manuscript, University of Michigan, Ann Arbor, 1975.

Dail Fields, Mary Pang, and Catherine Chiu. "Distributive and Procedural Justice as Predictors of Employee Outcomes in Hong Kong." *Journal of Organizational Behavior* 21, no. 5 (2000): 547–62. doi:10.1002/1099-1379(200008)21:5<547::aid-job41>3.0.co;2-i.

Diane Kobrynowicz and Nyla R. Branscombe. "Who Considers Themselves Victims of Discrimination?: Individual Difference Predictors of Perceived Gender Discrimination in Women and Men." *Psychology of Women Quarterly* 21, no. 3 (1997): 347–63. doi:10.1111/j.1471-6402.1997.tb00118.x.

Diane Kobrynowicz and Susan Owen. "Perceiving Discrimination against One's Gender Group Has Different Implications for Well-Being in Women and Men." *Personality and Social Psychology Bulletin* 28, no. 2 (2002): 197–210. doi:10.1177/0146167202282006.

Donna Bobbitt-Zeher. "Gender Discrimination at Work." *Gender & Society* 25, no. 6 (2011): 764–86. doi:10.1177/0891243211424741.

E. Holly Buttner and Kevin B. Lowe. "Addressing Internal Stakeholders' Concerns: The Interactive Effect of Perceived Pay Equity and Diversity Climate on Turnover Intentions." *Journal of Business Ethics* 143, no. 3 (2015): 621–33. doi:10.1007/s10551-015-2795-x.

Ed Diener. "Subjective Well-Being." *Psychological Bulletin* 95 (1984): 542–75. doi:10.1037/0033-2909.95.3.542.

Elizabeth A. Klonoff, Hope Landrine, and Robin Campbell. "Sexist Discrimination May Account for Well-Known Gender Differences in Psychiatric Symptoms." *Psychology of Women Quarterly* 24, no. 1 (2000): 93–99. doi:10.1111/j.1471-6402.2000.tb01025.x.

Firooz Ahmad Ganji and Bhavesh P. Joshi. "Impact of gender discrimination on the employees (Ghalib Private University in Herat, Afghanistan as a Case Study)." *European Journal of Molecular & Clinical Medicine* 7, no. 6 (2020): 1967–80. https://ejmcm.com/pdf_4006_3bc4cd62cefd0f562ae4281d1438bd0c.html.

Gökçen Sayar Özkan and Bülent Özkan. "Kadın çalışanlara yönelik ücret ayrımcılığı ve kadın ücretlerinin belirleyicilerine yönelik bir araştırma." *Çalışma ve Toplum Dergisi* 1, no. 24 (2010): 91–103. https://www.calismatoplum.org/makale/kadin-calisanlara-yonelik-ucret-ayrimciligi-ve-kadin-ucretlerinin-belirleyicilerine-yonelik-bir-arastirma.

Gökhan Özer and Mehmet Günlük. "The Effects of Discrimination Perception and Job Satisfaction on Turkish Public Accountants' Turnover İntention." *African Journal of Business Management* 4, no. 8 (2010): 1500–509.

H. Andaç Demirtaş. "Sosyal Kimlik Kuramı, Temel Kavram Ve Varsayımlar." *İletişim: Araştırmaları Dergisi* 1, no. 1 (2003): 1. doi:10.1501/iltaras_0000000023.

Hai-Anh H. Dang and Cuong Viet Nguyen. "Gender Inequality during the Covid-19 Pandemic: Income, Expenditure, Savings, and Job Loss." *World Development* 140 (2021): 105296. doi:10.1016/j.worlddev.2020.105296.

Henri Tajfel and John Turner. "An İntegrative Theory of İntergroup Conflict." In W. G. Austin & S. Worchel (eds.), *The Social Psychology of İntergroup Relations* (pp. 33–47). Monterey, CA: Brooks-Cole, 1979.

Hestia Jacomina Elmes "Age and Gender and Perceived Discrimination in South Africa." PhD diss., Grand Canyon University, 2021.

Ho Kwan Cheung, Eden King, Alex P. Lindsey, Ashley Membere, Hannah M. Markell, and Molly Kilcullen. "Understanding and Reducing Workplace Discrimination." *Research in Personnel and Human Resources Management* 34 (2016): 101–52. doi:10.1108/s0742-730120160000034010.

Hope Landrine, Elizabeth A. Klonoff, Jeannine Gibbs, Vickie Manning, and Marlene Lund. "Physical and Psychiatric Correlates of Gender Discrimination: *an Application of the Schedule of Sexist Events*." *Psychology of Women Quarterly* 19, no. 4 (1995): 473–92. doi:10.1111/j.1471-6402.1995.tb00087.x.

Jacob Mincer and Solomon Polachek. "Family Investments in Human Capital: Earnings of Women." *Journal of Political Economy* 82, no. 2, Part 2 (1974): 76–108. doi:10.1086/260293.

James Deconinck and Duane Bachmann. "The İmpact of Equity Sensitivity and Pay Fairness on Marketing Managers' Job Satisfaction, Organizational Commitment and Turnover İntentions." *Marketing Management Journal* 17, no. 2 (2007): 134–41. https://d0192efdd77670f7012d3fece2c7c0fc720c897f.vetisonline.com/10.1108/S0742-730120160000034010.

Josephine E. Olson. "Human Capital Models and the Gender Pay Gap." *Sex Roles* 68, no. 3–4 (2012): 186–97. doi:10.1007/s11199-012-0208-5.

Juan I. Sanchez and Petra Brock. "Outcomes of Perceived Discrimination among Hispanic Employees: Is Diversity Management a Luxury or a Necessity?" *Academy of Management Journal* 39, no. 3 (1996): 704–19. doi:10.5465/256660.

Kate Cooper, Laura G. Smith, and Ailsa Russell. "Social Identity, Self-Esteem, and Mental Health in Autism." *European Journal of Social Psychology* 47, no. 7 (2017): 844–54. doi:10.1002/ejsp.2297.

Marcia P. Miceli, Iljae Jung, Janet P. Near, and David B. Greenberger. "Predictors and Outcomes of Reactions to Pay-for-Performance Plans." *Journal of Applied Psychology* 76, no. 4 (1991): 508–21. doi:10.1037/0021-9010.76.4.508.

Margaret S. Stockdale and Joel T. Nadler. "Paradigmatic Assumptions of Disciplinary Research on Gender Disparities: The Case of Occupational Sex Segregation." *Sex Roles* 68, no. 3–4 (2012): 207–15. doi:10.1007/s11199-012-0228-1.

María del Triana, Mevan Jayasinghe, Jenna R. Pieper, Dora María Delgado, and Mingxiang Li. "Perceived Workplace Gender Discrimination and Employee Consequences: A Meta-Analysis and Complementary Studies Considering Country Context." *Journal of Management* 45, no. 6 (2018): 2419–47. doi:10.1177/0149206318776772.

Mary Ann Cejka, and Alice H. Eagly. "Gender-Stereotypic Images of Occupations Correspond to the Sex Segregation of Employment." *Personality and Social Psychology Bulletin* 25, no. 4 (1999): 413–23. doi:10.1177/0146167299025004002.

Matt L. Huffman. "Organizations, Managers, and Wage İnequality." *Sex Roles* 68 (2012): 216–22. https://link.springer.com/content/pdf/10.1007/s11199-012-0240-5.pdf.

Michael T. Schmitt, Nyla R. Branscombe. "The Meaning and Consequences of Perceived Discrimination in Disadvantaged and Privileged Social Groups." In W. Stroebe & M. Hewstone (eds.), *European Review of Social Psychology* (Vol. 12). Chichester, UK: Wiley, 2002.

Michele Gelfand, Lisa Hisae Nishii, Jana L. Raver and Benjamin Schneider. *Discrimination in Organizations: An Organizational-Level Systems Perspective.* CAHRS Working Paper Series. Paper 470, 2005. http://digitalcommons.ilr.cornell.edu/cahrswp/470.

Mindi D. Foster. "Positive and Negative Responses to Personal Discrimination: Does Coping Make a Difference?" *The Journal of Social Psychology* 140, no. 1 (2000): 93–106. doi:10.1080/00224540009600448.

Mindi D. Foster and E. Micha Tsarfati. "The Effects of Meritocracy Beliefs on Women's Well-Being after First-Time Gender Discrimination." *Personality and Social Psychology Bulletin* 31, no. 12 (2005): 1730–38. doi:10.1177/0146167205278709.

Nancy Krieger and Stephen Sidney. "Racial Discrimination and Blood Pressure: The Cardia Study of Young Black and White Adults." *American Journal of Public Health* 86, no. 10 (1996): 1370–78. doi:10.2105/ajph.86.10.1370.

Nilüfer Yörük Karakılıç. "Valuation of Glass Ceiling Syndrome in Terms of Gender Discrimination Perception." *Yönetim ve Ekonomi Araştırmaları Dergisi* 17, no. 2 (2019): 214–33. https://dergipark.org.tr/tr/download/article-file/757077.

Nyla R. Branscombe and Daniel L. Wann. "Collective Self-Esteem Consequences of Outgroup Derogation When a Valued Social Identity Is on Trial." *European Journal of Social Psychology* 24, no. 6 (1994): 641–57. doi:10.1002/ejsp.2420240603.

Oi-ling Siu, Paul E. Spector, Cary L. Cooper, and Chang-qin Lu. "Work Stress, Self-Efficacy, Chinese Work Values, and Work Well-Being in Hong Kong and Beijing." *International Journal of Stress Management* 12, no. 3 (2005): 274–88. doi:10.1037/1072-5245.12.3.274.

Patricia Gauci, Kath Peters, Kate O'Reilly, and Rakime Elmir. "The Experience of Workplace Gender Discrimination for Women Registered Nurses: A Qualitative Study." *Journal of Advanced Nursing* 78, no. 6 (2021): 1743–54. doi:10.1111/jan.15137.

Peter Warr. "A Study of Psychological Well-Being." *British Journal of Psychology* 69, no. 1 (1978): 111–21. doi:10.1111/j.2044-8295.1978.tb01638.x.

Phyllis Tharenou. "The Work of Feminists Is Not Yet Done: The Gender Pay Gap—A Stubborn Anachronism." *Sex Roles* 68, no. 3–4 (2012): 198–206. doi:10.1007/s11199-012-0221-8.

Richard M. Ryan and Edward L. Deci. "On Happiness and Human Potentials: A Review of Research on Hedonic and Eudaimonic Well-Being." *Annual Review of Psychology* 52, no. 1 (2001): 141–66. doi:10.1146/annurev.psych.52.1.141.

Robert P. Tett and John P. Meyer. "Job Satisfaction, Organizational Commitment, Turnover Intention, and Turnover: Path Analyses Based on Meta-Analytic Findings." *Personnel Psychology* 46, no. 2 (2006): 259–93. doi:10.1111/j.1744-6570.1993.tb00874.x.

Rodger W. Griffeth, Peter W. Hom and Stefan Gaertner. "A Meta-Analysis of Antecedents and Correlates of Employee Turnover: Update, Moderator Tests, and Research Implications for the next Millennium." *Journal of Management*. No longer published by Elsevier, March 1, 2005. https://www.sciencedirect.com/science/article/pii/S014920630000043X.

Salustiano Martínez-Fierro and María Paula Lechuga Sancho. "Descriptive Elements and Conceptual Structure of Glass Ceiling Research." *International Journal of Environmental Research and Public Health* 18, no. 15 (2021): 8011. doi:10.3390/ijerph18158011.

Sharon Foley, Ngo Hang-Yue and Wong, Angela. "Perceptions of discrimination and justice." *Group & Organization Managemen* 30, no. 4 (2005): 421–50. doi:10.1177/1059601104265054.

Sneha Singh Munda, "Gender Discrimination: A Sting Which Affects Nurses Work Attitudes in Indian Hospitals." *ANVESHAK-International Journal of Management* 4, no. 2 (2015): 110. doi:10.15410/aijm/2015/v4i2/67722.

Süheyla Erikli. "Çalışma yaşamında toplumsal cinsiyet ayrımcılığının görünümü." *Hacettepe Üniversitesi Sosyal Bilimler Dergisi* 2, no. 1 (2020): 39–60.

Trond Petersen, and Laurie A. Morgan. "Separate and Unequal: Occupation-Establishment Sex Segregation and the Gender Wage Gap." *American Journal of Sociology* 101, no. 2 (1995): 329–65. doi:10.1086/230727. https://papers.ssrn.com/sol3/papers.cfm?abstract_id=3379209.

Vidhyalakshmi Ramesh and Ashok Srivastava. "Critical Evaluation of Gender Discrimination and Glass Ceiling Effect in the Indian and International Universities in UAE." *SSRN Electronic Journal* (2016). doi:10.2139/ssrn.3379209.

Violetta Khoreva and Aino Tenhiälä. "Gender Differences in Reactions to İnjustice." *Journal of Managerial Psychology* 31, no. 4 (2015): 790–804. doi:10.1108/JMP-07-2013-0230.

Women in Work Index 2021: *The İmpact of Covid-19 on Women in Work.* https://www.strategyand.pwc.com/de/en/functions/organisational-strategy/women-in-work.html.

World Economic Forum (2021). *Global Gender Gap Report 2021.* https://www3.weforum.org/docs/WEF_GGGR_2021.pdf.

Xiaoming Zheng, Weichun Zhu, Haixia Zhao, and Chi Zhang. "Employee Well-Being in Organizations: Theoretical Model, Scale Development, and Cross-Cultural Validation." *Journal of Organizational Behavior* 36, no. 5 (2015): 621–44. doi:10.1002/job.1990.

Yanjing Qu, Jo WooMi, and Chris Choi Hwansuk. "Gender Discrimination, Injustice, and Deviant Behavior among Hotel Employees: Role of Organizational Attachment." *Journal of Quality Assurance in Hospitality & Tourism* 21, no. 1 (2019): 78–104. doi:10.1080/1528008x.2019.1619498.

Zahid Ali Channar, Zareen Abbassi and Imran Anwar Ujan. "Gender Discrimination in Workforce and İts İmpact on the Employees." *Pakistan Journal of Commerce and Social Sciences (PJCSS)* 5, no. 1 (2011): 177–91. http://hdl.handle.net/10419/188023.

Zoua M. Vang, Feng Hou, and Katharine Elder. "Perceived Religious Discrimination, Religiosity, and Life Satisfaction." *Journal of Happiness Studies* 20, no. 6 (2018): 1913–32. doi:10.1007/s10902-018-0032-x.

7

Domestic Workers from Global Migration to Internal Migration

What about a Pandemic

M. Zaenul MUTTAQIN

Introduction

In the study of international relations, there are various views on migration. Lee (1966) stated that migration is the mobility of people to other places with short- and long-term goals. Castles (2009) through the lens of political economy, described cross-border migration as a reflection of globalization which offers economic development in the global south and north. Southern countries lack adequate bargaining power apart from relying on dominant northern countries. The dependence of the global south on the north is marked by the migration of cheap labor, especially women from southern countries, in frame of global economic system (Asriani and Amalia, 2014).

Another definition of migration on a regional scale is put forward by sociologists Harris and Todaro (1970), suggesting that migration offers balanced growth with the allocation of rural labor, which is identical from agriculture to the industrial sector in urban areas. Based on this purpose, migration in IOM (2019:132–137) states that migration has the objectives of finding work, being forced, fleeing, and seeking asylum. Workers in this category have legal and illegal characteristics, with and without documents. For official workers, the purpose of migrating within a certain period is determined based on the contract agreement. Furthermore, forced migration occurs due to external factors such as natural disasters. Meanwhile, refugee migration aims to avoid conflict or violence. Then cross-country migration aimed at seeking asylum refers to efforts to seek protection but does not meet the requirements under the 1951 convention.

This chapter further examines the purpose of migration on a regional scale, called internal migration. Based on data UN DESA in 2016, the record of internal migration in all parts of the world is around 768 million people (Marta et al., 2020a, 2020b). In the World Migration Report released by IOM (2020), Indonesia is among the 10 countries that have the largest migrant workers in the Asian region. Data released by Bank Indonesia (2019) shows 3,742 Indonesian migrant workers with the diaspora in 39 countries in 2019. The National Agency for the Placement and Protection of Indonesian Migrant Workers (BNP2TKI) shows different data, Indonesian migrant workers with a diaspora of around 21 the country numbered 283,640 people, and the domestic sphere dominated the work of migrant workers with a total of 93,124 people (BNP2TKI, 2019). In 2013 Indonesia's total remittances from migrant workers were estimated at IDR 73 trillion, and most of these domestic migrant workers were women (Asriani and Amalia, 2014).

The discussion of domestic workers (PRT) in Indonesia received much attention from researchers. Various approaches and disciplines provide several insights regarding the correlation of migrant workers, especially domestic workers, in the body of international relations and policy studies. Soetjiptio (2017) says that the phenomenon of domestic workers is identical to the migration of third-world women to developed countries with private-sector job classification. Domestic workers are equated with the feminization of migration as a developing country that has received less attention than other economic sectors. Then Makmur and Mohamad (2021), in their study, describe the legal instruments for the protection of domestic workers in Indonesia, which are still gray. Minister of Manpower Regulation (Permenaker) No. 2/2015 concerning the protection of domestic workers is a derivation of Law (UU) No. 23/2014 on Regional Government which has different roots. Ministerial Regulation (Permen) should be derivative of Law no. 13/2003 concerning Manpower in the regulatory review.

Law no. 13/2003 has contained eight fundamental rights to work relations, social security, health, wages, hours of work and leave, work agreements, strikes, special rights for women, and protection for Termination of Employment (PHK). Meanwhile, Permenaker No. 2/2015 contained the rights of domestic workers, including a good treatment of users and their family members; wages according to work agreements; healthy food and drinks; rest periods; leave according to the agreement; opportunities for worship; holiday allowances; and communication with family. The fundamental difference between the two legal products lies in the protection of wages, social security, work safety, health protection, and layoffs.

Afifah (2018) shows that although there is no specific derivative regulation for the protection of domestic workers in Indonesia, the Indonesian government has a concrete substance for the protection of Human Rights (HAM). It contained in the 1945 Constitution of the Republic of Indonesia and ratified the convention, which includes the Universal Declaration of Human Rights. Ratification of the convention includes the International Covenant on Economic, Social and Cultural Rights (ICESCR), Covenant on the Elimination of All Forms of Discrimination against Women (CEDAW), ILO Convention No. 189 on the Decent Work Convention for Domestic Workers.

Sonhaji (2020) said that the weak national legal system to protect domestic workers has made the discriminatory gaps lasting. These domestic workers are generally women and are still haunted by discrimination in carrying out their work. Dhewy (2017) is more straightforward in explaining that apart from the weak legal umbrella of protection, discrimination against domestic workers still often occurs because the average has low education and is considered less talented.

While tossing and turning over protection policies, the COVID-19 pandemic has added to the long list of problems faced by domestic workers. This chapter aims to explore the phenomenon of protecting Indonesian domestic workers during the pandemic. Previous studies have become a significant knowledge base for international relations studies and a significant setting for exploring further studies on domestic workers. In addition, this chapter aims to explore the possibility of advocating the problems domestic workers face during the pandemic (Afifah, 2018).

The writing design uses a qualitative approach compiled from various literature and searches for various information on the internet (Hamzah, 2020). Exploring the issues underlying internal migration in this chapter refers to informal domestic workers, the time context during the pandemic, and the regional context. The analysis refers to the steps developed by Miles and Huberman (1992), including reduction during the data search, codification of the data to draw interpretation, presentation of the data, and concluding the data carefully. This chapter consists of several sections: first, the migration motives of domestic workers; second, the pandemic and layoffs; and third, feminism optics to unravel the roots of discrimination against domestic workers, including the challenges and opportunities for advocating policies to protect domestic workers.

Migration Motives

The International Labor Organization (ILO) states that until 2012, 2.6 million Indonesians were working as domestic workers, dominated by women with

TABLE 7.1
Motives Driving Migration

No.	*Background*	*Explanation*
1	Employment	Narrow job opportunities followed by job requirements based on education level.
2	Development	Cities tend to experience rapid development than villages which are relatively sluggish.
3	Lack of choice	The average migrant who cannot be absorbed in the industrial sector has no other choice to survive in the city.

Source: Created by the authors.

low education (Muhtadi, 2014). The domestic workers who are women are mostly scattered in various big cities in Indonesia. Meanwhile, on a global scale, the migration of Indonesian domestic workers in the ILO's 2009 prediction reached 6 million people (90%) (Soetjiptio, 2017).

The background of the migration of third-world people rests on several motives. As seen in table 7.1,

First, limited employment opportunities in rural areas, because employment tends to rely on the traditional agricultural sector (Makmur and Mohamad, 2021). They are a subcommunity lacking skills and education modalities amid a labor sector that absorbs workers from educated and skilled circles (Pribadi et al., 2020). Second, inequality in rural and urban development (Afifah, 2018). However, the urban area is a parameter for the development of a region. In Indonesia, most migrant workers are concentrated in big cities such as Jakarta, which reach 801,566 people.

On the other hand, the destination cities for migrants have not accommodated all migrants, especially workers with low talent. Third, there is no choice (Afifah, 2018; Soetjiptio, 2017). Migrants who have already arrived at their destination and are not absorbed by the industrial sector have no choice but to work in the informal sector. They choose the informal sector for three reasons: it does not require particular skills, is relatively easy to enter, and relies on relationships or networks of friends (Afifah, 2018; Pribadi et al., 2020).

Pandemic and Termination of Employment

During the pandemic, data on Termination of Employment (PHK) that afflict domestic workers is rarely disclosed because the classification of workers is published in general. There are at least two urgent and essential aspects of unemployment caused by the pandemic. First, layoffs that befell domestic workers are part of gender issues. Second, they work in sectors with weak guarantees of protection. Agustina et al. (2021) stated that previously fertile gender inequality was exacerbated during the pandemic because of the semi-closed nature of their work in the domestic sphere, challenging to reach by protective regulations.

Based on UN Women's data through the Rapid Gender Assessment (RGA), more than 15% of women lost their jobs during the pandemic. Meanwhile, the decrease in wages for women reached 41% of cases. Agustina et al. (2021) explain that the pandemic has brought multiple adverse effects on social life; the exploitation of domestic workers increased, the workload heavier, the absence of additional wages, and the shadow pandemic problems such as embedding labels as spreaders of the viruses.

Since the Indonesian government stipulates Government Regulation (PP) No. 21 of 2020 concerning Large-Scale Social Restrictions (PSBB), many companies cut the number of workers on the grounds of force majeure, which is one indicator of natural disasters. Juaningsih (2020) denied the reason for the layoff using force majeure. One of the requirements for force majeure in the legal framework is if a natural disaster occurs for two years. Meanwhile, on the facts on the ground, mass layoffs were carried out for one year. Bappenas data shows the unemployment rate due to the pandemic reached 4.2 million people in 2020. On the other hand, even during the pandemic, some companies continued to carry out production as usual. So the reason for force majeure does not meet the requirements to reduce workers (Juaningsih, 2020).

Bangun (2017) explains that layoffs are organizational members who leave due to limited ability to meet organizational needs. Layoffs for companies are synonymous with budget efficiency. Meanwhile, for workers, layoffs are a form of loss of work and a source of income. Muslim (2020) explained a unique mechanism for layoffs during a pandemic. Before doing layoffs, the company first laid off workers, followed by salary cuts. The reflection of the many layoffs resulted in soaring unemployment during 2020. The disqualified group of male workers from the informal sector reflected women's initiation to jump in to replace their husbands to earn a living amid the COVID-19 pandemic (Firmansyah, nd). Thus, the pandemic landscape adds to women's motives to work in the informal sector as domestic workers.

However, domestic workers as informal sector workers are more disadvantaged than formal sector workers. In general, domestic workers earn less than working in large companies (Triastari et al., 2021). In the informal sector, it is recorded that around 189,000 workers have been laid off and become victims of layoffs (Yazid, 2020). Based on LIPI survey data (2020), about 2% of laid-off victims received severance pay.

The informal sector during the COVID-19 pandemic was considered a work sector that was prone to acts of gender-based violence. Based on data from the Ministry of Women's Empowerment and Child Protection (KPPPA), around 417 cases of violence are experienced by women in the informal employment sector, especially domestic workers. Violence experienced by women's groups in the informal sector includes physical violence, psychological violence, and sexual violence (KEMENPPPA, 2020).

Agustina et al. (2020) consider that the risk of women's work in the domestic and public spheres is greater than that of male workers. Amid the lack of rules for protecting domestic workers, women need to equip themselves with strategies to deal with threats such as human rights education and building affiliations (Afifah, 2018; Sonhaji, 2020). This provision of skills goes beyond the ILO formulation, which reveals that domestic workers need an adequate skill base in the domestic sphere of the home. These skills include cooking, cleaning the house, washing, taking care of children and the garden (Ajrin, 2016).

Tracing the Roots of Domestic Worker Discrimination, Policy Challenges, and Advocacy Opportunities

Exposure to a feminist lens provides a comprehensive and more precise understanding of the phenomena of gender inequality and violence against domestic workers. There are two feminist thinkers that I use in looking at the phenomenon of domestic workers migrant workers. First, Mies (2007, 2014: 39–40), one of the socialist feminist thinkers who see women as not having equal opportunities in access to work. In employment, women are fragmented in jobs with low wages. The identification of women as non-productive workers is rapidly accumulating on a global scale. Second, Enloe (2014: 184) describes the relationship between global economic theory and the migration of women workers, especially domestic workers. In his view, the IMF debt regime is the main factor in the rapid migration of domestic workers from their hometowns to cities and other countries. Women from developing countries, including Indonesia, are under pressure financially due to the rising cost of living. Remittances sent to their countries of origin continue to increase from year to year so that migrant workers, especially domestic workers, are often referred to as the foreign exchange. Women domestic workers with closed and intimate characteristics in the domestic household sector tend to be at greater risk and are not infrequently the target of violence. Midgley (2004) believes that economic equity and gender equality in international migration are the resonant reasons that cause the significant demand for domestic workers in developed countries: substitution of homework due to the deficit in care work in rich countries, elderly care services, and limited child care. However, the phenomenon of gender bias, as in the view of the international political economy, does not only occur in developed countries.

In developing countries, exploiting women domestic workers is common, especially in urban areas. Inequality is commodified when middle- and upper-class women can pay for gender equality by attracting domestic workers, presenting new inequalities. Put, middle- and upper-class women need a replacement for the domestic tasks they leave at home. The debate on domestic affairs seems to invite us to question the feminist movement since the 1960s.

Meanwhile, from the perspective of Indonesian policy, the situation is exacerbated by the lack of available regulatory tools to protect domestic workers from threats of violence and harassment. The Indonesian government does not have a solid legal umbrella (Pribadi et al., 2020). The rules for the protection of domestic workers do not detail the forms of protection for domestic workers, which include employee relations, discrimination, violence, wages, and others (Afifah, 2018). Data from the net of domestic workers cited by the National Commission on Violence against Women shows that domestic workers were 2,148 cases against domestic workers from 2015 to 2019 (Komnas Perempuan, 2021). Therefore, this situation becomes a severe challenge for policies to protect domestic workers in the future.

Digital media, as the only option during physical distancing, has an essential role in distributing information to the public. With the increase in layoffs during the pandemic, disclosure exploitation of domestic workers places the media as the center of the discourse of sense of crisis. Almond and Powell (1980) explained that interest groups aimed at the public interest have an orientation to urge the government to take specific actions related to the public interest. Maiwan (2016) explains that media companies are one of the interest groups that aim to amplify the public interest. Vertically, the role of the media is in line with the objectives of the policy assessment, namely to provide relevant information about policies and the policy design process (Ramdhani and Ramdhani, 2017).

Online media such as Tirto took part to discuss the issue of domestic workers, describing the results of critical investigations about the violence faced by domestic workers during the pandemic. Tirto focuses on visualizing data on violence against domestic workers during the pandemic. The data released in this media not only comes from the story of domestic workers being stigmatized as spreading COVID-19, but Tirto also displays data belonging to Komnas Perempuan without making a detailed assessment. In addition, the data shown is cited from groups that focus on women's issues, NGOs, and paralegal institutions such as the Legal Aid Institute (LBH). Based on a Komnas Perempuan survey, the weak protection for domestic workers makes them vulnerable to being exposed to the virus and being neglected from social assistance such as health insurance (Iswara, 2021).

Cases of violence during the pandemic that hit domestic workers until the end of December 2020 jumped significantly. In 2019, there were 467 cases of violence against domestic workers, increasing in 2020 to 842 cases (Iswara, 2021). According to data from the Domestic Worker Advocacy Network (Jala PRT), cases reported by domestic workers are varied, such as unpaid wages, unilateral layoffs without severance pay, no holiday allowance (THR), wage cuts, and not receiving social security (Iswara, 2021). The mass media have the power to roll the issue of domestic violence into the public sphere to urge policy makers to pay attention to the protection of domestic workers. Media companies or the press become agents of interest groups who have the power to bring policy issues to the level of agenda-setting and policy formulation (Nugroho, 2011:24–28).

Conclusion

The phenomenon of migration is identical to the discourse of economic and political development. The high demand for living in developing countries such as Indonesia causes migration to reach millions and increases every year. Most of these workers work in the domestic sector, which women migrants engage. This is because of low educational background and limited talent. The metaphor of the distinction between domestic and public sector jobs resembles the different positions of the state and society (Okin, 1989). Domestic sector workspaces tend to be closed, and the nature of interpersonal relationships makes it difficult to identify protection against domestic work. The discussion has described how exploitation often targets women in the informal sector of domestic workers. This chapter opens an extended discussion of violence against women domestic workers. The study of international relations, especially feminism theory, provides a repetitive picture of the feminist debate from the beginning about unfinished domestic work, including international economic theory. In the economic landscape, the presence of migrant workers in developed countries, on the one hand, is a remittance asset for the country of origin. Nevertheless, on the other hand, the protection rules are challenging to reach the closed nature of domestic work.

The portrait of the dominance of labor in the domestic sector authentically opens up a new exploitation space for women. A similar situation occurs in internal migration; the gray rules regarding the protection of domestic workers make the exploitation of women a mysterious ghost. Then the pandemic confirmed that domestic violence had increased significantly from 467 cases in 2019 to 847 cases during 2020 (Iswara, 2021).

The media is a crucial center for amplifying violence cases against domestic workers before the public and stakeholders during the pandemic (Maiwan,

2016). In addition, during the lockdown, the media fills the gaps in transmitting information in the online form (Sudibyo, 2019). The mass media is one of the interest groups that can urge the government to take certain actions (Almond and Powell, 1980). Therefore, the media in cases of violence against domestic workers can pressure policy makers to design effective protection strategies in the future.

On the one hand, this chapter does not describe in detail how the relationship between exploitation and violence uses a domination perspective, even though the description of domination is related to power relations, time, context, and background. In Vrousalis's (2021) opinion, exploitation in specific contexts does not come from one's domination. On the other hand, workers who only rely on labor-capital may be exploited. Further studies need to use the knife of power analysis to uncover the veil of violence domestic workers face.

References

Afifah, W. (2018). The existence of legal protection for domestic workers in Indonesia. [In Indonesian]. *DiH: Jurnal Ilmu Hukum*. doi:10.30996/dih.v0i0.1594

Agustina, E., Ernawati, E., Irvita, M., & Putri, C. P. (2021). The Impact of the Covid-19 Pandemic in the Perspective of Gender Equality. [In Indonesian]. *UNUSIA Conference*, *1*(1), 89–100.

Ajrin, S. (2016). Self-Acceptance to Domestic Helpers. [In Indonesian]. *Kafa`ah: Journal of Gender Studies*, *6*(1), 111. doi:10.15548/jk.v6i1.122

Almond, G., & Powell, B. (1980). *Comparative Politics: A Developmental Approach*. Little, Brown and Co.

Asriani, D. D., & Amalia, E. (2014). Footprints of Women Migrant Workers in the 2015 ASEAN Community. [In Indonesian]. *Jurnal Ilmu Sosial Dan Ilmu Politik*, *18*(2), 147–159. doi:10.22146/jsp.13129

Bangun, W. (2017). *Industrial Relations HR Management*. [In Indonesian]. Erlangga.

BNP2TKI. (2019). Placement of Indonesian Migrant Workers by Country. [In Indonesian]. Available online at: http://portal.bnp2tki.go.id/uploads/data/data_12-03-2019_094615_Laporan_Pengolahan_Data_BNP2TKI_2018.pdf. Accessed on 13 December 2021.

Castles, S. (2009). Development and Migration or Migration and Development: What Comes First? *Asian and Pacific Migration Journal*, *18*(4), 441–471. doi:10.1177/011719680901800401

Dhewy, A. (2017). Local and Migrant Domestic Workers. *Jurnal Perempuan*, *22*(3), iii–iii. doi:10.34309/jp.v22i3.197

Enloe, C. (2014). *Bananas, Beaches and Bases*. University of California Press.

Firmansyah, R. J. A. M. (n.d.). Indonesian Women's Vulnerability to Gender Based Violence during the COVID-19 Pandemic: The Case of Layoffs. *Dancing in a*

Storm (Gender And Hope Amid the COVID-19 Pandemic), 127. [In Indonesian]. Available online at: http://eprints.mercubuana-yogya.ac.id/14016/1/E-Book_Menari%20Dalam%20Badai%20-%20PSW%20UPNVY.pdf#page=137. Accessed on 13 December 2021.

Hamzah, A. (2020). *Literature Research Methods: Philosophical Studies, Applications, Processes, and Research Results*. Literasi Nusantara.

Harris, J. R., & Todaro, M. P. (1970). Migration, Unemployment and Development: A Two-Sector Analysis. *The American Economic Review*, *60*(1), 126–142.

Huberman, Miles. (1992). *Qualitative Data Analysis: A Resource Book on New Methods*. UI Press.

ILO. (2020). COVID-19 and the World of Work: Impact and Responses. Department of International Labor Standards (ILO). Versi 1.2. Available online at: https://www.ilo.org/wcmsp5/groups/public/---asia/---ro-bangkok/---ilo-jakarta/documents/publication/wcms_742033.pdf. Accessed on 20 January 2022.

IOM. (2019). *Glossary on Migration, IML Series, No. 34*. IOM Geneva.

IOM. (2020). World Migration Report 2020. Available online at: https://www.un.org/sites/un2.un.org/files/wmr_2020.pdf. Accessed on 13 December 2021.

Indonesia, B. (2019). *Indonesian Economic and Financial Statistics: Number of Indonesian Migrant Workers (IMWs) by Host Country*. [In Indonesian]. bi.go.id. Available online at: https://www.bi.go.id/seki/tabel/TABEL5_30.pdf. Accessed on 13 December 2021.

Iswara, M. A. (2021). *Domestic Workers' Rights Are Getting Circumcised, Violence Rises During the COVID-19 Pandemic*.[In Indonesian]. Tirto.Id. https://tirto.id/hak-hak-prt-semakin-disunat-kekerasan-naik-selama-pandemi-covid-19-gavM.

Juaningsih, I. N. (2020). Policy Analysis of Layoffs for Workers During the Covid-19 Pandemic in Indonesia. [In Indonesian]. *Adalah*, *4*(1), 189–196. doi:10.15408/adalah.v4i1.15764.

Kementerian PPPA. (2020). Women Friendly Houses Prevent Women from Experiencing Gender-Based Violence in Disasters. [In Indonesian]. Kemenpppa.go.id. Available online at: https://kemenpppa.go.id/index.php/page/read/29/2299/rumah-ramah-perempuan-cegah-perempuan-alami-kekerasan-berbasis-gender-dalam-bencana. Accessed on 13 December 2021.

Komnas Perempuan. (2021). Komnas Perempuan Press Release Commemorating National Domestic Workers (PRT) Day (15 February 2021). [In Indonesian] Available online at: https://komnasperempuan.go.id/siaran-pers-detail/siaran-pers-komnas-perempuan-peringatan-hari-pekerja-rumah-tangga-prt-nasional-15-feb-ruari-2021. Accessed on 12 January 2022.

Lee, E. S. (1966). A Theory of Migration. *Demography*, *3*(1), 47–57. doi:10.2307/2060063.

LIPI. (2020). Results of the Survey on the Impact of the Covid-19 Pandemic on Workers. [In Indonesian]. lipi.go.id. Available online at: http://lipi.go.id/siaran-press/hasil-survei-dampak-pandemi-covid-19-pada-pekerja/22011. Accessed on 13 December 2021.

Maiwan, M. (2016). Interest Groups, Their Power and Position in the Political System. [In Indonesian]. *Jurnal Ilmiah Mimbar Demokrasi, 15*(2), 75-91. doi:10.21009/jimd.v15i2.8815.

Makmur, S. M., & Mohamad, I. R. (2021). Review of the Protection of Domestic Workers. [In Indonesian]. *At-Tanwir Law Review*, *1*(1), 43–51.

Marta, J., Fauzi, A., Juanda, B., & Rustiadi, E. (2020a). Rural-Urban Migration in Indonesia: "Risk Coping Strategy vs Investment." *Jurnal Ekonomi Dan Pembangunan Indonesia*, *20*(2), 160–173. doi:10.21002/jepi.v20i2.1337.

Marta, J., Fauzi, A., Juanda, B., & Rustiadi, E. (2020b). Understanding Migration Motives and Its Impact on Household Welfare: Evidence from Rural–Urban Migration in Indonesia. *Regional Studies, Regional Science*, *7*(1), 118–132. doi:10.1080/21681376.2020.1746194.

Midgley, J. (2004). Arlie Russel Hochschild, The Commerialization of Intimate Life: Notes from Home and Work. *Journal of Sociology & Social Welfare*, *31*(3), 188–191.

Mies, M. (2007). Patriarchy and Accumulation on a World Scale Revisited. (Keynote lecture at the Green Economics Institute, Reading, 29 October 2005). *International Journal of Green Economics*, *1*(3–4), 268–275. doi:10.1504/IJGE.2007.013059.

Mies, M. (2014). *Patriarchy and Accumulation on a World Scale: Women in the International Division of Labour*. Bloomsbury Publishing.

Muslim, M. (2020). Layoffs During the Covid-19 Pandemic. [In Indonesian]. *ESENSI: Jurnal Manajemen Bisnis*, *23*(3), 357–370.

Nugroho, R. (2011). *Public Policy* (Edisi keti). PT Elex Media Komputindo.

Okin, S. M. (1989). *Gender, the Public and the Private*. Faculty of Law, University of Toronto.

Pribadi, L. E., Budiartha, I. N. P., & Arini, D. G. D. (2020). Legal Protection for Domestic Workers in Full-Time Employment Relations. [In Indonesian]. *Jurnal Interpretasi Hukum*, *1*(1), 89–94. doi:10.22225/juinhum.1.1.2192.89-94.

Ramdhani, A., & Ramdhani, M. A. (2017). General Concept of Public Policy Implementation. [In Indonesian]. *Jurnal Publik*, *11*(1), 1–12. doi:10.35448/jrat.v11i2.4261.

Soetjiptio, A. (2017). State Policy Against Migrant Domestic Workers in Indonesia: A Study of Gender and International Relations. [In Indonesian]. *Jurnal Masyarakat Dan Budaya*, *19*(1), 45–58. doi:10.14203/jmb.v19i1.388.

Sonhaji, S. (2020). Protection of Domestic Workers in the National Legal System. [In Indonesian]. *Administrative Law and Governance Journal*, *3*(2), 250–259. doi:10.14710/alj.v3i2.250-259.

Sudibyo, A. (2019). *Digital Universe: Liberation and Mastery*. [In Indonesian]. KPG (Kepustakaan Populer Gramedia).

Triastari, R., Krisnanik, E., & Zaidiah, A. (2021). Domestic Worker (PRT) Search Database Design. [In Indonesian]. *Senamika*, *2*(1), 178–186.

Vrousalis, N. (2021). How exploiters dominate. *Review of Social Economy*, *79*(1), 103–130. doi:10.1080/00346764.2019.1618483.

Yazid, E.K. (2020). Challenges and Adaptation of Employment in the Era of the COVID-19 Pandemic. [In Indonesian]. CSIS Commentaries DMRU046-ID. Available online at: https://www.csis.or.id/publications/tantangan-dan-adaptasi-lapangan-kerja-di-era-pandemi-covid-19. Accessed on 12 January 2022.

8

Locked Down and Left Behind

The Impact of COVID-19 on Refugees' Private Businesses in Granada City (Southern Spain)

Mohammad HASSOUNA, Iyad S. M. KHAMAYSA, and Javier Tamayo TORRES

Introduction

COVID-19 is spreading worldwide, with more than 300 million confirmed cases and more than 5 million deaths reported across almost 200 countries (John Hopkins University, National Public Health Agencies 2022). The rapid global spread of the COVID-19 has been unprecedented, and despite the government's measures to prevent its spread and minimize its economic consequences, things got out of control. Statistics in various countries of the world confirmed the inability of governments to control the negative effects accumulated as a result of the coronavirus at all levels and sectors (Ashraf 2020). Consequences led us to question the extent of its impacts on the refugees' private businesses. Let us specifically address the impact of this pandemic on a segment of society, the refugees, and how it affected their business. Some of the difficulties migrants and refugees face in the host countries are social, cultural, and economic. When we address the economic aspect, we mean the opportunities available in the labor market, whether in job positions (public/private) or private businesses. Some studies indicated the difficulties refugees face in obtaining job opportunities, so the majority tend to work on their accounts through small projects that provide them with what they can provide of a decent human life (Miller 2015, 2019; Zetter and Ruaudel

2018). Small businesses contribute to local economies by achieving growth and innovation in the community businesses established (Kobe and Schwinn 2018). It helps stimulate economic growth by providing job opportunities for people who are not employable in large companies. Small businesses were a fundamental building block in forming some sectors, including the tourism sector. It is considered one of the most important economic sectors at the level of the global economy and the most dynamic one. It represents one of the most important sectors contributing to generating GDP and creating job opportunities.

In 2019, the World Tourism Organization (WTO) produced reports on the economic and employment impact of travel and tourism for 185 countries and 25 geographic or economic regions in the world. The sector experienced 3.5% growth in 2019, where the contribution of the tourism sector to the global gross product was about US$8.9 trillion to the world's GDP. Europe had a share of 9.1% of the total GDP contribution with 2.0 TN (World Tourism Organization 2019). Moving to Spain in 2019, the contribution of the travel and tourism sector to GDP was 14.3% of the total economy (Instituto Nacional de Estadística 2020). In addition to its impact on public health, coronavirus disease in 2019 (COVID-19) has caused a major economic shock. The outbreak of the COVID-19 epidemic had a significant impact on the tourism sector worldwide due to travel restrictions and reduced movement of travel demand among travelers. The hospitality sector was one of the sectors most affected by this crisis (Yang et al. 2020); due to this crisis, a significant impact was created on the small business in Granada (where most small businesses are in the tourism and hospitality sector).

The remainder of the chapter is organized as follows. Section 2 describes the COVID-19 and Granada City, impacts of COVID-19 on refugees' private businesses, impacts of COVID-19 on refugees' incomes, and refugees' owners and governments have multiple issues to solve, and data presents the methodology of the applied study; section 3 results; section 4 concludes and references.

COVID-19 and Granada City

Since the beginning of March, the renewed corona epidemic has spread throughout the country, varying according to the country. At the beginning of the matter, people did not think it would spread. No one would be excluded, and the consideration of the virus as a dangerous disease initially was not very. The economic measures taken in the beginning were not in line with the magnitude of the disaster on the ground, particularly the owners of projects in general. But pandemic that suddenly came to their business and affected their trade; and led to a drop in small business owners was the largest on record in light of the Corona crisis and its developments (Fairlie 2020). The most affected business of this crisis is the restaurant sector (where most immigrants work). It is strongly linked to public health, how the consumers' perception changed after this pandemic, and the steps taken by restaurant owners. And it specially mentioned a small business that concerns refugees and immigrants in particular.

Granada is a tourist city that receives an approximately large number of tourists annually according to the International Tourism Statistics for Andalusia; the city of Granada received nearly 2 million tourists in 2019—opening a small business, a substantial opportunity for refugees, since Granada is always filled with students and tourists due to cheap prices (restaurant-accommodation) and various cultures. Because of the corona pandemic, the government took decisions that caused a complete closure of the city, which led to the non-arrival of tourists and the transfer of studies to students remotely. Since the beginning of the global shutdown, and the health crisis in Italy, anxiety has increased in the surrounding communities, especially refugees and migrants; life has become a most incredible difficulty. They have to face the corona crisis alone, and no one cares about their needs.

Coronavirus was a reason for not continuing refugees in their work; they became without a source of living. The actual effect on their business appeared, as the percentage of work decreased suddenly. The project became not capable of accommodating more than one person to work. The owners started working alone to cover the expenses until Spain entered the closure phase. The state declared a state of emergency for 15 days from March and extended it according to the health situation in the country.

Impacts of COVID-19 on Refugees' Private Businesses

From various pieces of literature that dealt with the economic impact of previous epidemics, Barro et al. (2020) measured the impact of the Spanish flu epidemic and the First World War on economic growth, expressed in growth rates of both actual outcomes and per capita consumption. Influenza and war mortality rates from 1918 to 1920 have been used for 48 countries. The regression results showed an inverse relationship between mortality rates and output and consumption, indicating the harmful effect of the Spanish flu and the war on economic growth. Cuddington (1993) inferred AIDS epidemic was expected to reduce the output per capita until 2010 by 10% compared to the situation without this epidemic. This study added that the policies adopted in the labor market might mitigate some of the adverse economic effects resulting from the AIDS epidemic, but without compensating the individual and social costs resulting from this epidemic. Bloom et al. (2005) developed scenarios based on previous experiences of influenza and SARS outbreaks. It also dealt with the impact of the bird flu epidemic on economic activity in Asia in the short term, finding that this epidemic has led to a slowdown in economic growth and a significant decline in trade, especially in services trade.

The corona pandemic is considered an unprecedented epidemic due to its evolution from a health shock to an economic and social crisis (Bonaccors et al. 2020) that will worsen in the long term with a decline in economic growth and high unemployment rates (Baert et al. 2020). The majority of global institutions unanimously agree that the crisis resulting from this pandemic is, at the economic level, more severe than all the previous ones. McKibbin and Fernando (2021) presented—according to the possible development of the disease—a set of scenarios for the impact of the corona epidemic on economic outcomes or outputs based on the experience gained from evaluating the economic effects of the SARS epidemic in 2003. This study aimed to measure the potential economic costs of the corona pandemic in different scenarios through exposure to several economic shocks represented in the decrease in the supply of work (illness and death); the high cost of doing business in each sector, including the disruption of production networks in each country; and reduced consumption due to changes in consumer preferences for each commodity from each country; high-risk premiums for stock price volatility in every sector in every country; And increases in the risk premium in a country according to its degree of exposure to disease, as well as the degree of its vulnerability to changing conditions at the macroeconomic level. The study finds that with the development of coronavirus into a pandemic at the global level, the economic costs resulting from this are rising rapidly.

The study of Kurman et al. (2020) showed new estimates of the impact of the corona crisis on employment and working hours in the United States by focusing on the entertainment and hospitality sectors and retail trade, which are two of the sectors most affected by the crisis, as it reached four main results: first, the decrease in employment in these two sectors by 60% between mid-February and the end of April 2020; second, that a third of this decrease is due to companies reducing employment to zero; and third, a decrease in the average number of hours per week for workers still working by about 10%; fourth, the first signs of recovery appear in the form of the return of 15% of the establishments that had previously ceased activity and in the increase in the average working hours of employees. In another study in the United States conducted by Bartik et al. (2020), showed that small companies employed almost 50% of American workers, they found that 43% of businesses were temporarily closed and that employment had fallen by 40%. Also, it indicated small businesses' responses that many are likely to fail absent financial assistance. Firms in particularly exposed industries—such as restaurants, tourism, and personal services—a project that they will find it extremely difficult to stay in business if the crisis lasts for longer than four months.

It is clear from these previous studies how the corona pandemic can negatively affect economic variables, including the unemployment rate; these results underscore the financial fragility of many small businesses, and how deeply affected they are by the current crisis. As in many other crises, migrants may be particularly vulnerable to the direct or indirect effects of the COVID-19 crisis, as their ability to receive health care or deal with the economic and social impacts of the pandemic may be affected (Liem et al. 2020). When we discuss the extent of the impact of the corona epidemic on the work of refugees and migrants in the host countries, we must first refer to the difficulties and obstacles faced by migrants in obtaining employment opportunities. Some previous literature findings indicated that the time an asylum seeker spends in refugee camps or other places of residence has a substantial impact on the chances of finding work in the future (Bakker et al. 2014). For example, in a study conducted in Switzerland by researchers Hainmueller et al. (2016), each additional year that an asylum seeker waits for reduces the employment rate by several percentage points. In the same vein, a study in Denmark by Hvidtfeldt et al. (2018) demonstrated that each additional year of waiting time in the asylum system reduces employment opportunities by an average of 3.2 percentage points.

In Germany, Brücker et al. (2019) find that prolonged asylum procedures inhibit subsequent job findings; while Marbach et al. (2018) show that temporary employment bans after arrival in Germany have significant adverse effects on subsequent employment trajectories of refugees. Exposure to adverse economic shocks and health risks associated with the COVID-19 pandemic is greater among immigrant workers than native-born people in high-income Western European countries (Bossavie et al. 2022). In April 2020, immigrant men had lower employment rates than native men in the United States (Borjas and Cassidy 2020). Fairlie (2020) presents a preliminary analysis of the epidemic's effects on several small companies in the United States using representative data for April 2020. The results were that immigrant business owners were exposed to huge losses amounting to 36%.

Impacts of COVID-19 on Refugees' Incomes

COVID-19 is causing widespread loss of livelihoods among refugee populations, affecting their self-reliance and increasing protection anxieties. Losing jobs and access to income, many refugees may suffer from raised food insecurity (Alzoubi et al. 2019), inability to pay rent, debt emerging from vital health care costs, and a lack of ability to cope with shocks. Thus, refugees are more likely to turn to negative coping strategies, including skipping meals and doing exploitative work (UNHCR 2019). Moreover, their status as refugees makes them subject to xenophobia and abuse, which often translates into worse working conditions than their national peers. Undoubtedly, COVID-19 has laboriously disrupted refugees' livelihoods and forced many to choose between earning a living and prioritizing their health. Despite quarantine efforts, the need to earn a living pushes refugee workers to keep working as COVID-19 affects businesses and economic activity worldwide. Refugees facing challenges to their economic inclusion will remain among the most powerless. The pandemic will only magnify their lack of access to the countries' social protection and economic systems that host them.

Refugees' Owners and Governments Have Multiple Issues to Solve

The maximum economic impact of the COVID-19 pandemic will be partially confined by how effectively policy makers and business authorities can mitigate structural crack to the economy while controlling the coronavirus. While the crisis is overgrowing, it is clear that helping the employees and businesses to address losing income during the lockdown is a priority. Policy makers have formed consequential financial help programs to support hirelings and businesses; the challenge represents organizing government support between public and private sectors. Alike will need to acclimate and innovate (Lund et al. 2020).

The Issues Facing Businesses

The last downturn lesson is that entirely severing the relationship between employers and workers extends unemployment. The actual economy will position for a faster and fuller recovery to the extent that enterprises can execute temporary layoffs, reduced hours, or creative job-sharing and redeployment programs instead of outright furloughs. The Payroll Protection Program, for example, is indicated to cover payroll costs for small businesses that will keep refugee workers employed (McKinsey Global Institute 2020). When firings and layoffs are inevitable, employers can take steps to help the newly unemployed land on their feet, such as share to pay rent. Experiencing social media can help furloughed workers link with companies that need temporary help to meet pouring demand. Some downsizing companies are already developing direct collaborations with organizations hiring to help make these workforce shifts faster and more seamless. Layoffs can also provide a window for employees to develop skills through online course training.

The Issues Facing Policy Makers

Many countries have reduced the pileup by counting staff or upgrading online processing. If lockdown needs to extend to protect public health, policy makers may consider extending the alarm period (Lund et al. 2020). However, freelancers and temporary workers are now eligible for unemployment. Many have found it challenging to steer application processes that the government did not develop with their situations. The refugees get information about COVID-19 and the lockdown period from social media. Spain is trying to address this problem by setting up portals specifically for independent workers.

Methodology

Study Procedure and Recruitment

This study was conducted in the city of Granada in southern Spain, where this city is considered in the province of Andalusia, and it is one of the cities that receive about 2 million tourists annually. We chose Granada for two reasons: first of all, it is a tourist destination for tourists and students, where the tourism and hospitality sector is one of the largest sectors in the city of Granada, where the work of refugees is concentrated in this sector, whether in restaurants, tourist attractions, or tourism offices. Second, Granada is a destination for many refugees and immigrants from different countries and enjoys great cultural and ethnic diversity due to its relatively low prices, be it the real estate sector or the costs of living in general.

The survey depends on a descriptive approach, involving 30 small- and medium-sized businesses (SMBs), owners, immigrants, and refugees whose field of work is concentrated in restaurants, tourism companies, and tourist bazaars in Granada city center. COVID-19 Business Impact Survey developed by the Weber County Economic Development in the United States of America was used to collect data. The comprehensive survey was conducted in September 2021; we collected data through an online questionnaire due to the prevailing concerns about the necessity of social distancing. Despite that, some interviews were conducted face-to-face interviews, taking into account the social distancing at that time. Collecting data was not accessible due to the difficulty of accessing employers due to businesses being closed because of the COVID-19; it was challenging to meet owners due to social distancing. However, I was explaining the scientific objective of the article to interview the business owners. They have felt some discomfort answering the questions, such as giving some information about their projects and feeling frustrated with the current economic situation. We have chosen this sample very carefully to represent almost all the existing segments that meet the requirements for this research according to the foundations of scientific research.

Results

Study participants have reported that revenues have decreased by 37.9% due to COVID-19 since March 1, 2020. They also faced a decrease in the workforce of 1–5 persons, at a rate of 75.9%. While they indicated they share 58.6% of their employees with information related to COVID-19 via social media, 55.2% receive information about the COVID-19 from social media as employers. The study also revealed that 69% of companies do not have a remote or teleworking policy implemented regarding COVID-19. The survey results also show that 93.1% of employers have a strong desire to get information about financial aid related to COVID-19 to overcome the repercussions of the virus. 62.1% have an interest in other business development services. Besides, 41.4% decided to reduce working hours due to the consequences of the pandemic and lockdown, while 20.7% closed temporarily, compared to 17.2% permanently and laid off workers. 93.1% need to receive information and financial assistance related to COVID-19 to improve their business. The majority of business owners immediately need help to face COVID-19 and need governmental support to open borders to bring in tourism and facilitate business help. After the pandemic, the business needs economic recovery through tax deductions and financial needs (rental help and paying bills). Owners indicated that COVID-19 impacted their company's workforce through school and daycare cancellations due to the physical and psychological impact. The cancellation led to the accumulation of social responsibilities; the lockdown even in the short periods proposed by the government and lack of movement led to poor sales. The leaving of university students from Spain, specifically Granada, towards their countries due to the uncertainty when the problem of the Corona pandemic will end, and the absence of tourists caused a lack of purchasing movement because the city of Granada depends mainly on students and tourists. On the other hand, the closure of boarding schools (private, public, and language schools) led to a decrease in sales. Finally, we can say that COVID-19 has affected all aspects of life for owners, workers, and their families.

Conclusion

This chapter provides knowledge of the work of refugees and their integration into the labor market with all its changes. The impact of the corona pandemic on their business, how they faced it, what are the lessons learned, and how the host country can contribute to the integration of refugee businesses into the labor market and consider it one of the essential and inspiring elements of the economy. The key to successful refugee integration depends on the quality and speed of entry into the labor market. Numerous refugees are still young and do not have the necessary qualifications or experience. That is why we must consider the expenditures and efforts we make on refugees as an investment, just as the expenditures we spend on nurseries and schools that we consider as an investment for our children, who will repay these expenditures in 10 or 20 years. The more we invest in refugees today, the more outstanding their contribution to the future. The results imply that the refugees need encouragement and support from the Spanish government to be productive people and not a burden on the state. This support helps them stimulate tourism and the economy, on the one hand. On the other hand, it helps them integrate socially and into the labor market. The COVID-19 can be considered a job shock that seriously impacts refugees' work and small businesses. We hope that these insights will encourage scholars, owners of companies, and policy makers alike to study and understand the work and employment implications of COVID-19 as a job shock and support refugees in dealing with this shock and integrating into the labor market and community.

References

Alzoubi, Fatmeh Ahmad, Ahmed Mohammad Al-Smadi, and Yazeed Mohammad Gougazeh. "Coping Strategies Used by Syrian Refugees in Jordan." *Clinical Nursing Research* 28, no. 4 (May 2019): 396–421. https://doi.org/10.1177/1054773817749724.

Ashraf, Badar Nadeem. "Economic İmpact of Government İnterventions During the COVID-19 Pandemic: International Evidence From Financial Markets." *Journal of Behavioral and Experimental Finance* 27 (2020): 100371. https://doi.org/10.1016/j.jbef.2020.100371.

Baert, Stijn, Louis Lippens, Eline Moens, Philippe Sterkens, and Johannes Weytjens. "How Do We Think the COVID-19 Crisis Will Affect Our Careers (If Any Remain)?" (2020). GLO Discussion Paper, No. 520, Global Labor Organization (GLO), Essen.

Bakker, Linda, Jaco Dagevos, and Godfried Engbersen. "The İmportance of Resources and Security in the Socio-Economic İntegration of Refugees. A Study on the Impact of Length of Stay in Asylum Accommodation and Residence Status on Socio-Economic İntegration for the Four Largest Refugee Groups in the Netherlands." *Journal of International Migration and Integration* 15, no. 3 (2014): 431–448. https://doi.org/10.1007/s12134-013-0296-2.

Barro, Robert J., José F. Ursúa, and Joanna Weng. "The Coronavirus and the Great Influenza Pandemic: Lessons From the "Spanish Flu" for the Coronavirus's

Potential Effects on Mortality and Economic Activity." No. w26866. National Bureau of Economic Research, 2020.

Bartik, Alexander W., Marianne Bertrand, Zoe Cullen, Edward L. Glaeser, Michael Luca, and Christopher Stanton. "The Impact of COVID-19 on Small Business Outcomes and Expectations." *Proceedings of the National Academy of Sciences* 117, no. 30 (2020): 17656–17666. https://doi.org/10.1073/pnas.2006991117.

Bloom, Erik, Vincent De Wit, and Mary Jane Carangal-San Jose. "Potential Economic Impact of an Avian Flu Pandemic on Asia." *ERD Policy Brief* (42), Asian Development Bank, 2005.

Bonaccorsi, Giovanni, Francesco Pierri, Matteo Cinelli, Andrea Flori, Alessandro Galeazzi, Francesco Porcelli, Ana Lucia Schmidt, et al. "Economic and Social Consequences of Human Mobility Restrictions Under COVID-19." *Proceedings of the National Academy of Sciences* 117, no. 27 (2020): 15530–15535. https://doi.org/10.1073/pnas.2007658117.

Borjas, George J., and Hugh Cassidy. "The Adverse Effect of the COVID-19 Labor Market Shock on Immigrant Employment." No. w27243. National Bureau of Economic Research, 2020.

Bossavie, Laurent, Daniel Garrote-Sanchez, Mattia Makovec, and Çağlar Özden. "Do Immigrants Shield the Locals? Exposure to COVID-Related Risks in the European Union." *Review of International Economic* (2022): 1–32. https://doi.org/10.1111/roie.12609.

Brücker, H., J. Hainmüller, D. Hangartner, P. Jaschke, and Y. Kosyakova. "Refugee Migration to Germany Revisited: Lessons on the Integration of Asylum Seekers." In *Proceedings of the XXI European Conference of the fRDB on How to Manage the Refugee Crisis*, Reggio Calabria, Italy, vol. 15, 2019.

Conceiçao, P., J. Hall, A. Jahic, M. S. Kovacevic, S. Nayyar, A. Ortubia, and H. Tapia. "COVID-19 and Human Development: Assessing the Crisis." *Envisioning the Recovery*, United Nations Development Programme, 2020.

Cuddington, John T. "Further Results on the Macroeconomic Effects of AIDS: The Dualistic, Labor-Surplus Economy." *The World Bank Economic Review* 7, no. 3 (1993): 403–417. https://doi.org/10.1093/wber/7.3.403.

Fairlie, Robert W. "The Impact of COVID-19 on Small Business Owners: Continued Losses and the Partial Rebound in May 2020." NBER Working Paper (w27462), 2020.

Hainmueller, Jens, Dominik Hangartner, and Duncan Lawrence. "When Lives Are Put on Hold: Lengthy Asylum Processes Decrease Employment Among Refugees." *Science Advances* 2, no. 8 (2016): e1600432.

Hvidtfeldt, Camilla, Marie Louise Schultz-Nielsen, Erdal Tekin, and Mogens Fosgerau. "An Estimate of the Effect of Waiting Time in the Danish Asylum System on Post-Resettlement Employment Among Refugees: Separating the Pure Delay Effect From the Effects of the Conditions Under Which Refugees Are Waiting." *PLoS One* 13, no. 11 (2018): e0206737. https://doi.org/10.1371/journal.pone.0206737.

Instituto Nacional de Estadística-INE. "World Travel & Tourism Council, Economic Impact 2019 (2019)." https://www.ine.es/en/index.htm.

John Hopkins University, NPHA. "Covid Map: Coronavirus Cases, Deaths, Vaccinations by Country (2022, January)." https://www.bbc.com/news/world-51235105.

Kobe, Kathryn, and Richard Schwinn. *Small Business GDP 1998–2014.* US Small Business Administration, 2018.

Kurmann, André, Etienne Lalé, and Lien Ta. "The Impact of Covid-19 on Us Employment and Hours: Real-Time Estimates With Homebase Data." May, 2020. http://www. andrekurmann. com/hb_covid.

Liem, Andrian, Cheng Wang, Yosa Wariyanti, Carl A. Latkin, and Brian J. Hall. "The Neglected Health of International Migrant Workers in the COVID-19 Epidemic." *The Lancet Psychiatry* 7, no. 4 (2020): e20. https://doi.org/10.1016/S2215-0366(20)30076-6.

Lund, Susan, Kweilin Ellingrud, Bryan Hancock, and James Manyika. *COVID-19 and Jobs: Monitoring the US Impact on People and Places.* McKinsey Global Institute, 2020.

Marbach, Moritz, Jens Hainmueller, and Dominik Hangartner. "The Long-Term Impact of Employment Bans on the Economic Integration of Refugees." *Science Advances* 4, no. 9 (2018): eaap9519. https://doi.org/10.1126/sciadv.aap9519.

McKibbin, Warwick, and Roshen Fernando. "The Global Macroeconomic Impacts of COVID-19: Seven Scenarios." *Asian Economic Papers* 20, no. 2 (2021): 1–30. https://doi.org/10.1162/asep_a_00796.

McKinsey Global Institute. "Safeguarding Europe's Livelihoods: Mitigating the Employment Impact of COVID-19." April 2020. www.McKinsey.com.

Miller, David. "Justice in İmmigration." *European Journal of Political Theory* 14, no. 4 (2015): 391–408. https://doi.org/10.1177/1474885115584833.

Miller, David. "Our Responsibilities to Refugees." In *Proceedings of the 2018 ZiF Workshop "Studying Migration Policies at the Interface Between Empirical Research and Normative Analysis"*, eds. Matthias Hoesch and Lena Laube, ULB Münster (miami.uni-muenster.de), 2019, 37–49. https://doi.org/10.17879/95189441435.

UNHCR. "Monitoreo de Protección de las Americas: Perú." November 2019. https://data2.unhcr.org/en/documents/download/73326.

World Tourism Organization (UNWTO). "Covid-19 and Tourism; Tourism in Pre-Pandemic Time." 2020, February. https://www.unwto.org/covid-19-and-tourism-2020.

Yang, Yang, Hongbo Liu, and Xiang Chen. "COVID-19 and Restaurant Demand: Early Effects of the Pandemic and Stay-at-Home Orders." *International Journal of Contemporary Hospitality Management* (2020). https://doi.org/10.1108/IJCHM-06-2020-0504.

Zetter, Roger, and Héloïse Ruaudel. "Refugees' Right to Work and Access to Labour Markets: Constraints, Challenges and Ways Forward." *Forced Migration Review* 58 (2018): 4–7.

9

Educational and Social Aids Financed by Government Budget and Other Public Funds

Nihat AKBULUT

Introduction

The problem of the study is the inadequacy of educational aids for secondary school students in Turkey and lowness of the ratio of those who benefit from these aids. Within the framework of this problem, it is aimed to reveal the amount of resources allocated to educational aid financed by public resources and to what extent secondary school students can benefit from these aids. In the study, besides the resources allocated to education from the state budget, the resources allocated to education aids within the social aids transferred from the Social Assistance and Solidarity Encouragement Fund (called as SYDTF orj.) to the budget of the Ministry of Family and Social Services (Aile ve Sosyal Politikalar Bakanlığı) are discussed. Although Social and Economic Aids (SEA) are not direct educational aids, the payments made to secondary school students who benefit from these aids are also considered within this scope.

In the first part of the research, scholarships and economic support payments for secondary education students from the general budget and other public resources are revealed with the data of 2019. The second part compares the last two years' (2018–2019) data of the distribution of public social assistance based on public institutions providing these assistances, depending on data from the annual program of the Turkish Republic Presidency (Türkiye

Cumhuriyeti Cumhurbaşkanlığı) and the Ministry of Family and Social Services. In the third part, data on the amounts of resources allocated to education aids from the general budget and other public resources and also their ratios to national income are presented.

In the conclusion part, based on the results of the research on the determinant effect of socioeconomic reasons on school dropouts, the effectiveness of education aids financed by public resources within the solution-oriented public finance policies and programs is evaluated in terms of both the number of beneficiaries and the size of the budget allocated in this area. Thus, this study aims to reveal that economic policies and programs aiming to prevent school dropouts are crucial, and in this context, it brings forward the idea of more budgetary resources should be allocated for educational aids such as scholarships, dormitories, clothing, and meals for economically disadvantaged students as the main proposal.

Methodology

At first, the main findings of researches about the relationship between socioeconomic factors and early school leaving problems have been compiled from the literature. Regarding the findings revealing that socioeconomic factors are the main underlying reasons for school dropouts, it is focused on developing policies toward disadvantaged children to ensure their attendance to education. In this policy framework, educational and social aids for students and their households in Turkey are presented, and their sufficiency levels are evaluated in terms of numbers of beneficiaries of these aids and the amount of allocated budget and other public funds. In the meantime, these data are compared with European Union countries, and depending on these compared data, some public financial policy measures are recommended.

Theoretical Framework

Why Do the Governments Intervene in Education?

Increasing the level of education contributes to the realization of social cohesion by making individuals feel good and healthy, decreasing their tendency to delinquency. Education contributes to the realization of social cohesion for children from different socioeconomic backgrounds, and it increases women's labor force participation and contributes to the elimination of gender inequalities. In addition to the benefits that cannot be directly calculated in terms of money in the short term, some benefits can be directly calculated economically, such as higher wages for the qualified workforce thanks to increasing the level of education and the quality of labor.

The benefits of education that cannot be calculated (such as accelerating technology, increasing adaptability, reducing crime, providing socialization, and encouraging democratic participation) are called externalities (Karakütük, 2012: 181). On the other hand, among the externalities of education, there are also externalities with economical functions. Economical externalities of education; the effects on healthy living, bad habits, communicable diseases, tax system, child care, social aid support, crime, and crime-related expenditures, redistribution of social resources, efficient markets and adaptation to technical changes, economical development, productivity, local and national expansions in education (Toy, 2019: 37).

While some economists say that education is a public good, some economists point out that this service is essentially a private good (Stiglitz and Rosengard, 2015). Goods that are obliged to be consumed by the intervention of the state are considered as virtuous (assessed) goods, such as compulsory education, compulsory insurance, and health services (e.g., vaccination). These kinds of goods are close to public goods (Uçkaç, 2003: 18).

Musgrave is the first economist to call education services virtuous goods. For certain public goods, it is difficult to distinguish whether they are private or social goods. As it is for examples of education and health services, in addition to their private benefits, everyone can benefit (externally) thanks to living in a society composed of individuals who are relatively well educated and healthy (Musgrave, 1959).

Stiglitz (1988) also states that education is not pure public good, the marginal cost of education of an additional student is not zero, and its marginal cost and average cost are almost equal; therefore, it is not possible to calculate the cost of the service for each person who benefits from an education service (Stiglitz, 1988: 372).

Some of the modern economists argues that education is not a pure public good, because the main feature of a public good is that it cannot be easily externalized and priced, whereas private education expenditures can be priced and their benefits can be externalized (segregated), the marginal cost of providing education to an additional pupil comes close to its average cost (Gradstein et al., 2005).

Unlike general views of the schools of economics about the intervention of governments into the markets, their views about intervention in the field of educational services differ. Classics emphasized that, as a general view, the markets come into a balance automatically within itself, government intervention disrupts this balance, but education expenditures should be considered separately from government expenditures within this scope, and in the field of education government intervention is necessary, but it should be done strictly, taking into account the human and social development factors. Adam Smith in his reputable book *The Wealth of Nations* (1776) explains the general processes of economics and also government functions in free markets in strict term and economics in broad term (Smith, 1937). According to Smith, governments should produce services in areas that provide social benefit, especially in education, that the governments should offer education services such as building schools and employing teachers, in order not to deprive poor people of education services, so that education is important for the whole society in terms of welfare (Uçkaç, 2003).

In the welfare economics theory, the role of the governments in the economy is generally described as intervening against market failures such as imperfect competition, full or semipublic good characteristics, externalities, incomplete markets, lack of information, unemployment, inflation, and imbalances that prevent to reach Pareto Efficiency (Stiglitz and Rosengard, 2015).

The main approach that explains government intervention in education services in terms of ensuring a fair social income distribution is equality of opportunity. Particularly in primary and secondary education, the concept of "equality" is the main reason used to explain the existence of public interventions in education services. Equality of opportunity is accepted as a factor related to the concept of social justice and is used as an indicator of the existence of social justice (Barr, 1993: 250).

The fact that its social benefits are higher than its social costs and that it increases efficiency in the economy by ensuring the development of human capital distinguishes education expenditures from other public expenditures. The public intervenes in this area because a significant part of the education expenditures is considered as social justice expenditures aimed at ensuring equality of opportunity, its positive externality is high, and especially primary education is considered among the virtuous services (Yılmaz, 2006: 42).

As a brief, although there are discussions in the literature about the extent to which the government should support or intervene in education, for whom and how, it is possible to say that there is a consensus on the need for governments to intervene in education services for various reasons, particularly because of their external benefits.

School Dropouts and Underlying Socioeconomic Reasons

The relationship between school dropouts and socioeconomic reasons has been investigated in most of the domestic and foreign studies on the causes of school dropouts, and there has been found a direct or indirect relationship between the child's dropping out of school and the socioeconomic status

(SES) of their family; SES is a basic indicator in explaining school dropouts (Deschamps, 1992; Bradley and Renzulli, 2011; Marks, 2007; McHenry, 1997).

There are different definitions of SES in literature, but their content is almost similar. In literature, references, which are related to this issue, focus on the impact of SES, the primary factor is the family's income status, then education and occupation status of parents. To express the *SES* concept, some sources refer to it as *low-income families* (Aluede and Ikechukwu, 2003; Carlos and Pastor, 2000), some of them refer it as *lower socioeconomic groups* (Deschamps, 1992; Peng and Fetters, 1978; Peng and Lee, 1992; Prawatrungruang, 2002; Rumberger, 1983; Wayman, 2001), some of them refer it as *low SES* (Alexander et al., 1997; LeCompte and Dworkin, 1991; Caldas and Bankston, 1997; Seppala, 2000; Trusty, 1998), or some of them refer it directly as *lower social and economic class*.

In most of the studies on this subject, there has been stated that the SES variable and/or the factors such as family income and education level in the content of the SES variable have a significant relationship with school dropouts (Schreiber, 1964; Renzulli and Park, 2000; Bradley and Renzulli, 2011; Şahin et al., 2016; Chevalier et al., 2005; Hill, 1979; Marks and Fleming, 1999; Alexander et al., 1997; Gyönös, 2011).

In the studies conducted by Deschamps (1992), Peng and Fetters (1978), Peng and Lee (1992), Prawatrungruang (2002), Rumberger (1983), and Wayman (2001), students from families in the lower socioeconomic group are more likely to come up with school dropout risk. Many domestic and foreign researches demonstrate that dropouts are high among students with low income and ethnic minorities (Garnier et al., 1997; Traag Van der Veldan, 2008; Freeney and O'Connell, 2009). In Bloomer's (1997) study, it was stated that most of the children who dropped out of school were in a low economic situation, and therefore, they were in a disadvantaged position in terms of social, educational, and economic conditions (Bloomer, 1997).

In Bradley and Renzulli's (2011) research, working at a job and not being able to find the opportunity to work while studying, taking care of their family or supporting their family are seen as the reasons that cause the child to drop out of school. In the research of Renzulli and Park (2000), one of the reasons for school dropouts for children is working at a job. In the research of Rumberger (1983), it is stated that children from poor families are more likely to drop out of school because of they work in paid jobs. In McCoy and Symth's (2005) research, it is stated that the children of families with low SES start to work at an early age or some of them work in part-time jobs while studying at school.

In studies conducted in Turkey, the causes of school dropouts were investigated; in a study carried out in Çanakkale, it is concluded that in terms of school dropouts lack of economic resources, and working in a job for the children in their school age are among the most important causes of school dropouts. As mentioned before, the reason for not wanting to study or being unsuccessful at school is actually due to indirect economic reasons such as malnutrition due to lack of income, loss of motivation for health and school, and thus loss of the physical and moral working capacity of the children. In the mentioned study, it was stated that the most important reasons for school dropouts were lower-income or in other words lack of economic resources, and it was stated that this situation became more evident especially for the households below the poverty line, and 44.8% of children whose families are below the poverty line dropped out of school because of economic reasons (Yılmaz et al., 2015: 40).

In a research conducted by ERG (2014), for households, poverty is the most important determinant of student absenteeism (and thus of student school dropouts); the effect of the education level of the parents was found extremely limited compared to the effect of poverty. In this sense, poverty can increase the risk of school absenteeism due to the insufficient resources required for education and health problems arising from the quality of life due to low household income. It has been stated that poverty can boost absenteeism due to problems such as the fact that children have to work to provide additional income for their families (ERG, 2014).

According to the results of research conducted by UNICEF (2011) within the framework of a program conducted in Turkey for children at primary school age (called YSOP), it is concluded that the main economic reasons for school absenteeism or dropouts are: the poverty of the child and their family, working in a job in their school age, and their family being a seasonal worker which cause children to be absent in the short run or completely to be dropout in the long run (UNICEF, 2011). The research impact level of these reasons on school absenteeism and dropouts is over 50%.

In the study conducted by Akbulut (2021), to inquire the impact of socio-economic reasons for school dropouts, by categorizing the reasons two separate scales were developed; the first scale is *Economic and Social Reasons* (including 6 sub-scales and a totally of 26 reasons in these sub-scales) and the other scale is *School Environment, Education System and Health-Related Reasons* (including 3 sub-scales and 17 reasons in these sub-scales). Applying these two scales by using the survey data applied in the 5-point Likert Scale regarding the impact of the reasons or sub-causes, it was found that the average effect of the first scale (*the Economic and Social Reasons Scale*) was 3.24 which means partially effective in the 5-point Likert Scale, while the other scale (*the School Environment, Education System and Health-Related Reasons Scale*) was 3.00 (that means partially effective in the 5-point Likert Scale). So as a result the average impact of Economic and Social Reasons is seen to be higher than other reasons.

In this research, it was found that among the sub-scales the "Economic Reasons" sub-scale is the most statistically compatible one. So it is seen that to be able to evaluate the impact of the first scale this sub-scale includes the most important reasons/factors in the Economic and Social Reasons Scale (table 9.1).

The average impact score of these reasons/factors is 3.1 (partially effective), and the impact rates of these factors are respectively: *working in a job because he has to take care of his family, working in a job to contribute to the family budget, unemployment of his father, the family does not have a regular monthly income, the family's economic opportunities are not sufficient, the family's ability to pay for education and transportation to school is weak, the social and economic environment in which he lives, inadequate opportunities, having a large number of siblings who go to school, insufficient study environment at home, unemployment of his mother.*

Another important result of Akbulut's (2021) research on the impact of socioeconomic reasons is that there is a strong correlation (correlation) between two main scales (the Economic and Social Reasons Scale and the other Scale). These results reveal that 51.62% of the other reasons can be explained by Economic and Social Reasons. On the other hand, regarding the results of the research the impact level of the reasons in *the Economic and Social Reasons Scale* show difference in different regions (*at the NUTS-1 level*). It was found that the impact level of this scale is higher in regions with low socioeconomic development levels.

As the conclusion of Akbulut's (2021) research, socioeconomic factors are seen among the main reasons for school dropouts like almost all of the related researches available in domestic and foreign literature.

TABLE 9.1
Drop-outs_Economic and Social Reasons Scale_Economic Reasons Sub-Scale

	**Impact Level (%)*
His father is unemployed	46.0
The family does not have a permanent monthly income	45.3
Working in a job to contribute to the family budget	46.0
Their family has not got sufficient financial resources	43.8
Poor family ability to pay for the education and transportation expenses of children	38.1
Having many siblings going to school	31.8
Working at a job to take care of his family	49.1
His mother is unemployed	17.4
The insufficient study environment at home	26.5
Insufficient social and economic opportunities of the district they live	33.2

Source: Akbulut, 2021 (Impact level: Taken as the sum of those who said "effective" or "very effective")

Empirical Data about Educational and Social Aids toward Students

Regarding the results in literature revealing that socioeconomic factors are among the prominent reasons for school dropouts, there needs to develop policies to support particularly disadvantaged pupils to be able to attend their education. To be able to achieve this goal educational and social aids for pupils and their households are crucial. In this framework data about educational and social aids in Turkey are given in this part of the chapter.

Scholarships and Economic Support Payments for Secondary Education Students

The number of students who benefit scholarships within the budget of the Ministry of National Education (MoNE) in secondary education schools (these funds allocated as *Transfers to Households* within the *Current Transfers* in government budget) is 149,628 (including general secondary schools and vocational secondary schools, but excluding religious education schools because they are combined schools as secondary school and high school) (table 9.2). Within the budget of the MoNE, the number of students who benefit from the free dormitory in public schools (these funds allocated as *Transfers to Households* in the government budget) is 196,124 (including general secondary schools, vocational secondary schools, and special education and guidance schools, but excluding religious education schools for the abovementioned reason) (Milli Eğitim Bakanlığı/MoNE, 2020: 220–221).

The number of primary and secondary school students who benefit from the scholarships given by the General Directorate of Foundations is 21,453. Within the total beneficiaries of social aids, the number of pupils, at secondary school age, who benefit from the SEA aids given by the Ministry of Family and Social Services is 27,513. The total beneficiaries of all social aids in secondary school are 907,917. On the other hand, the total number reaches 1,036,438 when the student scholarships, given by the General Directorate of Foundations to the primary education schools students and the scholarships given by the MoNE to the religious education schools students, are included in these numbers (table 9.2).

On the other hand, since Conditional Cash Transfers for Education (CCTE) and scholarship payments are given only to the students who attend school as a requirement, these aids can only be offered within the SEA aids payments for open education school students. The number of pupils at the age of secondary school who benefited from these aids in 2019 is just 1,618 (table 9.3). The ratio of this number to the total students who leave school (who don't attend formal education) and pass to open education is 0.11%.

TABLE 9.2
Educational Scholarships and SEA Aids Payments in Social Expenditures (2019)

Social Aids and Students Benefit from Free Pension and Scholarship	*Primary Schools*	*Secondary Schools*
MoNE—Total Secondary Schools Students Benefit From Scholarship (Excluding (a))		149.628
MoNE—(a) Religious Education Schools Students Benefit From Scholarship	30.657	
MoNE—Total Secondary Schools Students Benefit From Free Dormitory (Excluding (b))		196.124
MoNE—(b) Religious Education Schools Students Benefit From Free Dormitory	76.411	
General Directorate of Foundations—Primary and Secondary Schools Students Benefit From Scholarship*	21.453	
Ministry of Family and Social Services—Conditional Cash Transfers for Education (CCTE) Payments*		534.652
Ministry of Family and Social Services—Social and Economic Assistance (SEA) Aids Payments*		27.513
Total Secondary Schools Students		907.917
Total Primary and Secondary Schools Students	1.036.438	

Source: Milli Eğitim Bakanlığı (MoNE). 2020. "Milli Eğitim İstatistikleri" Örgün Eğitim, 2019–2020.
* "Türkiye Cumhuriyeti Cumhurbaşkanlığı, Strateji ve Bütçe Başkanlığı 2020 Yıllık Programı" (data extracted from the Aile ve Sosyal Politikalar Bakanlığı. 2019 ve 2020 Yıllık Faaliyet Raporları).

The ratio of students attending secondary education and receiving SEA aids (27,513) to the total number of students at secondary education in public schools (3,677,964) is 0.7%.

SEA aids are provided to families of the pupils who are at risk of being taken into institutional/social care due to the poor economic condition of their families, thus pupils can live with their own family or relatives. In the meantime, families benefiting from these aids are directed to Turkish Employment Agency (İŞKUR) vocational and professional courses to provide available jobs for them.

In terms of this research topic, data on numbers of students at secondary education age but not attending school is crucial. It is seen that the number of students in this group benefiting from SEA aids is very low (1,618 people). When students attending secondary education are included in this number, it is seen that a total of 27,513 secondary school students benefited from these aids in 2019. Although the number of SEA aids recipients in 2018 is close to the 2019 figures, the number of students who did not attend secondary education decreased in 2019 (table 9.3).

TABLE 9.3
Number of Beneficiaries of SEA Aids at Secondary Education Level

	2018	*2019*
Pupils Attending Secondary Education Schools	24.678	25.895
Pupils At Secondary School Age But Not Attend School	1.684	1.618

Source: Aile ve Sosyal Politikalar Bakanlığı. 2018 ve 2019 Yıllık Faaliyet Raporları.

In the 2018–2019 academic year in Turkey, there are 5,649,594 secondary education students, 3,677,964 of whom are in secondary education in public schools, 581,693 in private schools, and 1,389,937 in open education schools (Milli Eğitim Bakanlığı/MoNE, 2019). The ratio of secondary school students (907,917) benefiting from the free dormitory facilities of the MoNE is 16%. This ratio is around 24% for only official school students. Considering that the amount of CCTE payments is very low, the ratio of those benefiting from aids other than CCTE aids (only the students benefit from free dormitory and scholarships) to total secondary education students (5,649,594) drops to 6.6%. This ratio is 10.1% only for official school students (3,677,964). Considering the 15.6% ratio of students not enrolled in formal education, which is calculated based on the net enrollment ratio (84.6%) for 2018–2019, it appears that the ratio of benefiting from educational aids is so low. Even if scholarships and free dormitory facilities are allocated only to students who are out of formal education due to socioeconomic reasons and only to students in public schools, it is seen that the ratio of those who are in secondary education and benefit from these benefits remains low.

Public Resources Allocated to Education within the Total Public Social Aids

Public resources allocated to education within the total public social aids are financed out of the general budget resources dedicated in the budget resources of *the Ministry of Family and Social Services, the MoNE, the General Directorate of Foundations, and the Credit and Dormitories Institution (YURTKUR)*, and *the resources transferred from the Fund (SYDTF) to the Ministry of Family, Labor and Social Services*. Among these resources allocated to social aids, it is observed that the payments made to poor children and families remain low in terms of both the number of beneficiaries and the total allowance (table 9.4).

As mentioned in the previous section SEA aids are being provided to poor families of the pupils who are at risk of living apart from their families unless they are supported economically. So, these aids are not classified as a kind of educational aid. But among the beneficiaries of these SEA aids, some students

TABLE 9.4
Public Social Aids for Education and SEA Aids for Children and Families (2017–2019)

Institutions	*Social Aids*	*2017*		*2018*		*2019*	
		Beneficiaries (1)	*Amount Allocated (000 TL)*	*Beneficiaries (1)*	*Amount Allocated (000 TL)*	*Beneficiaries (1)*	*Amount Allocated (000 TL)*
The Ministry of Family and Social Services	SEA (poor families)	161,493	834,691	185,766	1,096,121	198,907	1,389,135
	SYDV (Fon)						
	All Social Aids out of Fund (SYDTF)	*3,201,253	5,730,580	*3,494,932	5,957,458		7,371,671
The General Directorate of Foundations	Bursaries (primary and secondary school students)	21,290	20,302	20,741	29,730	21,453	32,068
The MoNE	Bursaries (primary and secondary school students)	142,205	330,228	386,413	665,572	147,166	472,765
The YURTKUR	Bursaries (high schools/ universities students)	548,156	2,053,739	557,475	2,253,784	569,747	2,401 727

Source: Data extracted from Türkiye Cumhuriyeti Cumhurbaşkanlığı., Strateji ve Bütçe Başkanlığı, 2021 Cumhurbaşkanlığı Yıllık Programı.
*Data extracted from Türkiye Cumhuriyeti Cumhurbaşkanlığı., Strateji ve Bütçe Başkanlığı, 2020 Cumhurbaşkanlığı Yıllık Programı.

attend their secondary education as well. Although it is an important support to ensure children can attend their school, the limitation of the prerequisites for getting the aids limits its function to ensure school attendance. However, since this research has revealed that the reasons for students dropping out of formal school education are mostly economic, it can be ensured that students who have almost complete lack of economic support of their families can continue their education thanks to getting these aids. To do so, it is necessary to determine pupils who need SEA aids by conducting statistical household research on this matter.

In Turkey, the largest share of social aids (5.9% of GDP in 2018) is allocated to pensioners and elderly allowances, followed by illness and health expenditures (3.2% of GDP in 2018). Pensions and elderly allowances (2018 forecast GDP) are in the first place in social protection aids (as a ratio of GDP) in EU countries, where the share of aids allocated to children and families are relatively low (0.5% of GDP in 2018). It is seen that the illness and health expenditures are in second order (9.8% of the GDP in 2018 projection) (table 9.5).

In the European Union countries, it is seen that the share of children and families as the EU27 average (2.2% of the GDP in 2018 forecast) is low when it is compared to the elderly pension and health expenses, but when the share of aids toward children and families compared with Turkey, EU has a much higher ratio in terms of GDP.

In a research conducted by Karadeniz and Yılmaz (2018), the distribution of social security expenditures in the EU and Turkey was compared; regarding this study, the share of resources allocated to family and child expenditures in Turkey is 3.12%; in the EU, it was 8.5%. After all, it was pointed out that a more effective distribution could be achieved by increasing

TABLE 9.5
Turkey-EU Comparative Social Protection Aids Expand GDP Ratios (2018)

	Allocated Amount (Million TL)	*Turkey As GDP Ratio (%)*	*AB27* As GDP Ratio (%)*
	2018	*2018*	*2018(t)*
Total Social Protection Aids**	442,027	11.8	26.7
Illness/Health Care	121,755	3.2	9.8
Disabled/Retired-Disabled	14,840	0.4	2.0
Pensioners and Elderly Allowances	219,939	5.9	10.7
Families/Children	16,986	0.5	2.2
Unemployement	10,358	0.3	1.2
Social Exclusion	5,887	0.2	0.6

Source: TÜİK (TURKSTAT). 2019. "Sosyal Yardım İstatistikleri, 2019," TÜİK Haber Bülteni, No: 33668. EUROSTAT, https://appsso.eurostat.ec.europa.eu/nui/submitViewTableAction.do (accessed:07.03.2021)
**All public or private institutions/organizations providing social protection services are covered.
(t): Forecast (provision)

the resources allocated to social aids in favor of families and children, as it is in the EU (Karadeniz and Yılmaz, 2018: 56). In a UNICEF report on this subject, it is emphasized that in Turkey the current social security programs are not effective in reducing child poverty, that more than 90% of the social protection expenditures committed by the public are allocated to premium system (regime) expenditures, which consist retirement expenditures and health expenditures have the second-biggest percentage in social protection expenditures. So it is concluded that the social security system is not effective in tackling poverty (UNICEF Çalışma Grubu, 2011: 63).

Educational Aids Financed by Public Resources

Educational aids financed out of public resources (*government budget and public funds*) for students are shown in table 9.6; most of them are financed out of resources transferred from the Fund (SYDTF) to the Ministry of Family and Social Services' budget. Educational aids financed out of this budget in the form of direct aids are: *educational material aids*, *CCTE*, *free meals (lunch)*, *free textbooks*, *student transport citation-accommodation and subsistence aids*, and *free transportation of disabled students*. Educational aids

TABLE 9.6
Education Aids with Public Resources (2018–2019)

(000 TL)	*2018*	*2019*
Educational Materials	11,860	11,450
Free Meals (Lunch)	805,000	962,000
Free Textbook Materials	350,000	881,000
Free Transportation for Disabled Students	368,000	692,000
Conditional Cash Transfers for Education (CCTE) (ŞEY as TR originally called)	643,100	614,460
Total Education Aids Financed out of the Fund (SYDTF as TR original institution name)*	**2.177.860**	**3.160.450**
MoNE Social Protection Expenditures****	1,855,437	2,293,879
YURTKUR (as TR original institution name) Student Payments** (toward Higher Education students)	2,253,784	2,401,727
General Directorate of Foundations Student Scholarships**	29,730	32,068
Total Educational Aids***	**6,316,811**	**7,888,124**
Ratio to GDP (percent)	0.168	0.182

Source: *Aile ve Sosyal Politikalar Bakanlığı. 2018 ve 2019 Yıllık Faaliyet Raporları.
** *Source*: Türkiye Cumhuriyeti Cumhurbaşkanlığı., Strateji ve Bütçe Başkanlığı, 2021 ve 2022 Cumhurbaşkanlığı Yıllık Programları.
***Educational aids within the social benefits of municipalities are not included.
**** Milli Eğitim Bakanlığı (MoNE). 2019 ve 2020 Bütçe Kesin Hesap Cetvelleri"
(1) Ministry of National Education budget/current transfers/5.4. Transfers to Households: excluding cash aids as scholarships and pocket money within the scope of free boarding and scholarship payments, and in-kind aids such as clothing-stationery and boarding expenses abroad, excluding postgraduate scholarship payments (MEB Social Protection Statistical data on expenditures submitted to TURKSTAT).

financed out of the budget of the MoNE are: *aids in the form of scholarships and pocket money being paid as cash, free dormitory and scholarship aids to primary and secondary school students, and direct aids as clothing, stationery, and hostel expenses.* Educational aids financed out of the budget of the General Directorate of Foundations are: *the scholarships offered to primary and secondary school students.* Educational aids financed out of the budget of the YURTKUR are: the scholarships offered to students in higher education. The public education aids offered in 2018–2019 are given in table 9.6.

All of these educational aids financed out of public resources (government budget and public funds) for students (as shown in table 9.6) were 1.68 per thousand in 2018; and 1.82 per thousand in 2019.

Most of the educational aids financed out of the resources transferred from the Fund (SYDTF) are in the form of direct aids or services. CCTE is given as cash aids. CCTE (ŞEY as TR originally called) payments budget were 29.5% of the educational aids transferred from SYDTF in 2018, while this rate decreased to 19.4% in 2019. The ratio of the CCTE payments budget to the total social protection expenditure budget allocated to educational aids also decreased from 10.2% to 7.8% (Akbulut, 2021).

The number of secondary school students who benefit from educational and social aids in secondary education in 2019–2020 is 907,917. The ratio of this number to total secondary school students (5,630,652) is 17%. When the CCTE beneficiaries are excluded (considering that the amount of CCTE payments remains very low and thus it seems far from being a scholarship to cover the educational needs of students), the total number of beneficiaries drops to 373.265. This corresponds to 6.6% as a ratio of total secondary school students. Even excluding private school students (in terms of having relatively average higher economic opportunities) this ratio for just public school students (3,712.013) remains at 10.1%.

As a result, the ratio of secondary school students who benefit from public educational and social aids, free dormitory and scholarships is below the ratio of 15% students who are not currently registered in a school (formal education) according to the net enrollment ratio for 2019–2020, even when only official school students are taken into account. This result shows that scholarships and free dormitory facilities are not sufficient even for students who are out of school mostly due to socioeconomic reasons. Therefore, the ratio of educational aids financed out of public resources for socioeconomically disadvantaged students needs to be increased.

Since pupils who are out of school (called formal education) do not have the right to get a scholarship from the MoNE, these pupils can only benefit from the SEA aids given by the Ministry of Family and Social Services. In 2019, the ratio of those pupils (who are out of school despite being at the age of secondary education, but who benefit from the SEA aids) is approximately one in a thousand.

Although SEA aids are not classified as direct educational aids among the beneficiaries of these aids, some students attend their secondary education. The ratio of students who benefit from SEA aids to the total secondary school students in public schools is 0.7%. This poor ratio seems to confirm the idea mentioned in previous sections that while SEA aids seem an important tool to support students in terms of school attendance, its prerequisites limit its function. However, since this research has revealed that students drop out of school mostly due to economic reasons, it looks crucial for pupils who completely have lacked their family's support. So it is a requirement to determine statistically those pupils and their households.

Conclusion and Discussion

Regarding the conclusions of researches in both foreign and domestic literature, socioeconomic factors are among the prominent reasons for school dropouts, so there needs to develop policies to improve the SES of individuals and the society as a whole, with economic and social policies to find solutions toward school dropouts matter. In this context, it is important to implement public finance policies to increase the efficiency of public education expenditures and education aids, particularly within the framework of social expenditures in broad definition and social protection expenditures in its strict definition.

Considering that the largest share of social protection aids in Turkey are allocated to general health insurance premiums, pensions for the elderly and disabled, and home care services, the share of aids allocated to children and families remain relatively low in terms of both the number of beneficiaries and the total allowance. In 2019, it is seen that the payments made for SEA aids to the elderly and disabled pensions are more than seven times both in terms of amount and the number of beneficiaries. When compared with EU countries, it is seen that the share of family and children in social protection expenditures remains low. As stated in the research of Karadeniz and Yılmaz (2018), a more effective distribution could be achieved by increasing the resources allocated to social aids in favor of families and children in Turkey, as it is in the EU.

Although the CCTE program, which is implemented particularly to ensure school attendance, has a positive effect on the absenteeism ratios in Turkey, it is seen that the amount of these payments per student is very low, and since there has been almost no increase over the years, its value has been decreasing because of inflation. It can be said that an inflation-indexed increase should be made for CCTE payments to be in reasonable amounts for students and their families. Thus, it is considered that detecting students in poor economic conditions and making their payments in more reasonable amounts considering their family's income level may be an effective way to prevent them from leaving school due to economic deprivations.

To prevent children from being dropped out of school, in addition to social aids, there needs to reach economical development at the macro-level and thus to improve individual income distribution throughout the country. Besides these precautions regional development disparities should be reduced among the regions. On the other hand, in order to ensure that disadvatagеd people may benefit significantly from this increase in welfare, available social aids, and financial transfers should be provided to them and thus they can easily reach these funds when they need.

In policies targeting to increase the effectiveness of educational aids, the existing education aids must be delivered to the economically disadvantaged pupils and their households more effectively. In this regard, the UNICEF (2011) report has focused on the difficulties experienced in reaching educational and social aids for children and their households. Regarding this report, 30% of poor households with children under the age of 19 do not receive any scholarship, direct social aids, or public aids, 30% of them do not receive any public or private transfers, and 62% of them do not receive student scholarships or any kind of aids. It was stated that the social aids for the households/individuals below the poverty line were not at the satisfactory level of effectiveness to be able to tackle poverty. In the mentioned report of UNICEF, some of the reasons for the ineffectiveness of social aids for children and their families include the lack of data about children who need aids, the absence of birth certificates for some of the children, differences in calculating the poverty threshold, and lack of information on educational and social aids. For these reasons, it is important to ensure that the available educational and social aids would reach those children and their households with more effective methods so that their SES would be getting better.

Overall it is crucial to reduce the socioeconomic difficulties against accessing education. To do so, it is a necessity to ensure that all children can attend school within equal opportunities. Disadvantaged children and their households should be supported socially and economically. Economical policies and programs aiming to prevent school dropouts are crucial. In this context, more budgetary resources should be allocated for educational aids such as scholarships, dormitories, clothing, and meals for economically disadvantaged students.

References

Aile ve Sosyal Politikalar Bakanlığı. 2012. "Türkiye'de uygulanan şartlı nakit transferi programının fayda sahipleri üzerindeki etkisinin nitel ve nicel olarak ölçülmesi projesi final raporu." Aile ve Sosyal Politikalar Bakanlığı ve Gazi Üniversitesi ortak araştırması.

Aile ve Sosyal Politikalar Bakanlığı. 2018. "2018 Yıllık Faaliyet Raporu."

Aile ve Sosyal Politikalar Bakanlığı. 2019. "2019 Yıllık Faaliyet Raporu."

Akbulut, Nihat. 2021. "Okul Terkleri Sosyoekonomik Nedenleri Çözüme Dönük Kamu Maliyesi Politika ve Programları." EfeAkademi Yayınları. ISBN: 978-625-8065-52-7.

Alexander, Karl, L.; Entwisle, Doris, R.; Horsey, Carrie, S. 1997. "From First Grade Forward: Early Foundations of High School Dropout." *Sociology of Education-American Sociological Association*, 70(2), 87–107. http://www.jstor.org/stable /2673158. Accessed at:04-04-2017 18:45 UTC.

Aluede, Oyaziwo; Ikechukwu, B. N. 2003. "Analysis of the Variables That Predispose Adolescents to Dropout of Schools." *International Journal for the Advancement of Counselling*, 25 (2–3), 181–192. https://doi.org/10.1023/A:1026284329850. Accessed at:01.12.2019.

Barr, James. 1993. *Biblical Faith, and Natural Theology: The Gifford Lectures for 1991*. University of Edinburgh Clarendon Press.

Bloomer, A. 1997. "The Athlone Youth Report." Unpublished Report, Athlone Community Services Council.

Bradley, Christen, L.; Renzulli, Linda, A. 2011. "The Complexity of Non-Completion: Being Pushed or Pulled to Drop Out of High School." *Social Forces-Oxford Academic*, 90(2), 521–545. https://doi.org/10.1093/sf/sor003. Accessed at:01.12.2019.

Caldas, Stephen, J.; Bankston, Carl. 1997. "Effect of School Population Socioeconomic Status on Individual Academic Achievement." *The Journal of Educational Research*, 90(5), 269–277. https://doi.org/10.1080/00220671.1997.10544583. Accessed at:01.12.2019.

Carlos, Peraita; Pastor, Margarita. 2000. "The Primary School Dropout in Spain: The İnfluence of Family Background and Labor Market Conditions." *Education Economics*, 8(2), 157–161. https://www.tandfonline.com/toc/vjer20/90/5.

Chevalier, Arnaud; Harmon, Colm; O'Sullivan, Vincent; Walker, Ian. 2005. "The Impact of Parental Income and Education on the Schooling of Their Children." *IZA DP No. 1496 Discussion Papers Series*, Institute for the Study of Labor, February.

Deschamps, Ann, Barnes. 1992. "An Integrative Review of Research on Characteristics of Dropouts." Unpublished Doctoral Dissertation, George Washington University.

ERG. 2014. "İlköğretimde Devamsızlığın Belirleyicileri ve İzlenmesi." ERG yayınları.

EUROSTAT (The Statistical Office of the European Union). 2019. "Statistics_Social Protection Aids." EUROSTAT Statistics, 72/2019. https://appsso.eurostat.ec.europa .eu/nui/submitViewTableAction.do. Updated:03.03.2021. Accessed at:07.03.2021.

Freeney, Yseult; O'Connell, Michael. 2009. *Psychological, Economic and Academic Predictors of the Intention to Leave School Early Among a Sample of Irish Students*. Combat Poverty Agency.

Garnier, Helen, E.; Stein, Judith, A.; Jacobs, Jennifer, K. 1997. "The Process of Dropping Out of High School: A 19-Year Perspective." *American Educational Research Journal*, 34, 395–419. https://doi.org/10.3102/00028312034002395 Accessed at:01.12.2019.

Gradstein, Mark; Justman, Moshe; Meier, Volker. 2005. "The Political Economy of Education: Implications for Growth and Inequality." In *CESifo Book Series*. Cambridge, Ma, London, England: The MIT Press.

Gyönös, Erika. 2011. "Early School Leaving: Reasons and Consequences Transylvania University, Braşov." *Theoretical and Applied Economics*, XVIII, 11(564), 43–52.

Hill, Russell C. 1979. "Capacities, Opportunities and Educational Investments: The Case of the High School Dropout." *The Review of Economics and Statistics*, 61(1), 9–20. The MIT Press. http://www.jstor.org/stable/1924826. Accessed at:03-04-2017 18:30 UTC.

Karadeniz, Oğuz; Yılmaz, Hakan, Hakkı. 2018. "İş Dünyasında Kadın, Cilt 3, Sorunlar-Çözümler-Öneriler." Turkonfed.

Karakütük, Kasım. 2012. "Eğitim Planlaması" Elhan Kitap Yayın Dağıtım.

LeCompte, Margaret, Diane; Dworkin, Anthony, Gary. 1991. *Giving Up on Schools Student Dropouts and Teacher Burnouts*. Corwin Press, Inc., ISBN-0-8039-3491-2, 313.

Marks, Gary. 2007. "Do Schools Matter for Early School Leaving? Individual and School Influences in Australia." *School Effectiveness and School Improvement*, 18(4), 429–450. https://doi.org/10.1080/09243450701712528. Accessed at:01.12.2019.

Marks, Gary; Fleming, Nicole. 1999. "Early School Leaving in Australia: Findings From the 1995 Year 9 LSAY Cohort." In *Australian Council for Educational Research,* Report No. 11. ISBN: 0 86431 328 4. Melbourne: ACER.

McCoy, Selina; Smyth, Emer. 2005. "At Work in School: Part-Time Employment Among Second-Level Students." *Research Series*. Economic and Social Research Institute (ESRI). https://ideas.repec.org/b/esr/resser/bkmnext49.html. Accessed at:01.12.2019.

McHenry, Nancy, Lynn. 1997. "An İntegrative Review of Research on Characteristics of Students Who Drop Out of School." Unpublished Doctorate Thesis, Seattle Pacific University.

Milli Eğitim Bakanlığı (MoNE). 2019a. "2019-2023 Stratejik Planı."

Milli Eğitim Bakanlığı (MoNE). 2019b. *Milli Eğitim İstatistikleri*. Örgün Eğitim, 2018–2019.

Milli Eğitim Bakanlığı (MoNE). 2019c. "2018 Bütçe Kesin Hesap Cetvelleri."

Milli Eğitim Bakanlığı (MoNE). 2020a. *Milli Eğitim İstatistikleri*. Örgün Eğitim, 2019–2020.

Milli Eğitim Bakanlığı (MoNE). 2020b. "2019 Bütçe Kesin Hesap Cetvelleri."

Musgrave, Richard, A. 1959. *The Theory of Public Finance; A Study in Public Economy*. Kogakusha Co.

Peng, Samuel; Fetters, William, B. 1978. "Variables Involved in Withdrawal During the First Two Years of College: Preliminary Findings From the National Longitudinal Study of the High School Class of 1972." *American Educational Research Journal*, 15(3). https://doi.org/10.3102/00028312015003361.

Peng, Samuel; Lee, Ralph M. 1992. "Home Variables, Parent-Child Activities and Academic Achievement: A Study of 1988 Eighth-Grader." Paper Presented at: *Congreso Anual de la American Educational Research.*

Prawatrungruang, Sittiporn. 2002. *Understanding Dropouts in Thai Private Vocational Schools: A Case Study.* Illinois State University.

Renzulli, Joseph, S.; Park, Sunghee. 2000. "'Gifted Dropouts: The Who and the Why'. The University of Connecticut." *Gifted Child Quarterly,* 44(2), 261–271.

Rumberger, Russell W. 1983. "Dropping Out of High School: The Influence of Race, Sex, and Family Background." *American Educational Research Journal.* https://doi.org/10.3102%2F00028312020002199. Accessed at:01.12.2019.

Şahin, Şeyma; Arseven, Zeynep; Kılıç, Abdurrahman. 2016. "Öğrenci Devamsızlıkları ve Okul Terklerinin Nedenleri." *International Journal of Instruction,* 9(1), 195–210.

Schreiber, Daniel, Ed. 1964. "Guidance and the School Dropout." In *American Personnel and Guidance Association, National Education Association.* Washington, DC: Ford Foundation, New York, NY, p. 64279. https://files.eric.ed.gov/fulltext/ED079643.pdf. Accessed at:01.12.2019.

Seppala, Marry F. 2000. "Dropping Out of High School: Students' Perspectives." Unpublished Doctorate Thesis, University of Massachusetts Amherst.

Smith, Adam. 1937. "The Wealth of Nations" [1776], Vol. 11937, na.

Stiglitz, Joseph, E. 1988. "Economic Organization, Information, and Development." *Handbook of Development Economics* 1, 93–160.

Stiglitz, Joseph, E.; Jay, Rosengard, K.. 2015. "Economics of the Public Sector." Fourth International Student Edition, W. W. Norton, Incorporated.

Toy, Hakkı. 2019. "Eğitimin Dışsallıklarına İlişkin Öğretim Elemanları ve Üniversite Öğrencilerinin Görüşleri." doktora tezi, 37. https://tez.yok.gov.tr, tez no: 550223.

Traag, Tanja; Van der Velden, Rolf, K. W. 2011. "Early School-Leaving in the Netherlands: The Role of Family Resources, School Composition and Background Characteristics in Early School-Leaving in Lower Secondary Education." *Irish Educational Studies,* 30(1), 45–62.

Trusty, Jerry. 1998. "Family Influences on Educational Expectations of Late Adolescents." *The Journal of Educational Research,* 91(5), 260–271. https://doi.org/10.1080/00220679809597553. Accessed at:01.12.2019.

TÜİK (TURKSTAT). 2019. "Sosyal Yardım İstatistikleri, 2019." *TÜİK Haber Bülteni,* No: 33668.

Türkiye Cumhuriyeti Cumhurbaşkanlığı. 2020. "Cumhurbaşkanlığı 2020 Yıllık Programı." Strateji ve Bütçe Başkanlığı.

Türkiye Cumhuriyeti Cumhurbaşkanlığı. 2021. "Cumhurbaşkanlığı 2021 Yıllık Programı." Strateji ve Bütçe Başkanlığı.

Uçkaç, Aynur. 2003. "Eğitimde Fırsat Eşitliği" master tezi." https://tez.yok.gov.tr, tez no:140334.

UNICEF. 2011. "Yetiştirici sınıf Öğretim Programı (YSÖP)-Ara Dönem Gözden Geçirme Raporu." UNICEF yayınları.

UNICEF Çalışma Grubu. 2011. "Kamu Politikaları Harcama Analizi Raporu: Çocuk Yoksulluğu ve Mali Alan Yaklaşımı." Ankara University-UNICEF Çalışma Grubu.

Wayman, Jeffrey, C. 2002. "The Utility of Educational Resilience for Studying Degree Attainment in School Dropouts." *Journal of Educational Research*, 95(3), 167–178.

Yılmaz, Hakan, Hakkı. 2006. "Türkiye'de 2000 Sonrası Dönemde Uygulanan İstikrar Programlarında Mali Uyumda Kalite Sorunu." doktora tezi. https://tez.yok.gov.tr, tez no:174981.

Yılmaz, Hakan, Hakkı; Erkan, Volkan; Peker, Uğur. 2015. "Çanakkale Belediyesi Gelir Dağılımı, Yaşam Koşulları ve Sosyal Yardımlar Alan Araştırması Final Raporu." PYB Araştırması.

10

An Empirical Analysis of the Determinants of Average Life Expectancy

Muhammet KUTLU and Şeyma ŞAHİN KUTLU

Introduction

One of the frequently used indicators in international comparisons of human development and well-being is the average life expectancy or, in other words, life expectancy at birth. Life expectancy can be expressed as the average number of years an individual is expected to live after birth (Bilas et al., 2014: 1). Life expectancy is a variable that is influenced by many other factors besides physical health factors and has gradually developed in parallel with technological transformation. With the increase in per capita income in countries, improvements observed in factors such as poverty, nutrition, literacy, clean water, disease burden, and life expectancy have been affected positively. However, in some countries (especially sub-Saharan African countries), there have been periods when life expectancy tended to decrease despite an increase in income and health expenditures (Kabir, 2008: 185). Changes in life expectancy can be influenced by long-term alterations in various factors, including the political regime and socioeconomic situation of a country. Considering that the rights of citizens to express themselves are more developed in more democratic countries, it is therefore expected that public services will be more responsive to social needs in these countries. Furthermore, as a result of the electoral system, politicians are expected to shape public policies on the labor market and welfare issues to avoid shortages, augment per capita income, increase and improve spending on public health and medical care (Lin et al., 2012: 1–2).

Despite its negative effects on the poor working class, the Industrial Revolution birthed significant improvements in income, education, living standards, and health indicators in Western countries with its technical innovations. However, in poorer countries, the development that occurred in the second half of the twentieth century did not lead to an increase in health standards, as witnessed in Western countries. Many developing countries have shown relatively small improvements in the health of their populations (Hertz et al., 1994: 105). In the last century, life expectancy has increased dramatically. In the early stages of this increment, rapid population growth with a decrease in mortality rates was witnessed (Zhang et al., 2001: 485). Changes in life expectancy have notable implications for individual and collective human behavior. This fluidity affects the fertility behavior of individuals, economic growth, human capital investment, intergenerational transfers, and incentives for pension compensation claims (Shaw et al., 2005: 768). Therefore, life expectancy, which varies depending on multiple economic, social, and environmental factors, can at the same time be represented as an explanatory variable for certain economic, social, and environmental variables.

As seen in figure 10.1, the average life expectancy on Earth has been on a constant increase. In the 1800s, the average life expectancy on Earth was 28.5 years. By 1913, the average life expectancy on Earth reached 34 years. In 1913, the average life expectancy on the Asian continent was 28.1, on the European continent it was 46.8, and on the American continent it was 45.1. After 1913, especially following the Second World War and the 1918 influenza pandemic, meaning from about 1920 to 1973, a rather swift improvement in average

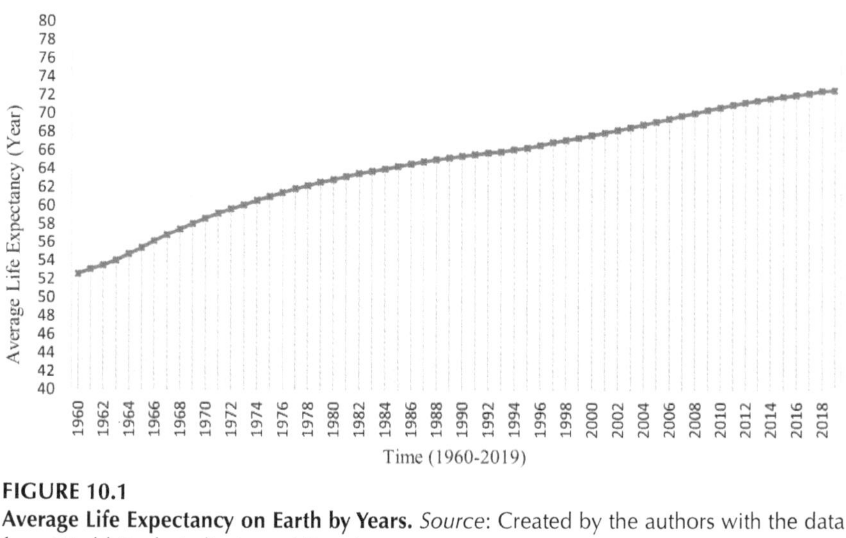

FIGURE 10.1
Average Life Expectancy on Earth by Years. *Source*: Created by the authors with the data from World Bank, Indicators of Development.

life expectancy was recorded. During this period, life expectancy on Earth increased by about half a year for each calendar year (Riley, 2005: 537). The life expectancy has reached 72.7 years as of 2019. However, this increase was not observed for all the countries of the world.

Figure 10.2 displays the trajectory of life expectancy for certain groups of countries and countries. As can be read from the graph, differences were observed in the trajectory followed by life expectancy for different countries and groups of countries. Accordingly, life expectancy in the European Union is seen to have steadily increased, reaching an average of 81.1 years in 2019. Similarly, the increase in life expectancy in countries such as Canada and Japan has been stable. As of 2019, the average life expectancy was 82 for Canada and 84.4 for Japan. Yet such numbers in terms of life expectancy are still far away for some countries and groups of countries. For instance, the average life expectancy as of 2019 was determined to be 62 years in sub-Saharan African countries where life expectancy has been stagnant for a long period of time. Likewise, Zimbabwe and Sudan are countries where life expectancy is observed to be an average of 61 and 65 years, respectively. Japan and Switzerland are countries with the highest life expectancy with an average of 84.4 and 83.7 years, respectively. Sierra Leone and the Central African Republic are countries with the lowest life expectancy with an average of 52.2 and 52.8 years, respectively.

As our examination exhibits, average life expectancy displays a significant difference between countries and groups of countries. According to data from the World Bank, a difference of 31.9 years is observed between the country with the highest life expectancy and the country with the lowest. Furthermore,

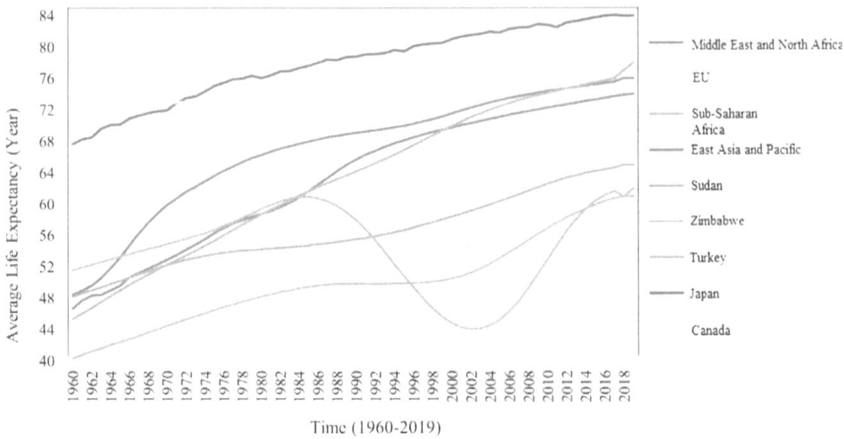

FIGURE 10.2

Expected Life Expectancy for Certain Countries and Groups of Countries. *Source*: Created by the authors with the data from World Bank, Indicators of Development.

87 countries—with rather strong economies among them—have an expected life expectancy below the world average of 72.2 years. Considering the fact that the global life expectancy data were presented for a total of 207 countries and independent regions, it can be stated that the corresponding time length showed high deviations for countries that fell below the average life expectancy of the world.

The aim of this study is to determine the average life expectancy, which differs drastically for countries, and the economic, social, and political factors that influence it. For this purpose, economic, social, and political factors affecting the average life expectancy in 38 countries selected according to varying levels of development were investigated for the period of 2000–2018. The second section of the study concerns the relevant literature, the third part deals with the data and methodology, the fourth part presents the findings, and in the last part, the results of the study are provided.

Literature Review

In studies investigating the potential determinants of average life expectancy, factors such as income, health expenditures, education level, urbanization, number of doctors, access to clean water, nutrition, and geographical location were considered as the main determinants and were modeled by multiple variables. Among the variables mentioned, income and health expenditures can be considered as variables that are expected to have a positive influence on life expectancy. However, in numerous developing countries, despite the increase in income and health expenditures, low life expectancy has been observed (World Bank, Indicators of Development). Therefore, empirical studies aimed at investigating the effects of these factors on life expectancy have revealed different results regarding the direction, size, and functional patterns of the variables.

Preston (1975) stated in his study that income level and life expectancy have a nonlinear relationship and that a higher life expectancy for the same income level at later points in life was observed due to improvements in health. Rodgers (1979), while confirming that there is a positive nonlinear relationship between income and life expectancy, stated that life expectancy increases at a decreasing rate with an increase in income. In addition, he stated in his study that income inequality is effective in accessing health and social services, education and some other aspects of society related to mortality, and that life expectancy may be 5 to 10 years longer in economies where income is relatively more evenly distributed than in economies with unequal distribution. Rogers and Wofford (1989) correlated life expectancy with socioeconomic factors that they considered to be indicators of development and found that the amount of population per doctor and the agricultural population were negative predictors and the literacy rate was one of the positive predictors. Wilkinson (1992) discovered the relationship between per capita income and life expectancy to be quite weak in developed countries. He revealed that the relationship between living standards and life expectancy disappears when countries reach a threshold income level, and that the increase in per capita income is not related to life expectancy. According to Rogot et al. (1992), interpersonal life expectancy at the national level is directly related to education level and family income, contributing to studies stating that income is one of the deciders of life expectancy. Anand and Ravallion (1993) found that the relationship between life expectancy and per capita income is positive, as established in previous studies. However, they reported that per capita income has an indirect effect on life expectancy through increasing health expenditures. When health and poverty expenditures were included in the study model, no significant relationship between life expectancy and per capita income was obtained. Wilkinson (1996) expressed that there is a relationship between income and life expectancy up to a certain threshold value of per capita income and that this relationship disappears after the threshold value in per capita income is reached. The research in question can be associated with studies which state that there is a nonlinear relationship between income and life expectancy. It can be seen that the general point of connection in the aforementioned studies in explaining life expectancy is income per capita. However, as already stated, per capita income alone may not be sufficient to explain life expectancy or differences may arise with regard to the nature of the impact of income on life expectancy. In these studies, more effective results were obtained in determining the factors affecting life expectancy when possible factors that may influence life expectancy were evaluated as explanatory variables either individually or as a whole. Barlow and Vissandjee (1999) found that literacy and per capita income are the strongest predictors in explaining life expectancy. However, it was underlined in the study that some of the explanatory power in question is related to factors such as fertility rate, access to clean drinking water, and nutrition. In the study, no relationship was detected between health expenditures and life expectancy. Gulis (2000) stated that literacy and access to safe drinking water are the most crucial variables that influence life expectancy. The results of the study in which the positive effect of education on life expectancy was expressed are similar to the studies conducted by Williamson and Boehmer (1997) and Sen (1999). Another variable that has direct and indirect effects on life expectancy is urbanization. Kalediene and Petrauskiene (2000) found that there is a positive correlation between life expectancy and the level of urbanization. They stated that this relationship is based on achieving better health services and better educational opportunities as the rate of urbanization accelerates.

In Hussain's (2002) study, public- and private-sector health expenditure per capita, total fertility rate, illiterate adult rate, daily calorie intake per capita, and the country's status as a sub-Saharan African country were found to have significant effects on life expectancy. De Vogli et al. (2005), sampling high-income countries, stated that the effect of income inequality on life expectancy is greater than the effect of per capita income and education variables. The study in question confirms that the impact of income inequality on life expectancy persists. Kabir (2008) established that socioeconomic variables, which are traditionally thought to be very effective in determining the life expectancy of developing countries, are not as significant as suggested in previous studies. In the study, which states that improvements in per capita income, education, health expenditure per capita, and urbanization may not lead to longer life expectancy among developing countries, it is revealed that most of the variables traditionally thought to be influential are insignificant, which is contrary to the findings of previous studies. According to the study results, it can be stated that an increase in the number of doctors, an increase in adult literacy, and an improvement in nutrition can increase life expectancy. Sufian (2013) stated that among countries categorized according to life expectancy differences, the most notable reason for life expectancy variation is infant mortality, followed by poverty and total fertility rate. Gilligan and Skerpnek (2015) found that GDP, health expenditures, literacy rate, and vaccination averages are the most essential determinants of life expectancy in developed countries. Furthermore, vaccination rates and physician density were found to be paramount for life expectancy in non-industrialized countries. Studies conducted to ascertain the determinants of life expectancy have often focused on economic and health factors. In addition to these factors, it has been stated that countries' forms of government, meaning their political regimes, have a significant impact on life expectancy. In their study for underdeveloped countries, Lin et al. (2012) determined the variables of educational status, per capita income, nutritional status, and political regime as explanatory variables. According to this study, although the effect of the political regime variable on life expectancy is less in the short term compared to other factors, it has a significant effect in the long term. Research shows that citizens of countries with a high level of democracy tend to live longer than citizens of countries governed by a lower level of democracy. However, this effect of democracy is less for societies with low-income levels (Franco et al., 2004; Ross, 2006).

When studies conducted to investigate the factors determining life expectancy are examined, income per capita, total health expenditure per capita, level of urbanization, level of accessibility to clean drinking water, adequate nutrition level, fertility rate, infant mortality rate, number of doctors per capita, and political regime variables are observed to be significant factors in the studies. The functional form, size, and significance of the related variables differ according to the methods and samples of the studies. In addition, it is likely that there is a high multi-linearity between the variables used in these studies. Expressing variables with high interaction with each other as meaningless in the study does not make it possible to state with certainty that the variable expressed as meaningless has no effect on life expectancy. Furthermore, this situation cannot be justified to exclude the variables in question. For, the increase in health expenditures, which is expressed as an important determinant of life expectancy, can of course be expected to follow the increase in per capita income. However, income growth may not lead to an increase in health expenditures for all country groups. Therefore, each of the aforementioned variables, their coefficients and magnitudes, and marginal effects are significant for explaining the current situation and putting forward appropriate policy proposals.

Data and Methodology

Undoubtedly, statistical data is the most important issue for econometric studies, in which statistical tests and estimation methods are employed to explain the relationship patterns between economic variables. While the accuracy of this data is essential in terms of the results of the econometric research, the structure of the data is crucial for the selection of statistical testing and forecasting methods to be used. In line with the purpose of the study, a panel dataset was used to investigate the factors affecting average life expectancy. A panel dataset consisting of data from 38 countries for the period of 2000–2018 was created.

Average life expectancy was taken as the dependent variable in the study. Based on the inference that they may have an effect on the dependent variable in line with the reviewed economic literature and expectations, independent variables such as per capita income, urbanization rate, carbon dioxide emissions, health expenditures per capita, rate of access to electricity, education expenditures, the presence of the country in the Middle East or in sub-Saharan Africa, and the status of being a member of the European Union were included in the model. The countries included in the analysis are listed in table 10.1. The variables, the data representing the variables, and the data sources are summarized in table 10.2.

Econometric analyses using panel datasets, that is, panel data econometrics, have shown a rapid spread and progress with advantages such as more accurate estimation of model parameters, more realistic behavioral hypotheses, ability to model dynamic relationships, control for the effects of neglected variables, creation of micro-bases for aggregate data analysis, production of

TABLE 10.1
Countries Included in the Analysis

Germany	*Czech Republic*	*Sweden*	*Mali*	*Chile*
Australia	China	Italy	Egypt	Tunisia
Austria	Denmark	Japan	Mozambique	Uganda
Belarus	Indonesia	Cameroon	Peru	Uruguay
Belgium	Gana	Canada	Portugal	Jordan
United Kingdom	Morocco	Qatar	Senegal	Greece
Brazil	India	Kenya	Slovenia	
Bulgaria	Spain	Hungary	Sudan	

Source: Created by authors.

more accurate predictions for individual outcomes, and ease of computation (Hsiao, 2014: 1–10). Considering the advantages of panel data econometrics and the content of the study, the panel regression model was preferred in the study. In order to test the factors affecting average life expectancy, a panel regression model was established with variables determined. The basic panel regression model established for the analysis of factors affecting average life expectancy can be expressed as follows:

$$i = 1, 2, \ldots, N \ and \ t = 1, 2, \ldots, T$$

$$LE_{it} = \beta_0 + \beta_1 GDP_{it} + \beta_2 HE_{it} + \beta_3 UR_{it} + \beta_4 CE_{it} + \beta_5 AE_{it} + \beta_6 ANS_{it} + \beta_7 ME_{it} + \beta_8 SA_{it} + \beta_9 EU_{it} + \varepsilon_{it} \quad (1)$$

TABLE 10.2
Variables, Data Representing Variables, and Data Sources

Variable	*Data and Unit*	*Source*
Average Life Expectancy (LE)	Life Expectancy at Birth (Year)	World Bank
Income (GDP)	GDP per Capita (Thousand $)	World Bank
Health Expenditures (HE)	Health Expenditures per Capita ($1,000)	World Bank
Urbanization Rate (UR)	Urban Population (Total Population %)	World Bank
Carbon Dioxide Emissions (CE)	Carbon Dioxide Emissions Per Capita (Metric Ton)	World Bank
Access to Electricity (AE)	Access to Electricity (Total Population %)	World Bank
Education Expenditures (ANS)	Adjusted Savings for Education Expenditures (GNP %)	World Bank
Presence in the Middle East (ME)	Presence in the Middle East (0, 1)	
Presence in sub-Saharan Africa (SA)	Presence in sub-Saharan Africa (0,1)	
EU Membership (EU)	EU Membership (0, 1)	

Source: Created by authors.

Equation (1), where i represents the horizontal cross-section of the data and t represents time.

In the estimation of the panel regression model, there are three different models: the classical model, the fixed-effects model, and the random-effects model. The classical model used in Equation (1), in which the model related to the study is written, is based on the assumption that both constant and slope parameters are stable with respect to units and time; in other words, all observations are homogeneous (Tatoğlu, 2018: 38–40). The classical model can be rewritten in the following form using general econometric terminology.

$$y_{it} = x_{it}'\beta + z_i'\alpha + \varepsilon_{it} \quad (2)$$

Here, x_{it} represents the explanatory variable vector without constant terms and β represents the parameter vector of the explanatory variables. z_i contains a set of unit- or group-specific variables and a constant term. In the case of the classical model, z_i can be observed for all units and estimated as an ordinary linear model. If z_i is not observable but is related to x_{it}, then $z_i'\alpha = \alpha_i$ is treated as if it were a unit-specific constant. The said model, which is expressed as the fixed-effects model, can be written as follows to express the constant that can change from α_i unit to unit (Greene, 2018: 374–377).

$$y_{it} = x_{it}'\beta + \alpha_i + \varepsilon_{it} \quad (3)$$

With the assumption that the unobserved unit and group-specific variables will be unrelated to the explanatory variables in the model, the case where the units have common constants and the differences between the units are explained with error terms is handled with the random-effects model. The said model, to represent the zero mean and constant variance error terms specific to u_i unit, can be expressed as follows:

$$y_{it} = x_{it}'\beta + \alpha + \varepsilon_{it} + u_i \quad (4)$$

Here, α represents the mean of the unit-specific constants, while u_i represents the deviations of these constants from the mean (Gujarati, 2009: 592–602; Greene, 2018: 374–377). It is important to note that the fixed effects and random effects shown in Equations (3) and (4) are based on interunit differences in the models. The alternative to the situation known as one-way unit effects panel data models in the econometrics literature is two-way panel data models, that is, panel data models with both unit effects and time effects. The case of having only time effects is quite limited. Two-way fixed-effects and random-effects models, which include unit effects and time effects at the same time, λ_t being a variable representing the effects according to time, which does not change according to units and is not represented in the regression model, are shown in Equations (5) and (6), respectively. (Tatoğlu, 2018: 133–141).

$$y_{it} = x'_{it}\beta + \alpha_i + \lambda_t + \varepsilon_{it} \tag{5}$$

$$y_{it} = x'_{it}\beta + \alpha + \varepsilon_{it} + u_i + \lambda_t \tag{6}$$

Findings

In order to test the factors affecting average life expectancy, the panel regression model seen in Equation (1) was estimated. The model was estimated using the least squares method and the vitality of the variables in the model were evaluated. Based on the econometric inference, variables related to the location of countries (whether they are located in the Middle East or Sub-Saharan Africa) were excluded from the model in order to avoid the multicollinearity problem. In the following process, in order to determine which of the panel regression models is suitable, the choice between the classical model and the fixed-effects model was tested with the likelihood ratio (LR) test in the context of the basic hypothesis that there is no fixed effect based on units/time; that is, the classical regression model is suitable. In order to test the classical model against the random-effects model, the Breusch-Pagan LM test was performed with the hypothesis that the standard errors of the unit/time effects are equal to zero; that is, the classical model is suitable. In the choice to be made between the fixed-effects model and the random-effects model, the explanatory variables and the basic hypothesis of "there is no correlation between the unit/time effects" and the Hausman specification test were used (Baltagi, 2005: 66–70; Tatoğlu, 2018: 165–190). The relevant test results are summarized in table 10.3.

The basic hypothesis, which states that the classical regression model should be preferred over the fixed-effects model according to the results of the LR test summarized in the table, was rejected at 1% significance level for unit and unit-time effects. This suggests that the fixed-effects model should be preferred to the classical model. However, the fact that the basic hypothesis could not be rejected for time effects at the level of importance examined allows the evaluation of the unit effect being preferred in the fixed-effects model to be used. The following Breusch-Pagan LM test was used to test the random-effects model against the classical model. It must be noted that the basic hypothesis established for the suitability of the classical model was rejected for unit and unit-time effects at 1% significance level. Yet, the basic

TABLE 10.3
Results of the Fixed-Effects Model

	Impact	Statistical Value	Probability Value
Likelihood Ratio (LR) Test	Unit	109.005	0.000
	Time	1.619	0.049
	Unit-Time	110.519	0.000
Breusch-Pagan LM Test	Unit	3795.390	0.000
	Time	0.291	0.058
	Unit-Time	3795.681	0.000
Hausman Test	Unit	79.809	0.000
	Time	28.783	0.000

Source: Created by authors.

hypothesis could not be rejected at the level of importance for time effects. If the random-effects model is preferred, it can be estimated that it cannot be predicted by time effects. As a result of these two tests, it was concluded that the fixed-effects or random-effects models should be preferred to the classical model in the estimation of the economic model established to determine the factors affecting average life expectancy. The Hausman test was used to determine the preference between the fixed-effects model and the random-effects model. As a result of the test made with the basic hypothesis of the suitability of the random-effects model, the hypothesis was rejected at 1% significance level in terms of unit and time effects. Accordingly, it was concluded that it is appropriate to use a fixed-effects model in the estimation of the relationship that is the subject of the study.

It was determined that the appropriate model for the estimation of the economic model established in testing the factors affecting average life expectancy is the fixed-effects model. Thus, the fixed-effects model was estimated. The estimated model was tested according to econometric criteria and autocorrelation *(Baltagi-Wu locally best invariant test, LBI = 0.443 < 2)*, variable variance (ANOVA) *Modified Wald test, prob = 0.000)* and cross-sectional dependence *(Pesaran horizontal section independence test, prob = 0.000)* findings were found in the model. At this stage, the Driscoll-Kraay estimator, which produces efficient and consistent estimations by producing resistant standard errors with Newey-West type correction, was used for the issues of autocorrelation, varying variance, and cross-section dependence. The results of the fixed-effects model are summarized in table 10.4. The statistical value of F for the model is 1270.3 *(probe = 0.000)* and R^2 the value was obtained as 0.78. Based on these values, it can be stated that the model is generally meaningful and the model's explanatory power is sufficient.

The model in which average life expectancy is considered as the dependent variable and socioeconomic factors are included as independent variables is estimated with the help of the fixed-effects model. According to the findings,

TABLE 10.4
Results of the Fixed-Effects Model

Variable	*Coefficient*	*Drisc./Kraay Standard Errors*	*t-value*	*Probability Value*
Stable	33.72864	0.6676431	50.52	0.000
GDP	0.0000622	0.0000149	4.180	0.001
HE	0.2074291	0.0765991	2.71	0.014
UR	0.2953015	0.0322287	9.16	0.000
CE	−0.1941008	0.0569211	−3.41	0.003
AE	0.2070707	0.0190472	10.87	0.000
ANS	0.0622673	0.0907083	0.69	0.501
EU	1.146432	0.2520361	4.55	0.000

Source: Created by authors.

per capita gross domestic product, per capita health expenditure, urbanization rate, access to electricity rate, and the country's membership to the European Union were determined as the factors that positively affect average life expectancy and whose effects were found to be statistically significant. On the other hand, a negative relationship between carbon dioxide emission and average life expectancy was discovered. The effect of the education expenditure variable on average life expectancy was found to be meaningless.

Conclusion

Although average life expectancy is not considered to be a variable employed to directly evaluate the economic profile of countries, it is an outcome of the welfare provided by the economic profile in question. As a matter of fact, it is a predictable reality that positive developments in the economic variables that are determined to judge the economic performance of countries will lead to an increase in human living standards, that is, welfare levels of countries. The expected result of the positive changes in human living standards due to economic developments is that the average life expectancy, that is, the average value of time spent from birth to death of individuals residing in a country, increases. However, there are discussions about the degree and validity of the positive relationship between economic performance and average life expectancy, which can be based on the expected and said pattern. As a matter of fact, Wilkinson (1992) and Kabir (2008) revealed that the positive relationship, which is also confirmed in the economics literature and traditionally dominant studies such as Rodgers (1979) and Gilligan and Skerpnek (2015), may not be valid. This situation is not a case of the decisiveness of the hypothesis that economic developments do not impact life expectancy, but a problem of constrained transitivity between economic performance and life expectancy. The issue in question can be evaluated as a result of the inability of economic development to increase welfare. Consequently, the tested relationship between life expectancy and economic performance can be the answer to the question of whether economic development leads to increases in welfare when the life expectancy variable is taken as the outcome variable of prosperity. In this study, it is aimed to test the expected and generally accepted hypothesis that improvements in economic performance and in socioeconomic and political variables that develop in conjunction with economic performance will increase average life expectancy. Accordingly, a panel regression model was created using annual data for the period 2000–2018 for 38 countries selected according to different levels of development. In the study, in which average life expectancy was determined as the dependent variable, various economic, social and political variables (such as per capita income, per capita health expenditures, urbanization rate, carbon dioxide emissions, access to electricity, education expenditures, presence in the Middle East, presence in sub-Saharan Africa, and membership to the European Union) were included in the model as independent variables. The appropriateness of the fixed-effects model for the estimation of the generated panel regression model was determined.

According to the findings of the study, per capita income, per capita health expenditures, urbanization rate, electricity access rate, and the country's membership status in the European Union have a positive impact on average life expectancy. However, the effect of carbon dioxide emission on average life expectancy was reported as negative. Moreover, the effect of the education expenditure variable on average life expectancy was found to be meaningless. The findings obtained from the study support the prevailing view that socioeconomic and political indicators have a positive impact on life expectancy. As expected, increases in income and health expenditures have a positive influence on life expectancy. On the other hand, the fact that the relationship between education expenditures and life expectancy is not statistically significant can be explained by evaluating education expenditures as a human capital factor that has long-term consequences and will affect life expectancy in the long run. Modeling the long-term relationships between education expenditures, or human capital investments as a whole, and life expectancy can be put forward as the research proposal of the study. Based on the significant positive effect of membership in the European Union on life expectancy, which is another finding obtained from the study, it is deduced that international cooperation, which has the function of standardization of economic and social life with certain legal regulations, is significant for welfare level and, ultimately, average life expectancy. This is a sufficient inference for the European Union membership to be suggested as a policy proposal.

The study reports the effect of carbon dioxide emission rate, which is one of the important variables discussed in the field of carbon economy that has been frequently mentioned in the recent economic literature, on life expectancy is negative. This can be considered as an outcome of the environmental Kuznets curve, which is often confirmed in the economic literature. In accordance with this hypothesis, it is expected that environmental pollution will decrease after a certain threshold level of economic development is passed. When the positive effect of economic development on life expectancy and the environmental pollution that decreases with the threshold income level are evaluated together, the result obtained could be in line with the expectations. Ultimately, it has been evaluated that the carbon emission rate is not a determinant of life expectancy through the impact it will have on human health. Similarly, the increase in life expectancy and the decrease in carbon emissions are also a result of economic growth.

References

Anand, S., & Ravallion, M. (1993). Human development in poor countries: On the role of private incomes and public services. *The Journal of Economic Perspectives*, 7(1), 133–150.

Baltagi, B.H. (2005) *Econometric Analysis of Panel Data*. 3rd ed. New York: John Wiley & Sons Inc.

Barlow, R., & Vissandjee, B. (1999). Determinants of national life expectancy. *Canadian Journal of Development Studies*, 20, 9–29.

Bilas, V., Franc, S., & Bošnjak, M. (2014). Determinant factors of life expectancy at birth in the European Union countries. *Collegium Antropologicum*, 38(1), 1–9.

De Vogli, R., Mistry, R., Gnesotto, R., & Cornia, G. A. (2005). Has the relation between income inequality and life expectancy disappeared? Evidence from Italy and top industrialised countries. *Journal of Epidemiology and Community Health*, 59(2), 158.

Driscoll, J. C., & Kraay, A. C. (1998). Consistent covariance matrix estimation with spatially dependent panel data. *Review of Economics and Statistics*, 80(4), 549–560.

Dünya Bankası (2021). *Gelişmişlik göstergeleri*. Erişim Tarihi: 17.03.2021, https://data.worldbank.org.

Franco, Á., Álvarez-Dardet, C., & Ruiz, M. T. (2004). Effect of democracy on health: Ecological study. *British Medical Journal*, 329(7480), 1421.

Gilligan, A. M., & Skrepnek, G. H. (2015). Determinants of life expectancy in the Eastern Mediterranean Region. *Health Policy and Planning*, 30(5), 624–637.

Greene, W.H. (2018). *Econometric analysis*. 8th ed. New York: Pearson.

Gujarati, D. (2009). *Basic Econometrics*. 5th ed. The McGraw–Hill Companies.

Gulis, G. (2000). Life expectancy as an indicator of environmental health. *European Journal of Epidemiology*, 16(2), 161–165.

Hertz, E., Hebert, J. R., & Landon, J. (1994). Social and environmental factors and life expectancy, infant mortality, and maternal mortality rates: Results of a cross-national comparison. *Social Science & Medicine*, 39(1), 105–114.

Hsiao, C. (2014). *Analysis of Panel Data*. 3rd ed. Cambridge: Cambridge University Press.

Husain, A. R. (2002). Life expectancy in developing countries: A cross-section analysis. *The Bangladesh Development Studies*, 28(1/2), 161–178.

Kabir, M. (2008). Determinants of life expectancy in developing countries. *The Journal of Developing Areas*, 41(2), 185–204.

Kalediene, R., & Petrauskiene, J. (2000). Regional life expectancy patterns in Lithuania. *European Journal of Public Health*, 10(2), 101–104.

Lin, R. T., Chen, Y. M., Chien, L. C., & Chan, C. C. (2012). Political and social determinants of life expectancy in less developed countries: A longitudinal study. *BMC Public Health*, 12(85), 1–8.

Preston, S. H. (1975). The changing relation between mortality and level of economic development. *Population Studies*, 29(2), 231–248.

Riley, J. C. (2005). Estimates of regional and global life expectancy, 1800–2001. *Population and Development Review*, 31(3), 537–543.

Rodgers, G. B. (1979). Income and inequality as determinants of mortality: An international cross-section analysis. *Population Studies*, 33(2), 343–351.

Rogers, R. G., & Wofford, S. (1989). Life expectancy in less developed countries: Socioeconomic development or public health? *Journal of Biosocial Science*, 21(2), 245–252.

Rogot, E., Sorlie, P. D., & Johnson, N. J. (1992). Life expectancy by employment status, income, and education in the national longitudinal mortality study. *Public Health Reports*, 107(4), 457–461.

Ross, M. (2006). Is democracy good for the poor? *American Journal of Political Science*, 50, 860–874.

Sen, A. (1999). Economic policy and equity: An overview. In T. Vito et al. (eds.), *Economic Policy and Equity*. Washington, DC: International Monetary Fund.

Shaw, J.W., Horrace, W.C., & Vogel, R.J. (2005), The determinants of life expectancy: An analysis of the OECD health data. *Southern Economic Journal*, 71(4), 768–783.

Sufian A.J.M. (2013). Life expectancy and its socioeconomic determinants-a discriminant analysis of national level data. *International Journal of Humanities and Social Science*, 3(12), 303–312.

Tatoğlu, Yerdelen, F. (2018). *Panel veri ekonometrisi*, 4. Baskı, İstanbul: Beta Yayıncılık.

Wilkinson, R.G. (1992). Income distribution and life expectancy. *BMJ: British Medical Journal*, 304(6820), 165–168.

Wilkinson, R.G. (1996). *Unhealthy Societies: The Afflictions of İnequality*. London: Routledge.

Williamson, J. B., & Boehmer, U. (1997). Female life expectancy, gender stratification, health status, and level of economic development: A cross-national study of less developed countries. *Social Science & Medicine*, 45(2), 305–317.

Zhang, J., Zhang, J., & Lee, R. (2001). Mortality decline and long-run economic growth. *Journal of Public Economics*, 80, 485–507.

11

Asset Prices and Monetary Policy

An Empirical Investigation for Turkey

Cem ŞAHİN

Introduction

Inequality has been the interest of public attention and focus of policy debate along with the deterioration of income distribution following economic and financial crisis. Inequality itself is not the sole concern but the implications of policy response bring serious headwinds. Following crisis, expansionary monetary policies have been at the forefront in terms of its implications on income distribution and wealth. In this line, the impact of monetary policy on asset prices is an important research question considering the reflections of change in asset prices over wealth and income distribution.

Since the transmission of monetary policy decisions on macroeconomic variables like asset prices is indirect at best known, a significant part of the literature has been dedicated to understand and describe the channels of transmission. Transmission doesn't function directly and the change in monetary policy tool doesn't affect immediately the final targets like inflation and growth. In this line, transmission mechanism is evaluated on the basis of different channels like asset price channel, credit channel, and so on, depending on the direction of the path and a large number of studies have been produced to enlighten the inside of the "black box," which is just at the center between the monetary policy and economic variables.

Understanding monetary policy transmission mechanism in detail carries importance not only for the policy makers' side and academic environment but also for the financial sector in order to assess how inflation and output respond to monetary policy decisions in order to make appropriate risk measurement analysis (Rigobon and Sack, 2004). The transmission mechanism of monetary policy attracts more attention in Turkey following the introduction of inflation targeting regime in 2002 together with reforms on the institutional side of the monetary policy and other structural reforms, especially on fiscal policy. On the other hand, the number of studies on the transmission mechanism of monetary policy in Turkey is limited. Even, this number is lower for the asset price channel. In this context, the aim of this study is to make an empirical analysis on the impact of monetary policy over asset prices in Turkey.

The econometric method used in this study is the same as the one in Rigobon and Sack (2002) that has similarities with event study methodology. Treasury bills and bonds at 3-month, 6-month, 9-month, and 12-month, and Istanbul Stock Exchange 100 Index are the assets used in this study. This study applies the identification through heteroscedasticity methodology of Rigobon and Sack (2002) for Turkey and a candidate to be a member of limited number of studies on the impact of monetary policy decisions on asset prices in Turkey. The results reveal that the unexpected part of the monetary decisions affects the interest rates of Treasury papers at all maturities and the impact of monetary policy decision increases as the maturity of the Treasury paper lengthens. However, monetary policy decisions have no effect on the stock market index.

This study is structured as follows. Section 1 gives a theoretical background on monetary transmission channels with a special focus on asset price channel and summarized the literature on the general functioning of the asset price channel. Section 2 and 3 summarize data and methodology, respectively. Section 4 presents the results and the final section concludes.

Theoretical Framework and Literature Review

Theoretical Framework

In view of the effects of asset prices on demand conditions through changes in wealth and borrowing costs, monetary policy authority should closely follow the response of asset prices to policy decisions so as to formulate effective monetary policy rules. Beside the importance of movements of asset prices with respect to effects on economic activity from the perspective of policy makers, the influence of monetary policy decisions on asset prices also attracts the attention of financial market actors by means of risk evaluations and decision making in investment decisions (Rigobon and Sack, 2004).

Accordingly, the change in asset prices in response to monetary policy decision put its influence on economy via change in wealth, mainly through change in the price of capital and reallocation of portfolios, and the borrowing costs, thereby investment decisions (B. S. Bernanke and Kuttner, 2005). The literature mainly considers the bonds and stocks prices in the analysis of the impact of monetary policy actions on asset prices. This impact passes through different channels. One of them is the interest rate channel that works mainly via the impact of central bank policy rate on market interest rates.

Interest Rate Channel

Tightening of monetary policy pushes up short-term market interest rates and thereby changes the prices of assets. On the other hand, long-term interest rates are the key variable in asset prices. At this point, the relation between short-term and long-term interest rates is explained by the expectations theory. The idea behind expectations theory relies on that long-term interest rates are the average of future short-term interest rate. Higher long-term interest rates lead to lower spending in interest rate sensitive sectors of the economy such as consumer durables and business sector investment (Roley and Sellon, 1995). In this framework, the expectations on future monetary policy actions are important for central banks to control the demand conditions.

Roley and Sellon (1995) examined the link between monetary policy and long-term interest rates in the United States by drawing attention to the impact of market expectations about future monetary policy actions on long-term interest rates. They found that the impact of monetary policy decisions on long-term rates vary depending on the business cycle and the perception of market participants whether the policy action is persistent. Therefore, transmission channel of monetary policy is very complicated, so it is not easy to reconcile exactly the link between market interest rates and monetary policy decisions, although there is close relationship between monetary policy decisions and market interest rates.

Asset Price Channel

The simple description of the asset price channel is the transmission of monetary policy decisions on asset prices and subsequently to total demand. One of the important components of asset price channel is the wealth effect. Simply, the change in monetary policy rate and its impact on short-term interest rate implies a change in the price of asset and the wealth regarding the negative relation between the price of assets, bonds and bills, and their interest rates. Furthermore, some part of the wealth is held as stocks so the change in stock prices in response to monetary policy decisions affects the demand conditions.

There are several channels from monetary policy rate to stock prices. The famous one of them is the Tobin's q theory that indicates contraction of monetary policy, for example, due to increasing inflation, increases the market interest rates that put pressure on the net present value of future cash flows and thereby pressure on equity returns and stock market indices. Bernanke and Kuttner (2005) confirm that the response of stock prices is highly dependent on the expected future cash flows.

Additionally, contractionary monetary policy is expected to drag down the economic activity and weaker demand would pull down the future cash flow that is an important component of the cost and risk-benefit analysis in investment decisions. Especially, this is more vital for the firms supplying products in markets to which the demand conditions are highly cyclical and sensitive to interest rate. Actually, these effects are not passed through the interest rate channel, but they are related to the outcomes related with the interest rate channel (Ehrmann and Fratzscher, 2004).

Literature Review

There is an extensive research on examining the link between monetary policy actions and asset prices, and in this part, a summary of the literature will be given without going into deep details but with a focus on the pros and cons of the methodologies. The studies could be gathered under three headlines according to the empirical approach they used; single factor regression models, Vector Auto Regression (VAR) models, and event study models.

Single Factor Regression Models

The early literature back to the 1970s and 1980s about the impact of monetary policy on asset prices was based mainly on the relation between monetary aggregates and market interest rates (Reichenstein, 1987). The analysis generally use single equation regressions with monthly data and conclude the weak relation between monetary policy decisions and asset prices contrary to the general beliefs of the controlling capability of central banks on market interest rates. However, these studies utilize mostly money supply aggregates such as M1, M2, and other aggregate monetary measures. Regarding the discussions on monetary policy implementation and choosing intermediate targets, utilizing monetary aggregates is questionable because money supply aggregates are highly dependent on liquidity of the banking sector and the technological developments especially for the long run analysis. Therefore, using directly monetary policy target rate rather than monetary aggregates could improve the analysis and eliminate the shortcomings of using monetary aggregates as the indicator of monetary policy stance. Another problem in regression models is utilizing monthly data of the variables. Here, empirical shortfalls could be gathered under three heading: endogeneity, omitted variable bias, and using an appropriate proxy for monetary policy change.

Vector Autoregression Models

The literature has used VAR to overcome endogeneity and omitted variable bias problems. Endogeneity could be analyzed under two subtitles that the first one is related with the question whether the monetary policy decisions are purely exogenous. In other words, change in monetary policy stance could be the result of excessive changes in asset prices, and the relation between monetary policy decision and asset prices could be simultaneous. Rigobon and Sack (2003) claim that stock market changes increase the probability of change in interest rate in the United States. Bernanke and Gertler (2000) conclude that central banks should actively follow the financial markets and react to excessive and speculative asset price movements if these movements are expected to be a threat to outlook of inflation.

In this context, rather than using single equation regression in order to measure the effect of monetary policy on asset prices (Evans and Marshall, 1998), some of the studies have utilized VAR approach that has been used as a popular approach to identify the economic impulses since Sims (1980). Additionally, utilizing limited number of exogenous variables and limited number of restrictions in VAR approach are the reasons of popularity compared to other econometric methods containing structural equations (Brunner, 2000).

Thorbecke (1997) investigated the relation between monetary policy decision and stock indices for the United States by implementing VAR approach and concluded that contraction in monetary policy leads to decrease in stock indices. Similarly, Evans and Marshall (1998) used VAR analysis to study the relation between monetary policy decisions and treasury interest rates for the United States. The results show that tightening of monetary policy pushes up treasury interest rates at all maturities, but the impact diminishes as the maturity lengthens consistent with the results and discussions in Roley and Sellon (1995).

Despite the advantages of VAR approaches by solving endogeneity problem, it carries some drawbacks. For example, the datasets used in VAR analysis generally contain more than two variables like industrial production and inflation, and most of them are quarterly or monthly data; therefore, stock indices and treasury interest rates are used in average terms and this has high potential to lead misinterpretation of the results. Additionally, utilizing monthly or quarterly data could probably miss some of the effects of monetary policy changes because of aggregation. Ehrmann and Fratzscher (2004) criticized that the analysis extracted from VAR methodology contains still endogeneity bias stemming mainly from the frequency of the data, monthly or quarterly, and the analysis could not fully solve the problems about the endogeneity of the monetary policy decisions.

In addition to the critics about the aggregation of data and remaining endogeneity, using monthly and quarterly data also results in omit variables due to release frequency of the related data that may have impact on both monetary policy decisions and asset prices. At this point, the major concern in the studies that used VAR approach is the possibility of omitting the related variables, and this view is reinforced with the possibility of changes in the monetary policy response functions. This is more likely when one takes into consideration that the priorities of the central banks and the existing economic environment can alter the formulation of monetary policy. In this context, the coefficients that could change in each period will be suspicious and "fragile" (Rudebusch, 1998). Therefore, VAR analysis may contain the bias stemming from omitting the related variable with a high probability.

In summary, single factor regressions carry an important drawback that is known as the endogeneity of monetary policy responses and identification problem. However, the VAR studies seem not to be able to solve this problem exactly and carry some additional shortcomings.

Event Study Models

The second endogeneity problem is related with the other exogenous shocks, as introduced just earlier, such as news about unemployment or inflation to which central bank and financial markets could react simultaneously. This could create problems in identification of the responses of asset prices to monetary policy decisions apart from the impact of other exogenous shocks.

Cook and Hahn (1989) use a different methodology compared to the earlier studies known as event study to overcome the problems related with data frequency and availability, and endogeneity. The event study methodology is based on determining an appropriate time window around event which is monetary policy decision.

More explicitly, the difference between the relevant asset price such as treasury interest rate and stock price on the previous day of the monetary policy decision day and on the day following monetary policy decision is regressed over the change in monetary policy rate. The aim of this approach is to solve the endogeneity problem experienced in monthly data through limiting the period in which monetary policy and asset prices affect each other simultaneously and other exogenous shocks affect both monetary policy actions and asset price movements at the same time, and thereby lessening the endogeneity bias. In a more formal way, Kuttner (2001) summarized the event study approach as controlling the information released to markets that own potential impact on both monetary policy actions and asset prices by examining the impact on asset prices in a narrow time window surrounding monetary policy action.

At this point, the width of the window around the policy decision day is an important point. The measurability of the response of asset prices, the selection of data frequency, and the window around the monetary policy decision are crucial to set a balance between identification of exogenous monetary policy decisions and the complete impact on asset prices (Ehrmann and Fratzscher, 2004).

At lower frequencies like monthly and quarterly data, identification of exogenous monetary policy is difficult as discussed in the previous parts. On the other hand, at higher frequencies like intraday data, the risk of capturing overreactions or overshooting effects in asset prices, which might appear for a limited period after the decision, increases. In addition, the participants of the financial markets are not identical and the timing of response of each participant in the market could vary because all investors could not react to monetary policy decision within a couple of hours so using intraday data may be more sensitive to the time interval chosen compared to the daily window (Ehrmann and Fratzscher, 2004). Therefore, using event study approach with daily data seems to be more appropriate approach to identify the response of asset prices to monetary policy actions.

Cook and Hahn (1988) implemented the event study methodology and used a single factor regression to get the one-day response of treasury interest rates at various maturities up to 12 months to the federal funds target rate changes. The findings are consistent with the views of the capability of Federal Reserve in influencing the market interest rates and the impact of policy changes decreases as the maturity lengthen. Other studies implemented in the event study approach will be mentioned in the following pages.

Measuring Monetary Policy Surprises

Up to here, the discussions have focused on providing a solution to the endogeneity problem in the econometric models stemming from the semi-directional relationship between monetary policy and asset prices, and pure exogeneity of both monetary policy decisions and movements in asset prices. The event study approach seems to be successful to solve these phenomena.

However, recent literature focused more on the problem of extracting an appropriate measure for monetary policy decisions. The discussions center around the question whether utilizing monetary policy rate directly in the regression analysis provides a reliable estimation. Kuttner (2001) criticized the direct utilization of policy rate (i.e., federal funds rates for the United States) because change in asset prices like treasury interest rates and stock prices would not reflect the response of the markets in an appropriate manner. He explained this by rational expectations hypothesis. Accordingly, financial market participants and central banks use more or less same information set like unemployment and inflation during decision making. Hence, financial market participants already priced in the effects of change macroeconomic variables announced before to which the current monetary policy decision is probably a response to these variables. This infers that the response of asset prices on the day of monetary policy decision announcement don't reflect correctly the response of asset prices to monetary policy action. Furthermore, asset prices do not respond only when the central bank surprises the market but also when central banks make revisions in monetary policy stance (Bernanke and Kuttner, 2005). Therefore, the announced amount of change in policy rate is not the sole determinant of asset price change, as well; the wording of the announcement giving hints about the future course of monetary policy is equally important in market response (Gürkaynak et al., 2004).

In this framework, asset prices will respond to only the unexpected part of monetary policy, therefore, distinguishing the unexpected part of the monetary policy actions is critical to identify the impact of monetary policy on asset prices. Therefore, the conclusions of the works that don't separate monetary policy actions into expected and unexpected parts and utilizing absolute change in policy rate could be misleading because they contain errors in variables bias depending on how much the financial markets are capable of anticipating the monetary policy actions (Gürkaynak et al., 2004).

The literature separates the expected and unexpected parts of monetary policy decisions by focusing on market-based measures and using other asset prices. Kuttner (2001) used the current month federal funds futures for the United States as a proxy for the unexpected part of the monetary policy. The main idea lying behind using federal funds futures is the fact that it incorporates implicitly the forecasts of the investors with regard to the future path of policy actions. In that way, it already covers the information owned by the investors on anticipated part of future monetary policy actions together with the evaluations on previous policy actions and the perceptions on recent economic activity. A previous study of Krueger and Kuttner (1996) also proposes that federal funds futures is a good predictor of federal funds rate and concluded unanticipated changes in federal funds target could be identified by the movements in federal funds futures.

There are some critics on using futures or other assets owning short maturities for the representation monetary policy response, especially in the case of absence of preannounced monetary policy decision dates. Following a monetary policy action, market participants could respond not only to the surprise part of the decision but also to the timing of the decision (Rigobon and Sack, 2002). For example, if the announcement date of monetary policy was not set previously, the market participants are surprised not only by the monetary action but by the timing of the action. In this line, change in current month federal funds future or any other alternative asset representing the monetary policy action contains both monetary policy surprise and timing surprise. Rigobon and Sack (2002) argue that utilizing longer-term assets having maturity such as three months is more reliable because these longer-term assets would not be affected by timing surprise. From the opposite point of view, price of assets having longer maturity might not change following the monetary policy action as discussed previously due to liquidity concerns of these assets, which means the information content diminishes together with lengthening maturities (Ehrmann and Fratzscher, 2004). Rigobon and Sack (2002) and Gürkaynak et al. (2007) also propose that current month federal funds futures could be biased due to timing of the policy changes. Therefore, choosing the maturity of the proxy asset contains a critical balance.

After Krueger and Kuttner (1996), market-based measures of monetary policy decision have become popular, and the following studies persuade this approach but with different assets at different maturities because of the discussions on the predicting capability in monetary policy decisions and the availability of the asset. For example, Rudebusch (1998) and Brunner (2000) use current month federal funds future like Kuttner (2001) and use VAR models. Poole and Rasche (2000) measure the expectations of financial market participants by one-month ahead federal funds future in a contemporary policy analysis framework to examine the impact of monetary policy on asset prices.

Alongside federal funds futures, other financial asset prices have also been used to embody the surprise component of monetary policy in the studies focusing on the United States. Cochrane and Piazzesi (2002) and Craine and Martin (2008) use one-month Eurodollar interest rate, Rigobon and Sack (2004) use the Eurodollar future rate having the closest maturity at the policy decision date, and Rezessy (2005) uses the three-month Treasury bill rate as Ellingsen and Söderström (2003). Bomfim (2003) also utilizes current month federal funds future to analyze the impact of monetary policy on stock market volatility in the United States by GARCH modeling. The results show that the volatility of the stock market increases following the monetary policy decisions.

Rigobon and Sack (2002) introduce identification through heteroskedasticity methodology, a similar approach to event study analysis, to examine the relation between monetary policy decisions in the United States and asset prices. The results confirm that monetary policy actions affect the stock prices negatively and treasury interest rates in the same direction but the effects diminish at longer maturity.

Craine and Martin (2008) pursue approximately the same approach as Rigobon and Sack (2002) and examined the impact of monetary policy surprise on equity and bond markets in the United States. The monetary policy shocks are measured by both 30 days Eurodollar rate, and one-month federal funds futures rate occur on event days in order to identify the monetary policy surprises and include also nonevent days. The results confirm that a positive monetary policy surprise increases the long-term bond yields and decreases equity returns.

Ehrmann and Fratzscher (2004) use a different approach compared to the studies using market-based measures (other asset prices) as a proxy for monetary policy surprise, and they measure the surprise component of monetary policy as the difference between the change in federal funds rate and the market expectations taken from the Reuters poll conducted before each Federal Open Market Committee meetings among market participants. The results of the study confirm that the monetary policy actions affect the stock prices in the United States.

The studies using other asset prices as a proxy to measure the monetary policy surprise component for other countries are relatively limited. For example, Bredin et al. (2009) used a regression consists of both expected and unexpected monetary policy variables similar to Kuttner (2001). They examine the effects of monetary policy in the UK and Germany on stock returns and proxy the unanticipated part of monetary decisions as three-month Euromark futures rate for the period and three-month Euribor futures rate for Germany, and three-month sterling futures for the UK. The results point out that unexpected monetary policy has negative effects on stock returns both in the UK and Germany.

Gregoriou et al. (2009) use the three-month sterling LIBOR futures contract rate as the proxy of unexpected monetary policy component within a panel GMM model and conclude that both expected and unexpected monetary policy actions affect negatively the stock returns in the UK. Actually, the results contradict with the theoretical perspective discussed previously because the response of asset prices to expected part of monetary policy action is not compatible with the arguments of rational expectations.

Corallo (2006) implements a similar approach of Rigobon and Sack (2002) for Germany and the UK to measure the effect of monetary policy on stock indices, and the results show unexpected monetary policy decisions have negative but not significant impact on stock indices. Rezessy (2005) also uses the methodology in Rigobon and Sack (2004) and examines the impact of monetary policy in Hungary to asset prices including treasury interest rates, stock prices, and exchange rate. The results are consistent with the literature and earlier studies that an unexpected policy rate cut pulls down treasury interest rates and affects stock prices positively.

Data

This study aims to analyze the impact of monetary policy decision on asset prices in Turkey between January 2002 and June 2008. The beginning of the period is chosen as 2002 considering the introduction of short-term interest rates as the monetary policy tool. The assets considered here consist of stocks and treasury papers. We include Treasury papers having maturity at 3, 6, 9, and 12 months traded in Istanbul Stock Exchange Bond and Bill Market, and Istanbul Stock Exchange 100 Index (ISE-100). All data are publicly available and taken from Istanbul Stock Exchange (ISE).

The sample consists of two groups of which details to be discussed in the methodology part. The first part consists of the policy days when the monetary policy decision is taken and the second part covers the non-policy days just before the policy days. In this line, the data of three days surrounding the policy day for each policy decision is gathered for Treasury paper having maturity approximately 3, 6, 9, and 12-month on the policy decision day, and ISE-100 index to calculate return. For treasury papers, the absolute differences between the interest rates' levels on policy and non-policy date are taken. The change in ISE-100 index is computed as the logarithmic return on policy and non-policy days. The unexpected part of the monetary policy decision is proxied by the treasury paper having a maturity of one month at the monetary policy decision date. Forming the sample of the unanticipated part of monetary policy decision is similar to the one made for other asset prices. To sum up, the sample consists of two subsamples, and each of them contains 58 observations for each asset and monetary policy proxy.

Model

Introduction to the Model

The methodology in this study is taken from the Rigobon and Sack (2002) who used identification through heteroskedasticity to examine the impact of monetary policy decisions in the United States on stock indices and treasury interest rates. This part will concentrate on introducing the merits of this methodology. As discussed extensively in the theoretical framework and literature review part, regression analyses carry some deficiencies in analyzing the impact of monetary policy on asset prices. The problems gather under three headlines as the semi-directional relationship between monetary policy and asset prices, the pure exogeneity of both monetary policy decisions and movements in asset prices and omitted variable bias. Event study approach seems to solve problems by examining the impact on asset prices in a narrow time window surrounding monetary policy action and thereby controlling the information released to markets that owns potential impact on both monetary policy actions and asset prices. Endogeneity problem leads OLS regression results to be biased and inconsistent.

The aim of the event study approach is limiting the bias stemming from the endogeneity discussions through the introduction of time window. However, Rigobon and Sack (2002) show that there is still bias in the estimations of event study analysis. First, they defined the relation between monetary policy actions and asset prices in a simultaneous equations framework to embody better the simultaneous relation.

$$\Delta i_t = \beta \Delta s_t + \gamma z_t + \varepsilon_t \tag{1}$$

$$\Delta s_t = \alpha \Delta i_t + z_t + \eta_t \tag{2}$$

In the equation system here, Δs_t and Δi_t show one-day change in asset price and monetary policy rate, respectively, z_t represents other exogenous shocks, and η_t and ε_t represent the shocks to monetary policy and asset prices, respectively. Also, the disturbance terms are assumed to be serially uncorrelated and to be uncorrelated with z_t. Finally, α is the interest of this study measuring the impact of monetary policy decision on asset prices.

Although monetary policy transmission is more complicated, the system in Eq. (1) and (2) provides an oversimplification of the relationship and the benefit of not imposing structural restrictions as in VAR analysis (Rigobon and Sack, 2002). Another important point is that z_t could be an unobservable variable, and it is difficult to identify all exogenous shocks. However, omitting relevant variables leads misleading inferences. According to the system of the aforementioned equations, the ordinary least square estimator of event study approach is specified in equation (3) under the orthogonality assumptions:

$$E(\hat{\alpha}) = \alpha + (1 - \alpha\beta)\frac{\beta\sigma_\eta^2 + (\beta + \gamma)\sigma_z^2}{\sigma_\varepsilon^2 + \beta^2\sigma_\eta^2 + (\beta + \gamma)^2\sigma_z^2} \tag{3}$$

The second part of the right-hand side of the equation constitutes the bias part of the estimator where σ_η^2, σ_ε^2, and σ_z^2 represent the variance of the socks of asset prices and monetary policy, and other exogenous shocks, respectively. On the other hand, introducing two additional assumptions can make the estimator asymptotically unbiased estimator. One of these assumptions necessitates the variance of the monetary policy shock (σ_{ε}^2) is greater than asset price shock (σ_{η}^2) and other exogenous shock (σ_z^2) on the policy date. In other words, the magnitude of the monetary shock is higher compared to asset price and other exogenous shocks on the event day. This assumption is acceptable because it is very likely that the dominance of monetary policy actions on financial markets is higher on policy decision date. However, this assumption is only an attempt to minimize the bias part of the estimator and doesn't dissolve entirely the identification problem. The second assumption is more restrictive than first one and requires that the relative importance of monetary policy shock compared to other shocks ($\sigma_{\varepsilon}^2 / \sigma_{\eta}^2, \sigma_{\varepsilon}^2 / \sigma_z^2$) goes to infinity. This assumption makes the event study approach very restrictive to get an unbiased estimator.

The Model: Identification through Heteroscedasticity

Rigobon and Sack (2002) introduce identification through heteroskedasticity methodology, and the assumptions are less restrictive than event study analysis. The methodology is based on the change of the variance of monetary shock on monetary policy decision days in estimating the asset price response to monetary policy decisions. There are two critical assumptions of the model. The first assumption is on the variances of structural shocks. Accordingly, monetary policy shock measure (σ_{ε}^2) shifts on policy decision date, and the magnitude of the asset price shock (σ_{η}^2) and other exogenous shock (σ_z^2) remains same on policy decision days compared to other days. The second assumption is the parameter stability during the sample period.

To integrate these assumptions into the model, identification through heteroskedasticity model is constructed by first defining two subsamples, the one for the policy date and the one for the non-policy dates. The approach incorporates the daily changes on monetary policy decision days similar to event study approach, but additionally the model introduced the second sample group consisting of the days just before the policy decision days to represent the non-policy days. Rigobon and Sack (2002) assigned F for the sample data from the days in which monetary policy decisions are taken and ˜F for the sample data from the non-policy days.

The advantage of this approach is that the shocks on non-policy dates still occur on policy dates, and they are included in the model contrary to event study approach. No change in asset price $((\sigma_{\eta}^2)^F = (\sigma_{\eta}^2)^{\sim F})$ and other exogenous shocks $((\sigma_z^2)^F = (\sigma_z^2)^{\sim F})$ together with shift in monetary policy shock on policy days $((\sigma_{\varepsilon}^2)^F > (\sigma_{\varepsilon}^2)^{\sim F})$ constitute the critical assumptions of the model aiming to focus more on the relative importance of monetary policy action on policy decision days. This assumption seems highly realistic when one considers that financial markets concentrate on monetary policy actions more on policy days.

Following the setting of the model assumptions and separating the sample into two subperiods as policy days and non-policy days, the first step is to get the reduced form equations from equations (1) and (2). The reduced forms of the equations for two subperiods are as in equation (4_i–4_iv),

$$\Delta i_t^F = \frac{1}{1-\alpha\beta}\left[(\beta+\gamma)z_t^F + \beta\eta_t^F + \varepsilon_t^F\right] \tag{4\_i}$$

$$\Delta i_t^{\sim F} = \frac{1}{1-\alpha\beta}\left[(\beta+\gamma)z_t^{\sim F} + \beta\eta_t^{\sim F} + \varepsilon_t^{\sim F}\right] \tag{4\_ii}$$

$$\Delta s_t^F = \frac{1}{1-\alpha\beta}\left[(1+\alpha\gamma)z_t^F + \eta_t^F + \alpha\varepsilon_t^F\right] \tag{4\_iii}$$

$$\Delta s_t^{\sim F} = \frac{1}{1-\alpha\beta}\left[(1+\alpha\gamma)z_t^{\sim F} + \eta_t^{\sim F} + \alpha\varepsilon_t^{\sim F}\right] \tag{4\_iv}$$

Δi_t^F shows the change in policy rate on the policy day, and it is the difference between the level of policy rate on the day just preceding the policy decision day and the level of policy rate on the decision day. Similarly, $\Delta i_t^{\sim F}$ represents the policy rate change in the non-policy day which is taken as the day prior to the decision day. Therefore, it is calculated by the difference between the level of policy rate on the day prior to the policy decision day and the level on two days before. To sum up, in order to calculate the differences of two subsamples, the study uses three days including the policy decision day, one day and two days before the policy decision day if the window around the release of monetary policy decision is chosen as one day.

The covariance matrices for two sub-periods are given in equations (5_i) and (5_ii). Under the assumptions made on the variance structure of the shocks previously and the parameter stability (α, β and γ), the difference between two covariance matrices is given in equation (5_iii). Equations (5_iv) and (5_v) give the estimates of variance covariance for two subsamples where Δx_t is the vector constructed by stacking the vectors of Δi_t and Δs_t. δ_t^F and $\delta_t^{\sim F}$ are dummy variables for the first subsample and the second subsample, respectively. T_F and $T_{\sim F}$ are the number of observations in each subsample.

$$\Omega_t^F = E\left(\left[\Delta i_t^F \, \Delta s_t^F\right]'\left[\Delta i_t^F \, \Delta s_t^F\right]\right) \tag{5\_i}$$

$$\Omega_t^{\sim F} = E\left(\left[\Delta i_t^{\sim F} \Delta s_t^{\sim F}\right]'\left[\Delta i_t^{\sim F} \Delta s_t^{\sim F}\right]\right) \tag{5\_ii}$$

$$\Delta\Omega_t = \Omega_t^F - \Omega_t^{\sim F} = \frac{\left(\left(\sigma_\varepsilon^2\right)^F - \left(\sigma_\varepsilon^2\right)^{\sim F}\right)}{(1-\alpha\beta)^2}\begin{bmatrix} 1 & \alpha \\ \alpha & \alpha^2 \end{bmatrix} \tag{5\_iii}$$

$$\hat{\Omega}^F = \frac{1}{T_F}\sum_{t=1}^{T} \delta_t^F \Delta x_t \Delta x_t' \tag{5\_iv}$$

$$\hat{\Omega}^{\sim F} = \frac{1}{T_{\sim F}}\sum_{t=1}^{T} \delta_t^{\sim F} \Delta x_t \Delta x_t' \tag{5\_v}$$

The estimates $\hat{\alpha}^i$ and $\hat{\alpha}^s$ are derived by instrumental variables regression and Rigobon and Sack (2002) utilize two possible instruments (w_i and w_s) as in equation (6). The estimators $\hat{\alpha}^i$ and $\hat{\alpha}^s$ are given in equation (7).

$$w_i \equiv \left[\Delta i_F' - \Delta i_{\sim F}'\right]' \tag{6}$$

$$w_s \equiv \left[\Delta s_F' - \Delta s_{\sim F}'\right]'$$

$$\hat{\alpha}^i = \left(w_i'\Delta i\right)^{-1}\left(w_i'\Delta s\right) = \frac{\Delta i_F'\Delta s_F - \Delta i_{\sim F}'\Delta s_{\sim F}}{\Delta i_F'\Delta i_F - \Delta i_{\sim F}'\Delta i_{\sim F}} \tag{7}$$

$$\hat{\alpha}^s = \left(w_s'\Delta i\right)^{-1}\left(w_s'\Delta s\right) = \frac{\Delta s_F'\Delta s_F - \Delta s_{\sim F}'\Delta s_{\sim F}}{\Delta i_F'\Delta s_F - \Delta i_{\sim F}'\Delta s_{\sim F}}$$

Testing the Assumptions of the Model

Rigobon and Sack (2002) introduce a hypothesis test to investigate whether the assumptions of the model are correct. If the assumptions on the variances of the shocks and parameter stability are correct, then $\hat{\alpha}^i$, $\hat{\alpha}^s$, and $\hat{\alpha}^{all}$ should be asymptotically equal and provide the true value of α. Accordingly, comparison of the estimators will provide information about the validity of the assumptions and overidentifying restrictions. The test is introduced in equation (8):

$$\hat{\Gamma}_{all,i} = \frac{1}{K}\left|\hat{\alpha}^{all} - \hat{\alpha}^{i}\right|\hat{M}_{all,i}^{-1}\left|\hat{\alpha}^{all} - \hat{\alpha}^{i}\right| \rightarrow F_{K,T-1} \quad (8)$$

$\hat{\alpha}^{all}$ is the vector of coefficients obtained from the model incorporating all asset prices, and the vector of coefficients ($\hat{\alpha}^{i}$) is made up by stacking all coefficients obtained from the single asset estimations with the instrument of policy rate. $\hat{M}_{all,i}^{-1}$ is the estimator of the variance of difference between the vectors of $\hat{\alpha}^{all}$ and $\hat{\alpha}^{i}$. The test statistic has F distribution where K is the number of assets and T is the sum of the number of observations in two subsamples. Rejection of the null hypothesis implies unstable parameters between the subsamples and invalid assumptions about the variance structures of the shocks.

In order to test the validity of the instruments and thereby the efficiency of the coefficients, Rigobon and Sack (2002) use Hausman test. Accordingly, the test could be defined in (9) where $\hat{\alpha}^{het}$ and $\hat{\alpha}^{es}$ show the vectors of coefficients obtained by instrumental variables regressions using all the instruments and OLS regressions. $\hat{M}_{het,es}^{-1}$ is the estimator of the variance of difference between $\hat{\alpha}^{het}$ and $\hat{\alpha}^{es}$, which is also asymptotically equal to the difference between the variances of coefficient vectors.

$$\hat{\Gamma}_{het,es} = \frac{1}{K}\left|\hat{\alpha}^{het} - \hat{\alpha}^{es}\right|\hat{M}_{het,es}^{-1}\left|\hat{\alpha}^{het} - \hat{\alpha}^{es}\right| \rightarrow F_{K,T-1} \quad (9)$$

Results

The summary statistics of the policy rate and asset prices are given in table 11.1. The variance of policy rate on policy days (F) is considerably higher than the variance on non-policy days (˜F), which is consistent with the arguments that the markets focus more on monetary policy decisions and the variance of policy rate shock shifts on policy days. Covariance structure of policy rate and other asset prices shows that the relation between policy rate and asset prices increases on policy days. Accordingly, increase in policy rate pushes up the interest rates of Treasury papers at all maturities. The relation between ISE-100 index and policy rate becomes negative on policy days, but the covariance on non-policy days is positive, which implies the dominance of exogenous shocks on non-policy days.

The estimation results are summarized in table 11.2. As mentioned in the methodology part, the estimation of the model is performed in two

TABLE 11.1
Variance/Covariance Structure of Policy Rate and Asset Prices

	Variance		Covariance with Policy Rate	
	F	*˜F*	*F*	*˜F*
Policy Rate	0.38	0.08	-	-
i_{3m}	0.33	0.07	0.26	0.03
i_{6m}	0.39	0.11	0.29	0.06
i_{9m}	0.60	0.38	0.38	0.09
i_{12m}	0.59	0.35	0.39	0.08
ISE-100	4.71	2.78	-0.22	0.10

ways, and the results are grouped according to the estimation methods. The model is estimated first for multiple assets by implementing three-stage least square (3SLS) estimation technique, and then the model is run for each asset separately by two-stage least square (2SLS). Beside the technical differences between two estimation methodologies such as inputting the covariance matrix of 2SLS in 3SLS coefficient estimation, here, in 3SLS estimation all instruments are included but in 2SLS only the instrument for monetary policy rate is utilized to test the overidentifying restrictions.

The coefficients for treasury interest rates are highly significant and show that monetary policy decisions raise the interest rates of treasury papers at all maturities (table 11.2). For example, 25 basis points unexpected increase in monetary policy rate leads to approximately 22.5 basis points increase in 3-month treasury interest rate. The results could seem a little confusing

TABLE 11.2
The Response of Asset Prices to Monetary Policy

	3SLS		*2SLS*	
	Coeff.	*Std. Err.*	*Coeff.*	*Std. Err.*
i_{3m}	0.91	0.09	0.85	0.09
$i_{6\,m}$	0.89	0.09	0.86	0.10
$i_{9\,m}$	1.13	0.13	1.06	0.13
$i_{12\,m}$	1.12	0.12	1.06	0.13
ISE-100	−0.45	0.50	−0.41	0.52
		F-Test	*P-Value*	
$\hat{\Gamma}_{all,i}$: *Test of Overidentifying Restrictions*		1.99	0.08	
$\hat{\Gamma}_{het,es}$: *Efficiency Test for Coefficients*		2.12	0.07	

Source: Author's calculations.

because the impact of monetary policy decision increases as the maturity of the Treasury paper lengthens according to the results of the literature. However, it is important to remind that the longest maturity of Treasury paper taken in this study is 12 months. Additionally, higher impact on 9-month and 12-month interest rates could be associated with the risk evaluations of the investors at different maturities and how the markets observe the explanations about rationale of the decision for the future monetary policy stance.

On the other hand, the impact of monetary policy on ISE-100 index is negative as expected, and a 25 basis points policy surprise is resulted in 0.1% decline in ISE-100. However, the coefficient is not statistically significant, and this shows that the relation between monetary policy decisions and stock prices is weak. The weak relationship could be explained by high foreign share in ISE-100 and that the evaluations of the investors on stock markets focus mostly on the riskiness at country group basis, independent from the country specific analysis.

The overidentification test ($\hat{\Gamma}_{\text{all},i}$) for the reliability of the model assumptions does not reject the hypothesis that the assumptions of the model about the parameter stability and variance structure of the shocks are not rejected at 10% significance level. Hausman test statistics ($\hat{\Gamma}_{het,es}$) for the efficiency of the estimators do not reject the null hypothesis that the probability limits of two estimators are equal.

Conclusion

A thorough understanding of monetary policy transmission mechanism has been the interest for all parts in the economy. The literature on the transmission mechanism is very extensive, and asset price channel is an important component of this mechanism. The empirical methodologies in investigating the relationship between monetary policy and asset prices have some difficulties to provide robust results.

The main problem related with the single factor regressions is the endogeneity problem stemming from semi-directional relationship between monetary policy decisions and asset prices and the identification of monetary policy response from other exogenous shocks. VAR approach solves to some extent the endogeneity problem but not completely that VAR analysis owns some deficiencies such as aggregation of the data and missing some variables because of the release frequency of the data. Furthermore, the formulation of monetary policy equation is a difficult task and increases the probability of omitting variables due to the variation of the priorities of central banks. The event study methodology is mainly based on determining an appropriate time window around the monetary policy decision date. The success of the approach is to solve the endogeneity problem by restraining the time period and thereby controlling the information released to markets having potential impact on both monetary policy actions and asset prices.

Apart from the discussion on the robustness of estimation methods, the recent discussions in the literature are focused on the reliability of using monetary policy rate directly in the analysis. According to rational expectations hypothesis, the financial market participants and central banks use more or less the same information set, and the response of asset prices on the day of monetary policy decision announcement reflects only the part of change that reflects the difference of reading the past macroeconomic data releases by monetary policy authority and financial market participants. The literature has distinguished the unexpected part from expected part of monetary policy decision by market-based measures, especially returns on future contracts.

Together with switching to formal inflation targeting in 2006 and amelioration of the distortions on transmission channel such as debt burden, double-digit inflation and dollarization, the link between monetary policy decisions and demand conditions, in other words, the transmission channel of monetary policy in Turkey raised the notice of the policy makers. This study examines the impact of monetary policy on asset prices for Turkey. Treasury bonds and bills at maturities 3-month, 6-month, 9-month and 12-month, and ISE-100 index are taken as the assets to be examined for the period between 2002 and June 2008. Treasury bond interest rate having one-month maturity on the policy day is taken in order to proxy the monetary policy surprise component.

The results show that the unexpected part of the monetary decisions affects the interest rates of treasury papers at all maturities, and the coefficients are statistically significant. On the other hand, monetary policy decisions affect the stock market negatively, but the coefficient is statistically insignificant. The results suggest that unexpected monetary policy changes reflect asset prices partly for Turkey.

References

Bernanke, B., and Gertler, M. (2000). Monetary policy and asset price volatility. *National Bureau of Economic Research Working Paper Series, No. 7559*. doi:10.3386/w7559.

Bernanke, B. S., and Kuttner, K. N. (2005). What explains the stock market's reaction to federal reserve policy? *Journal of Finance*, *60*(3), 1221–1257, June. doi:10.1111/j.1540-6261.2005.00760.x.

Bomfim, A. N. (2003). Pre-announcement effects, news effects, and volatility: Monetary policy and the stock market. *Journal of Banking and Finance*, 27(1), 133–151. doi:10.1016/S0378-4266(01)00211-4.

Bredin, D., Hyde, S., Nitzsche, D., and O'Reilly, G. (2009). European monetary policy surprises: The aggregate and sectoral stock market response. *International Journal of Finance and Economics, 14*(2), 156–171. doi:10.1002/ijfe.341.

Brunner, A. D. (2000). On the derivation of monetary policy shocks: Should we throw the VAR out with the bath water? *Journal of Money, Credit and Banking, 32*(2) (May, 2000), 254–279. doi:10.2307/2601242.

Cochrane, J. H., and Piazzesi, M. (2002). The fed and interest rates - A high-frequency identification. *American Economic Review, 92*(2), 90–95. doi:10.1257/000282802320189069.

Cook, T., and Hahn, T. (1989). The effect of changes in the federal funds rate target on market interest rates in the 1970s. *Journal of Monetary Economics, 24*(3), 331–351. doi:10.1016/0304-3932(89)90025-1.

Corallo, E. (2006). The effect of monetary policy on asset prices: Evidence from Germany and UK. *LIUC Papers in Economics 185, Cattaneo University (LIUC).*

Craine, R., and Martin, V. L. (2008). International monetary policy surprise spillovers. *Journal of International Economics.* doi:10.1016/j.jinteco.2007.06.005.

Ehrmann, M., and Fratzscher, M. (2004). Taking stock: Monetary policy transmission to equity markets. *Journal of Money, Credit, and Banking, 36*(4) (Aug., 2004), 719–737. doi:10.1353/mcb.2004.0063.

Ellingsen, T., and Söderström, U. (2003). *Monetary Policy and the Bond Market,* Stockholm School of Economics, Stockholm Sweden.

Evans, C. L., and Marshall, D. A. (1998). Monetary policy and the term structure of nominal interest rates: Evidence and theory. *Carnegie-Rochester Conference Series on Public Policy, 49,* 53–111. doi:10.1016/s0167-2231(99)00004-4.

Gregoriou, A., Kontonikas, A., MacDonald, R., and Montagnoli, A. (2009). Monetary policy shocks and stock returns: Evidence from the British Market. *Financial Markets and Portfolio Management, 23*(4), 401–410. doi:10.1007/s11408-009-0113-2.

Gürkaynak, R. S., Sack, B., and Swanson, E. T. (2004). Do actions speak louder than words? The response of asset prices to monetary policy actions and statements. *Finance and Economics Discussion Series.* USA. doi:10.17016/feds.2004.66.

Gürkaynak, R. S., Sack, B. P., and Swanson, E. T. (2007). Market-based measures of monetary policy expectations. *Journal of Business and Economic Statistics, 25*(2), 201–212. doi:10.1198/073500106000000387.

Krueger, J. T., and Kuttner, K. N. (1996). The fed funds futures rate as a predictor of federal reserve policy. *Journal of Futures Markets, 16*(8), 865–879. doi:10.1002/(SICI)1096-9934(199612).

Kuttner, K. N. (2001). Monetary policy surprises and interest rates: Evidence from the Fed funds futures market. *Journal of Monetary Economics, 47*(3), 523–544. doi:10.1016/S0304-3932(01)00055-1.

Poole, W., and Rasche, R. H. (2000). Perfecting the market's knowledge of monetary policy. *Journal of Financial Services Research, 18*(2), 255–298. doi:10.1023/a:1026555225089.

Reichenstein, W. (1987). The impact of money on short-term interest rates. *Economic Inquiry, 25*(1), 67–82. doi:10.1111/j.1465-7295.1987.tb00723.x.

Rezessy, A. (2005). *Estimating the Immediate Impact of Monetary Policy Shocks on the Exchange Rate and Other Asset Prices in Hungary* (Issue 38). Magyar Nemzeti Bank. MNB Occasional Papers. http://hdl.handle.net/10419/83543.

Rigobon, R., and Sack, B. (2002). The impact of monetary policy on asset prices. *Finance and Economics Discussion Series*. USA. doi:10.17016/feds.2002.04.

Rigobon, R., and Sack, B. (2003). Measuring the reaction of monetary policy to the stock market. *Quarterly Journal of Economics*, *118*(2), 639–669. doi:10.1162/003355303321675473.

Rigobon, R., and Sack, B. (2004). The impact of monetary policy on asset prices. *Journal of Monetary Economics*, *51*(8), 1553–1575. doi:10.1016/j.jmoneco.2004.02.004.

Roley, V. V., and Sellon, G. H. Jr. (1995). Monetary policy actions and long-term interest rates. *Economic Review*, *80*(4), 77–89.

Rudebusch, G. D. (1998). Do measures of monetary policy in a var make sense? *International Economic Review*, *39*(4), 943–948. doi:10.2307/2527344.

Sims, C. A. (1980). Macroeconomics and reality. *Econometrica*, *48*(1) (Jan., 1980), 1–48. doi:10.2307/1912017.

Thorbecke, W. (1997). On stock market returns and monetary policy. *Journal of Finance*. *52*(2), 635–654. doi:10.1111/j.1540-6261.1997.tb04816.x.

12

Can Removing Zeros from the Stock Market Index Be Used to Ensure Financial Stability and Sustainability?

Çağrı HAMURCU

Introduction

Investors are known as showing both rational and irrational behavior while making investment decisions. These irrational tendencies are the main focus of behavioral finance studies. One of the factors affecting decisions is the perception of investors. Their financial behavior occurs in parallel to their perception of events. The numerical indicators of investment instruments are counted among the factors that create investor perceptions and are revealed as an important factor in decision-making. The perception of the person about numbers could cause behavioral effects that might result in cluster formation in the markets by forming psychological barriers related to numbers (Mitchell, 2001). The psychological barrier could be seen as a mental obstacle created by the mind of the person and the decision-making process about certain issues, which prevents people from making rational decisions by restricting their access to mental processes and their ability to act in this way.

Investors are affected by certain indicators such as the size of the numerical data of the invested asset, the number of digits, and the last digits of these numbers. The perception created by these indicators in the investor could be considered a psychological barrier. Such barriers could be expected in financial markets built on numbers. Stock market indexes are one of the areas where these psychological barriers are seen. Many studies have revealed that the psychological barriers that occur in stock market indexes affect investors when they invest in stocks.

Donaldson and Kim (1993) examined whether the Dow Jones Industrial Average (DJIA) index has possible barriers to daily closing price movements. In their study, when the index closing values of the DJIA are examined, it is observed that the closing index values at the 100-level neighborhood are lower. It is also stated in that study that outside of the barrier points (support and resistance levels) in the index there are more upward or downward movements than normal. The results of their study, verified by AR (1), generalized autoregressive conditional heteroskedasticity (GARCH) (1,1), and Monte Carlo simulations, are interpreted as an indication that there might be barriers to pricing at 100 levels in the DJIA index.

The psychological barriers in stock markets are investigated by Koedijk and Stork (1994) in their study involving the Brussels Stock Exchange (Belgium), FAZ General (Germany), Nikkei Stock Average 225 (Japan), Standard and Poors Composite (United States), and FTSE-100 (United Kingdom). The results show that psychological barriers exist and are relatively rarely overcome in these stock markets, especially at the level of round index values.

The paper by Westerhoff (2003) discusses a basic model of the behavioral exchange rate in which traders use the closest round number as an underlying value proxy. According to the results, exchange rates are regularly misaligned due to anchoring bias, and this kind of conduct often generates support and resistance levels.

Bahng (2003) researched whether there are possible psychological price barriers in seven Asian financial exchanges' daily stock price indexes, that is, South Korea, Taiwan, Hong Kong, Thailand, Malaysia, Singapore, and Indonesia. The results showed the presence of a price barrier in the stock exchange of Taiwan. This barrier is not detected in the other markets.

In Cinko's (2014) study, the presence of psychological barriers was determined in thousands of digits in the BIST100 index of Borsa İstanbul (BIST). In that study, closing values of the BIST 100 index were analyzed over the 10-year period between 2003 and 2013.

A study conducted on the NASDAQ index investigated whether the stock market index levels have any behavioral tendencies depending on their proximity to psychological barriers (Woodhouse et al., 2016). In that study, it is stated that the market tends to stick to levels usually expressed in multiples of 100 before breaking out upward or downward. It is stated that not only do investors struggle with price and fundamental equity metrics but also their trading practices are impacted by index barriers.

Regarding the psychological barriers in stock market indexes, the homogeneity of the indexes in the last digits of the Greek, Italian, Portuguese, and Spanish stock markets is examined by Lobão and Pereira (2017). Their study analyzes whether the status of being above or below a possible barrier of the indexes has different effects or not using regression and GARCH methods. According to the results, in the Greek stock market, the psychological barriers are strong, and they are weak in the Iberian stock markets, while there is no evidence of psychological barriers in the Italian stock market. Psychological barriers were also determined in the stock exchanges of Germany, Finland, and the Netherlands in another study by Lobão and Pereira (2016).

Unlike the studies conducted so far, the number of digits of the stock market index might be thought to affect the perception of the investor, creating psychological barriers. It springs to mind that the perception of investors could be changed positively by removing the psychological barriers. Removal of zeros from the stock market index could be considered as one way to positively affect the perception of investors and create the potential to eliminate the psychological barriers that may have occurred regarding the index values.

Tversky and Kahneman (1974) stated that people are using some shortcuts in decision-making processes that will make the process simpler to reduce the complexity of the situations such as determining probabilities and predicting the future values. In light of this approach, it is assumed that reducing the number of digits in the index might reduce the complexity experienced by investors.

This study hypothesizes that "removing zeros from a stock market index could have a positive effect on returns and volatility," and it is thought that removing zeros might have a positive effect on psychological perceptions among investors. In order to investigate the accuracy of this hypothesis, the BIST 100 index (Istanbul Stock Exchange in Turkey), in which zeros are removed from the index value in two different periods, is discussed.

Volatility and ARCH Models

Volatility, which is defined as sudden fluctuations in financial asset values, brings about rises and falls in financial markets. Some modeling studies are needed to understand the volatility in markets. In this context, Mandelbrot (1993) stated that big changes are accompanied by big changes in the prices of assets traded in financial markets, while slight changes are followed by small changes. The autoregressive conditional heteroskedasticity (ARCH) model was developed by Engle (1982) to predict such movements and volatility in financial markets. ARCH models make the error terms of conditional variance at time t a function of system parameters, exogenous and delayed endogenous variables, and historical error terms. The formula of this ARCH model is given in equation (1). The motion of the conditional variance of the time series is explained by the ARCH model. In this formula, ξ_t is the prediction error and σ_t^2 is the variance of ξ_t given information at time t.

$$\sigma_t^2 = \alpha_0 + \sum_{i=1}^{p} \alpha_i \xi_{t-i}^2 \tag{1}$$

Following the ARCH model, the GARCH model was obtained by Bollerslev (1986) by adding the delayed value of conditional variance to equation (2).

$$\sigma_t^2 = \alpha_0 + \sum_{i=1}^{p} \alpha_i \xi_{t-i}^2 + \sum_{j=1}^{q} \beta_j \sigma_{t-j}^2 \tag{2}$$

In this equation, α_0, α_i, and β_j must be greater than zero, and the sum of the second and the third parts of it must be smaller than one. In this model, the conditional variance is modeled as an autoregressive moving average process, unlike the ARCH model. Higher α_i and β_j values imply a greater volatility reaction to market shocks and market shock persistence relatively. If α_i is high, there is high sensitivity to volatility from market movements. It can be surmised that the closer $\alpha_i+\beta_j$ is to 1, the more a shock at time t will have an effect in the future (Sosa and Ortiz, 2017).

Models expressed as autoregressive (AR) and moving averages (MA) and a combination of the two (ARMA) are utilized in the analysis of univariate time series, and the time series could be modeled by determining the most suitable approach with the Box-Jenkins method (Rojas et al., 2008). In the analysis, the order of the AR and MA is important. The formula for the ARMA (p, q) model is as follows:

$$y_t^2 = \alpha_0 + \sum_{i=1}^{p} \alpha_i y_{t-i}^2 + \sum_{i=1}^{p} \alpha_j \xi_{t-j}^2 \tag{3}$$

The exponential GARCH (EGARCH) model defined by Nelson (1991) deals with the asymmetric consequences of positive and negative volatility shocks and avoids some constraints on the GARCH model such as neglecting the nonnegative conditions of the coefficients and ignoring the asymmetry in volatility. The general formula of the EGARCH model is shown in equation (4). While the γ_k coefficient in the model enables the examination of asymmetric effects, the fact that the coefficient is not equal to zero indicates the presence of an asymmetric effect. In this model, the conditional variance might vary depending not only on the magnitude of the sudden event but also on its sign.

$$\log\ (\sigma_t^2) = \alpha_0 + \alpha_i \mid \xi_{t-i} / \sigma_{t-i} \mid + \beta_j \log(\sigma_{t-j}^2) + \gamma_k \xi_{t-k} / \sigma_{t-k} \tag{4}$$

Regardless of which model is established, the mean and variance equations obtained and their respective coefficients are evaluated and interpreted as indicators of the relation in the model between the variables.

Material and Methods

The BIST100 index values are obtained from the Electronic Data Delivery System of the Central Bank of Turkey (EVDS, 2020). The reference dates used in the study are given in table 12.1. The periods in which five-digit index values observed are determined as reference turning points in this study.

To evaluate the effect of removing zeros on the daily return rate of BIST100, a dummy variable was created (DZR—dummy zero removal). This variable is determined as "1" from the date of the first zero removal from the index (03.01.1997) until the date (07.12.1999) five-digit numbers are reached again. This variable was also added with a value of "1" in the period from the date of the second zero removal (27.07.2020) from the index to the last day of the study period (30.10.2020). The variable outside of these time intervals was entered as "0." In order to make the necessary analysis, ARCH, GARCH (1,1), and EGARCH models are established.

The steps in the analysis were carried out in the following order:

1. BIST100 index daily return values are calculated by taking the logarithmic difference between the index closing values for two consecutive trading days.
2. Augmented Dickey-Fuller and Phillips-Perron tests are conducted to determine whether or not the sequence is stationary.
3. ARCH, GARCH (1,1), and EGARCH models are established and analyzed with the variables to examine the relationship between the BIST100 index and zero removal from the index regarding return and volatility.

TABLE 12.1.
Important Dates Used in the Study and Their Explanations

Date	*Explanation*
18.06.1993	Index values reach 5 digits
03.01.1997	Two zeros are removed from the index
07.12.1999	Index values reach 5 digits
27.07.2020	Two zeros are removed from the index
30.10.2020	Date of the last index value included in the study

Source: Table created by author.

Results

Descriptive statistics of the daily rate of return of the BIST100 index are given in table 12.2. The skewness value shows that it displays left-hand skewness, and the distribution of this series is sharp according to the kurtosis value obtained. The Jarque-Bera and probability values of the series indicate that the series does not show a normal distribution.

According to the graph of the daily return rate of the BIST100 index series shown in figure 12.1, the series is stationary and shows a distribution around the constant average.

The outcomes of the augmented Dickey-Fuller and Phillips-Perron tests are given in table 12.3. The findings show that the BIST100 return variable is stationary at the zero-difference level and does not contain unit roots (prob. < 0.01).

According to the analysis, it is seen that the averages of the stock market index in the time intervals in which the zero removal operations are made and the effects of these continue are higher than the averages in the time intervals outside these periods (see table 12.4). Another result of this analysis is that there is a significant difference in terms of returns between the pre-removal and post-removal periods ($p = 0.024 < 0.05$), and the post-removal mean value reaches four times the pre-removal (0.0012/0.0003).

As a basis for ARCH models, the best ARMA model (AR and MA) is calculated in order to determine which the most suitable approach is. According to the calculations, it is concluded that the best model for this study was ARMA (1,1), and the analysis is based on this model.

TABLE 12.2
Descriptive Statistics for the Daily Return Rate of the BIST100 Index

	Daily Return Rate of BIST100 Index
Mean	0.0044
Median	0.0005
Maximum	0.0772
Minimum	−0.0868
Std. Dev.	0.0103
Skewness	−0.0886
Kurtosis	8.7555
Jarque-Bera	9441.539
Probability	0.0000
Sum	2.981492
Sum of Sq. Dev.	0.726654
Observations	6.834

Source: Calculated by author.

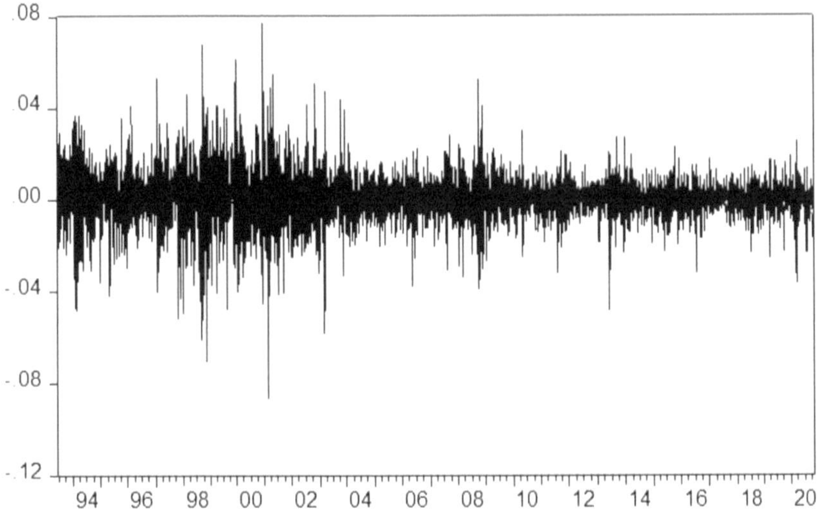

FIGURE 12.1
Graph of Daily Return Rate of the BIST100 Index Series. *Source*: Calculated by author.

It is seen in table 12.5 that the GARCH and EGARCH models are significant according to the probability values of the coefficients in terms of both mean and variance equations ($p < 0.05$). When the results for the heteroskedasticity tests are examined, to reject the null hypothesis, the p(Fs) values should be larger than 0.05. For this reason, only the GARCH (1,1) model was accepted.

Table 12.5 shows that all parameters in the equations of mean and variance in the GARCH (1,1) model are statistically significant ($p < 0.05$). In this model, the AR term is positive, implying that past returns have a positive impact. In this table, it is estimated that the parameter coefficients of α_1, β_1, and θ_1 are significant and positive.

According to the GARCH model obtained, two equations—mean and variance—are obtained. The first one is the mean equation (5). In this equation, r_t is the asset return at time t, μ is the average return, and ξ_r is a residual return.

$$r_t = \mu + \xi_r \qquad \text{Mean equation: (5)}$$

The second one is the variance equation (6). In the variance equation, σ_t^2 is the conditional variance, the GARCH term σ_{t-1}^2 is the variance on the previous day, and the ARCH term ξ_{t-1}^2 is the lag of the squared residuals or prediction error from the mean equation (Aliyev et al., 2020).

$$\sigma_t^{\,2} = \alpha_0 + \alpha_1 \xi_{t-1}^2 + \beta_1 \sigma_{t-1}^2 \qquad \text{Variance equation: (6)}$$

TABLE 12.3
BIST100 Index Daily Returns Unit Root Test Statistics

	None		*Intercept*		*Trend and Intercept*	
Method	*t-Statistic*	*Prob.*[*]	*t-Statistic*	*Prob.*[*]	*t-Statistic*	*Prob.*[*]
Augmented Dickey-Fuller	−78,13201	0,0001[***]	−78.25871	0,0001[***]	−78.33692	0,0001[***]
Test critical values 1% level	−2,565300		−3.431129		−3.959379	
5% level	−1,940871		−2.861769		−3.410461	
10% level	−1,616669		−2.566934		−3.126994	
	Adj. t-Stat	*Prob.*[*]	*Adj. t-Stat*	*Prob.*[*]	*Adj. t-Stat*	*Prob.*[*]
Phillips-Perron	−78.64849	0,0001[***]	−78.61138	0,0001[***]	−78.60509	0,0001[***]
Test critical values 1% level	−2.565300		−3.431129		−3.959379	
5% level	−1.940871		−2.861769		−3.410461	
10% level	−1.616669		−2.566934		−3.126994	

Source: Calculated by author.
Note: [*]MacKinnon (1996) one-sided p-values. [***] Significant at the 0.01 level.

TABLE 12.4
The Effect of the Zero Removal on Index Returns

Dummy Variable Zero Removing	*N*	*Mean*	*Std. Dev.*	*Std. Error*	*95% Confidence Interval for Mean*		*Min.*	*Max.*
					Lower Bound	*Upper Bound*		
0030	6053	0.0003	0.0096	0.0001	0.0001	0.0006	–0.0868	0.0772
1	786	0.0012	0.0145	0.0005	0.0002	0.0022	–0.0702	0.0679
Total	6839	0.0004	0.0103	0.0001	0.0002	0.0007	–0.0868	0.0772

Source: Calculated by author.

TABLE 12.5
Results of the ARCH, GARCH (1,1), and EGARCH Models

Parameter	*ARCH*			*GARCH (1,1)*			*EGARCH*		
	Coef.	*S.E.*	*p*	*Coef.*	*S.E.*	*P*	*Coef.*	*S.E.*	*p*
M.E.									
C	0.0004	0.0001	0.0039***	*0.0005*	*9.47E-05*	*0.0000****	0.0004	9.20E-05	0.0000***
AR (1)	0.0050	0.8237	0.9952	*0.5073*	*0.1925*	*0.0084****	0.5450	0.1486	0.0002***
MA (1)	0.0050	0.8270	0.9952	*−0.4673*	*0.1994*	*0.0191***	−0.4981	0.1555	0.0014***
V.E.									
α_0	0.0001	1.72E-06	0.0000***	*1.14E-06*	*1.20E-07*	*0.0000****	−0.3730	0.0217	0.0000***
α_1	0.1714	0.0115	0.0000***	*0.1001*	*0.0050*	*0.0000****	0.2137	0.0083	0.0000***
β_1				*0.8892*	*0.0049*	*0.0000****	−0.0365	0.0045	0.0000***
γ_1							0.9783	0.0020	0.0000***
Θ_1	0.0000	2.76E-05	1.0000	*2.59E-06*	*5.71E-07*	*0.0000****	0.0317	0.0042	0.0000***
H.T. p(Fs)		0.0000			*0.1636*			0.0353	

Source: Calculated by author.
*** Significant at the 0.01 level. ** Significant at the 0.05 level.

This dummy variable in the analysis appears as θ_1 in the variance equations of the results. When the dummy variable θ_1 is added to the GARCH (1,1) model, the new variance equation (7) is obtained:

$$\sigma_t^2 = \alpha_0 + \alpha_1 \xi_{t-1}^2 + \beta_1 \sigma_{t-1}^2 + \theta_1 \left(\mathrm{DZR}\right) \qquad \text{New variance equation: (7)}$$

According to the results of the variance equation obtained from the analysis, α_1 is significant and positive, and this means there is substantial volatility clustering. This implies that large returns/losses are followed by large returns/losses and small returns/losses are followed by small returns/losses. The value of α_1 is high, so it appears that there is high sensitivity to volatility arising from market movements. The value of β_1 is significant and positive; this is proof of the asymmetry volatility structure. According to the results, it is estimated that $\beta_1 > \alpha_1$; this result could signify that the effect of removing zeros continues for a long time and the volatility declines slowly over a long period (Sosa and Ortiz, 2017).

The dummy variable in the model shows the zero removing effect $\theta_1 > 0$. It is seen in the model that the dummy variable increases the volatility and shows a positive leverage effect. Thus, it could be surmised that the removal of zeros from the BIST100 index increases volatility and has a leverage effect. When this result is evaluated together with the average index returns that increase the effect of the event, it can be inferred that removing zeros from the index plays a leverage role to increase returns.

Discussion and Conclusion

It is found that removing zeros from the index creates a positive leverage effect on returns and causes an increase in the volatility. These results support the hypothesis of the study.

When these relations are analyzed from the perspective of investor perception, it is thought that removing zeros from the index could create a positive perception change among investors and provide significant benefits in terms of achieving stability and sustainability in financial markets.

The findings could imply that removing zeros from the index has a positive effect on the psychological perception among investors. It is estimated that this effect would last until the number of digits in the index increases again. According to this assumption, the number of digits in the index could be considered as a psychological barrier.

Cyree et al. (1999) studied the presence of psychological barriers in multiples of 100 in index levels in eight stock indexes. In their study, important conditional effects on variance associated with the barrier point were observed in seven of the indexes, in five of the eight indexes examined high returns were observed with the crossing of the barrier point, and significant effects in the mean sense were observed in the other two indexes as a part of the downward movement after the barrier. Moreover, it is stated that there are signs of autoregressive conditional heteroskedastic (ARCH), generalized ARCH (GARCH), and leverage effects in most series discussed in the study. In terms of the effects of the psychological barrier, it is seen that their results are consistent with ours.

In the study by Reyes (2004) investigating whether there is a 1,000 price level barrier in the DJIA index, the presence of significant positive abnormal returns before the barrier was revealed. It is also emphasized that no tendency for conditional volatility to be higher or lower was detected for the day when the stock market crossed a 1,000-level price barrier for the first time. While the results obtained in that study are consistent with our findings in terms of revealing the existence of a psychological barrier, they differ in terms of the direction of return and conditional volatility tendency.

In a study carried out by Lobão and Couto in 2019, the existence of psychological barriers in six important Asian stock markets was investigated. In that study, in which the GARCH model is used, it is concluded that there are strong barriers in the stock markets in South Korea and Taiwan, medium-level barriers in those in Japan and Hong Kong, and low-level barriers in those in Singapore and China. The findings of their study, in which the existence of the psychological barrier in the index is determined at different levels, support those of our study.

One of the limitations of the present study is that the effects of crises with global and domestic economic effects are not included. For this reason, it is considered that expurgating the analyses performed of these effects is important in terms of ensuring the validity of the results. It is among the limitations of the study that a short period has passed since the second incidence of removal of zeros from the index and that the analyses are conducted within this framework. Therefore, it is thought that it is important to expand the study to include longer periods for future studies and to investigate the validity of the findings. When other countries remove zeros from the stock market index, it will be useful to examine these practices in terms of psychological barriers and compare them with the findings of our study. The present study contributes to the literature since it offers a different perspective on psychological barriers in the stock market index.

References

Aliyev, F., Ajayi, R., & Gasim, N. (2020). Modelling Asymmetric Market Volatility with Univariate GARCH Models: Evidence from Nasdaq-100. *Journal of Economic Asymmetries*, *22*(April), e00167. doi:10.1016/j.jeca.2020.e00167.

Bahng, S. (2003). Do Psychological Barriers Exist in the Stock Price Indices? Evidence from Asia's Emerging Markets. *International Area Studies Review*, *6*(1), 35–52. doi:10.1177/223386590300600103.

Bollerslev, T. (1986). Generalized Autoregressive Conditional Heteroskedasticity. *Journal of Econometrics*, *31*, 307–327.

Cinko, M. (2014). Testing the Psychological Barrier in Borsa Istanbul. *Dogus University Journal*, *15*(2), 193–200.

Cyree, K. B., Domian, D. L., Louton, D. A., & Yobaccio, E. J. (1999). Evidence of Psychological Barriers in the Conditional Moments of Major World Stock Indices. *Review of Financial Economics*, *8*(1), 73–91. doi:10.1016/S1058-3300(99)00002-6.

Donaldson, R. G., & Kim, H. Y. (1993). Price Barriers in the Dow Jones Industrial Average. *Journal of Financial and Quantitative Analysis*, *28*(3), 313–330.

Engle, R. F. (1982). Autoregressive Conditional Heteroscedasticity with Estimates of the Variance of United Kingdom Inflation. *Econometrica*, *50*(4), 987–1007. doi:10.2307/1912773.

EVDS. (2020). *EVDS | All Series*. https://evds2.tcmb.gov.tr/index.php?/evds/serieMarket/collapse_1/5854/DataGroup/english/bie_mkbrgn/.

Koedijk, K. G., & Stork, P. A. (1994). Should We Care? Psychological Barriers in Stock Markets. *Economics Letters*, *44*(4), 427–432. doi:10.1016/0165-1765(94)90116-3.

Lobão, J., & Couto, M. (2019). Are There Psychological Barriers in Asian Stock Markets? *Asian Academy of Management Journal of Accounting and Finance*, *15*(1), 83–106. doi:10.21315/aamjaf2019.15.1.4.

Lobão, J., & Pereira, C. (2016). Looking for Psychological Barriers in Nine European Stock Market Indices. *Dutch Journal of Finance and Management*, *1*(1), 1–14. doi:10.20897/lectito.201639.

Lobão, J., & Pereira, C. (2017). Psychological Barriers in Stock Market Indices: Evidence from Four Southern European Countries. *Cuadernos de Economia*, *40*(114), 268–278. doi:10.1016/j.cesjef.2016.10.005.

Mandelbrott, B. (1993). The Variation of Certain Speculative Prices. *The Journal of Business*, *36*(4), 394–419.

Mitchell, J. (2001). Clustering and Psychological Barriers: The Importance of Numbers. *Journal of Futures Markets*, *21*(5), 395–428. doi:10.1002/fut.2.

Nelson, D. B. (1991). Conditional Heteroskedasticity in Asset Returns: A New Approach. *Econometrica*, *59*(2), 347–370.

Reyes, M. G. (2004). The Behavior of the Dow Jones Industrial Average Around 1000-Level Price Barriers: Some Preliminary Evidence. *Journal of Accounting & Finance Research*, *12*(2), 19–26.

Sosa, M. & Ortiz, E. (2017). Global Financial Crisis Volatility Impact and Contagion Effect on NAFTA Equity Markets. *Estocatica: Finanzasyriesgo*, *7*(1), 67–88.

Tversky, A., & Kahneman, D. (1974). Judgment under Uncertainty: Heuristics and Biases. *Science, 185*, 1124–113. doi:10.1016/0022-1031(70)90052-1.

Westerhoff, F. (2003). Anchoring and Psychological Barriers in Foreign Exchange Markets. *Journal of Behavioral Finance, 4*(2), 65–70. doi:10.1207/s15427579jpfm0402_03.

Woodhouse, S. A., Singh, H., Bhattacharya, S., & Kumar, K. (2016). Invisible Walls: Do Psychological Barriers Really Exist in Stock Index Levels? *North American Journal of Economics and Finance, 36*, 267–278. doi:10.1016/j.najef.2016.01.006.

13

Panoptic Power of the Politics versus Synoptic and Omniptic Power of the Marketing

Changing Consumption Patterns in the Transition from the Surveillance Society to the Consuming Society That Wants to Be Surveilled

Mahmut Nevfel ELGÜN and H. Çağatay KARABIYIK

Introduction

A correct understanding of the current social structure and the behaviors of individuals in this society is of great importance to develop the humanity. Because it is not possible to understand humanity, to realize its mistakes, and to guide humanity without understanding the structure of a society correctly. When evaluated in this context, the consumption structure and consumer behaviors are the factors that cannot be ignored to understand and guide the postmodern society. In this study, which was developed within the framework of this approach, postmodern consumer behaviors and the panopticon created by Foucault and the synopticon and omnipticon thoughts that emerged afterward were examined.

The panopticon emerged in 1787 as an architectural design to keep individuals in secluded places, especially prisons, under control, or when they are not controlled, the people there cannot be sure whether they are being surveilled (Steadman, 2012). Although it was not considered worthy of being built as an architectural project at that time, it gained great importance sociologically and philosophically after Foucault's study (*Discipline and Punish*) realized that the structure in which the society is located is already in a panoptic structure (Ziady, 1993: 25). Thus, the surveillance that power uses as a method and the ethical dimensions of this surveillance have been opened to discussion in the context of human freedom and security (Shearing & Stenning, 1985: 336). In other words, while this process creates a society that makes the individual feel safe, it also destroys privacy by causing surveillance to emerge. Although this process of change and awareness was disturbing for humanity at first, this panoptic structure that is turning to x-raying is accepted by people and turned into a social structure process that wants to be surveilled. Today, the society that enjoys being surveilled and the structure in which surveillance became autonomous are explained in a synoptic and omniptic structure. In other words, surveillance has become ubiquitous in the synoptic and omniptic eras, and this process is managed with an autonomous method. The technical background of this change is not the subject of this study. In this study, what and how individuals show or how individuals are surveilled are discussed. In addition, the effects of this situation on individuals were examined.

In a synoptic and omniptic society, it is necessary to examine the values of the postmodern society to correctly understand the images that individuals make themselves visible and the way they psychologically create themselves. Because every individual will be in an effort to show his existence according to the values of the society he lives in. In fact, this situation points to the phenomenon that Lyon (2001: 3) interpreted as classificatory power. While classificatory power was a political element in the panoptic era, today, in addition to this political element, there is an autonomous classificatory system over the structures in which individuals reveal their selves as a surveillance system. In these systems, the examination of the situations in which individuals want to be surveilled should also be done through consumption. Because, as Bourdieu stated, today individuals need mass consumption for self-fulfillment (Campbell, 2005: 35). In other words, in the postmodern society, the individual creates himself as much as he consumes and shows himself while consuming. For this reason, the dimension of this study in terms of consumer behaviours is postmodern consumer behaviors.

The importance of this study stems from the analysis of today's consumption phenomena through the panopticon, which was introduced by Foucault in a sociological sense, and the synopticon and omnipticon that emerged later, to understand consumer behaviors correctly. This study is of great importance especially in terms of the philosophical actuality of marketing science. In addition, the aim of this study is to philosophically examine the process of disclosing consumption in the digitalized synoptic and omniptic era. In this context, first of all, a literature review on the historical development of the panopticon and the synopticon and omnipticon was made. Then, as another variable of this study, the postmodern consumer behaviors literature was reviewed. Finally, by combining these variables in the literature review, today's consumer behaviors were discussed with a critical understanding, and as a result of these discussions, the synthesis of consumption understanding was revealed.

Theoretical Framework

The History of Panopticon

The primary source of the panopticon thought is the letters written by Jeremy Bentham in Crecheff, Russia, to his friend in England in 1787. These letters, which were not intended to be published, still appeared in the British and Irish press, and thus became public (Bentham et al., 2016: 9–12). The primary source of the panopticon as an idea is shown as Jeremy Bentham's brother, Samuel Bentham. Samuel Bentham, who was in Russia with Jeremy at that time, worked as a manager and engineer in a campus where many Russian workers were employed (Wallas, 1923: 51). In this process, he developed the idea of the panopticon to keep the workers under surveillance (Bentham et al., 2016: 78).

The idea of the panopticon was developed as an architectural design when it first appeared. Considering Samuel Bentham's mission in Russia, it is understood that it was an architectural design to control workers. Since Jeremy Bentham had studied law and also practiced law (Harrison, 1989), it should be considered normal for him to organize this project as a prison project. The idea developed by Samuel Bentham for the surveillance of workers was transformed into a prison by Jeremy Bentham and then tried to be adapted to many areas such as schools, hospitals, and factories (Galic, Timan & Koops, 2016: 22). However, after 20 years of Jeremy Bentham's efforts, he gave up the idea of the panopticon as an architectural work in 1813 as a result of pressure from the British government (Pease-Watkin, 2003: 2; Hume, 2008: 703).

When the panopticon drawings are examined, it is understood that the building has a completely surveillance-oriented purpose as a structure. The person in the watchtower in the center of the panopticon has an angle to see all the cells at the same time. Thus, the people in the cells do not know whether they are being surveilled or not at that moment. However, they still know that they can be surveilled at any time. This knowledge of the people in the cells forms the basis of the authority of surveillance.

Despite all the efforts of Bentham, both legally and economically, and Dumont's work in France (Steadman, 2009: 287), the panopticon was not accepted by the governments as a building. Thus, Bentham abandoned the project completely in 1813. However, this project, which did not become reality as a building, gained a sociological and philosophical dimension after Bentham's renunciation and gained great importance as a metaphor in the social structure.

Panoptic, Synoptic, and Omniptic Society

Although the panopticon does not exist as a structure in real life, an all-seeing surveillance world is a reality that people know well in daily life (Foucault, 1995: 205–208). For this reason, scientists who realized that the society and power they live in already have a panoptic structure started to examine the society in the panoptic structure again in the 1990s. In this period, the widespread use of cameras as a security tool in big cities draws attention. The cameras that became widespread in this period and in fact the surveillance over the panopticon again revealed the dichotomy between security and "x-raying."

In fact, a surveillance panoptic structure is a necessity for power. The important thing is how, and in which age, this necessity was realized. In other words, what the power needs to watch for control. For example, considering the relationship between the first emergence of the panopticon and the Industrial Revolution, it is understandable that Samuel Bentham put forward this design for the purpose of surveilling on the workers. However, with the resolution of the production problem, the panoptic structure became visible with a security outfit in order to protect the social status quo. Recently, the panoptic structure has turned into a capitalist form. The subject of this study is the philosophical transformation of the panopticon in the capitalist era.

While the surveillance power context of the panopticon was started by Bentham, the capitalist surveillance form was started by Foucault (Bentham et al., 2016: 111). The main source of this change is internet-based communication resources (D'Urso, 2006: 282). It is not possible to use internet-based surveillance tools, which were used for the surveillance of work areas at first, only for this purpose. Because the internet as a means of communication is an important revolution. For this reason, it did not take long for the power to start using internet technology as a surveillance tool (Lida, 2008: 4). In this context, the data obtained from the society, which was surveilled by internet-based technologies, were analyzed and reported (Nebeker & Tatum, 1993: 509).

Especially with the increase in communication-based technical possibilities, the use of power as a surveillance tool has revealed the panoptic society that Foucault envisioned. However, there is a process that should not be ignored at this point. When technological possibilities are invented and the subsequent developments are examined, it is seen that every technological invention is first in the hands of the few and then spread to the whole society. In this way, internet-based technological developments have spread to all segments of society and thus normalized surveillance, and ordinary people have had the opportunity to surveil with the same technology. In other words, with the spread of internet-based technologies to all segments of the society, a society in which the majority surveil, the minority emerged. This process is called synopticon (Demir, 2017: 59). As a matter of fact, this difference is also understood through the origin of the words "panopticon" and "synopticon." Panopticon is derived from the ancient Greek words "pan" meaning whole and "opticon" meaning visual and seeing and means that the whole is surveilled. The word "synopticon" is derived from the words "syn" meaning together-at the same time and "opticon" meaning surveillance (Mathiesen, 1997: 217–219).

However, the similarities of the application of panoptic and synoptic structures in terms of power should not be ignored. In the panoptic structure, while the power both surveilles and directly manages this process, the society neither watches nor manages. However, in the synoptic structure, power both surveilles and manages, and the society continues to be managed despite it can surveil (Doyle, 2011: 283). In other words, the fact that the majority has the ability to surveil on the minority in the synoptic society has not changed the reality of being governed. The reason why these changes are separated in different terms is that in the synopticon the society has become a surveillancer and at the same time the society has become exhibitionist. As Bauman (1999: 62) found, surveillance is accepted as voluntary in the synoptic society. The hegemonic surveillance practices of the panoptic structure made the society a voluntary exhibitionist. In other words, individuals in an omniptic society are willing to surveil or be surveilled.

After the synoptism, which emerged with the partial spread of surveillance tools in the society, with the complete spread of these tools, an omniptic society emerged where everybody surveils on everybody (Kavut, 2021: 76). In the omnipticon defined by Jeffrey Rosen (Sprague, 2007: 2), a society in which everyone surveils everyone has emerged (Yılmaz and Yengin, 2021: 234). The understanding of omniptic society, in which the surveillance process begun to be seen, has become exactly the prerequisite of postmodern society (Bitirim Okmeydan, 2017: 63).

In this study, postmodern consumer society was examined within the framework of omnipticonism. For this reason, the postmodern consumption issue is examined in the discussion part of this study. However, finally, the literature on postmodern consumer behaviors should be reviewed.

Disclosure in Postmodern Consumption

Postmodern society means a social structure identified with consumption as never before throughout human history. According to Baudrillard and

Jameson, postmodern society means a consumer structure that wants to compensate for itself through the symbolic values of consumption (Goulding, 2003: 153). This compensation process makes consumption one of the fundamentals of postmodern society. In other words, in the postmodern society, individuals form their own selves through consumption. This inevitably results in an increase in consumption. For this reason, first of all, it is necessary to conduct a literature review on the understanding of consumption in the postmodern society.

Postmodern consumer behaviors researched by marketing science and a literature have already been created that determine the characteristics of postmodern consumption. In this context, although the researchers who examine the modern period consumer behaviors have a more positivist approach, the fact that they turn to analyses that include the social and individual psychological behaviors of the consumers in the postmodern period shows how radical this change is (Tybout and Artz, 1994: 156). In other words, in order to explain consumer behaviors in the postmodern period, cultural, psychological, sociological, and philosophical factors should be taken into account more intensely. There are even studies examining consumer behaviors through hermeneutics to understand the postmodern consumer correctly (Arnold and Fischer, 1994). One of the most important results of consumption becoming a social image is the emergence of many types of marketing such as green marketing, social media marketing, and retro marketing in the postmodern era. The reason for this diversification should be seen as consumers, who make consumption a culture and self-creation process, demand a suitable marketing method for the self they want to create. For example, a consumer who has an environmentalist culture and wants to show himself like this to his social environment needs to be persuaded by green marketing. However, it is not possible to sell the same product to a consumer who has an image other than environmentalism with green marketing. In addition to these, consumption itself has become an experiential process in postmodern consumption (Raaij, 1993: 551–558; Addis, Holbrook, 2001: 50; Addis, Podesta, 2005: 398). At this point, one of the reasons why consumption itself becomes experiential, including certain rituals, is that consumers have to create a concept in which they can show the moment of consumption. For example, the disclosure of an ordinary dinner is not remarkable enough. But adding extraordinary rituals to the same dinner will make it worth to be surveilled. The rituals during the presentation have an important role in the global growth of the Nusret brand (Saltbae), which operates as a restaurant chain. For this reason, it is possible to attribute Nusret's success in marketing to meeting the expectations of the postmodern consumer.

Postmodern consumption literature shows that in this period, consumers position themselves in the social structure, as well as satisfying their needs by disclosing what they consume. In other words, consumption has become a communication tool that individuals use to say "This is I am!" to the society. The context of this study is the establishment of the relationship between the disclosure of consumption and the omnipticon. This relationship was established in the discussion and conclusion sections.

Discussion

First of all, it should be noted that in terms of architecture, the panopticon itself tends to expand in a structure similar to social networks as an architectural structure. In his fourth and fifth letters, Bentham mentions that if the panoptic blocks are expanded to form a circle, the blocks will also have a new bigger panoptic structure. This shows that the panopticon is similar to social structures in terms of architecture. When evaluated in this context, it is understood that it is normal for the panopticon to turn into a tool to explain the social structure as a metaphor. However, unlike today, when the panopticon was first used as a metaphor, it was seen as a method of violence and oppression used by power, but today individuals and societies have normalized this surveillance process. In addition, with the penetration of technical possibilities to the whole society, the surveillance process has become a voluntary surveillance process where everybody surveils everybody. In other words, being surveilled for a long time has made the society an exhibitionist. Zizek (2006: 288–289) evaluates this situation as the need for the camera's gaze to guarantee the existence of the subject in the postmodern society. Moreover, the fact that cameras are so numerous that everyone can carry their phone in their pocket and that every phone has internet access, making it easier to access display tools, has led to an explosion in exhibitionism. Moreover, many things have changed since the emergence of the idea of the panopticon in the "classical" sense. For example, the panoptic structure only expresses a physical surveillance process. This was interpreted as observing what people were doing at that time. However, today, with the society becoming exhibitionist, it is also possible for individuals to share their personal information. For example, a consumer fills out a questionnaire about consumption decisions and behaviors without thinking and voluntarily participates in the process of creating data about consumers (Campbell and Carlson, 2002).

It is an obvious fact that postmodern society has become exhibitionist. What needs to be discussed after this point is the issue of what to exhibit. Undoubtedly, the contents of the things that an individual who wants to position himself in the society and say to the society "This is I am!" must be compatible with the values of that society. For example, the content of surveillance that emerged in modern society was realized by the security and the control of workers. In the postmodern society, what is exposed has become consumption. This shows that the surveillance society has a capitalist origin.

Rebellion, one of the postmodern consumer characteristics in the marketing literature (Thomas, 1997: 56–57), should be reopened for discussion within the framework of the panopticon. The postmodern consumer's rebelliousness is valid for direct dictations that take place in the panoptic framework. In other words, while the postmodern consumer rebels against the directly dictated thoughts, they adapt to the dictations that take place indirectly through the values of the society. For example, in the early study of Wright Mills (1957: 298–324), it was stated that the postmodern society, which is called the mass society, is a structure that does not put forward an original view, acts according to the values of the society, and is shaped by the mass media. In the study of Berger et al. (1973: 90–91), it was stated that this situation arises from the indirect dictation of meanings to individuals by the mass structure as a social superconsciousness. This shows that consumers are not as individualistic and free as mentioned.

Conclusion

It is necessary to evaluate the conclusion part of the study from two perspectives, in the context of power and marketing. For this reason, as a secondary subject of this study, first the result of the power context was expressed. Finally, the results related to the subject of marketing, which directly constitutes the context of this study, were expressed.

Although there seems to be a change in the balance of power during the transition from panopticon to omnipticon, it should be noted that there was no such change. What changes in this process is the method of power. In the panoptic structure, power applies a direct dictation method, while in the omniptic structure, dictation takes place indirectly. This indirectness is realized through cultural influences. In other words, the omniptic structure differs from the panoptic structure only in terms of who made the surveillance. However, in a society in which everyone surveils everyone, although the power centers do not change, a society of transparency emerges from social exhibitionism. This change reveals the Transparency Society as expressed by Byung-Chul Han (2017).

When the omniptic society is examined in terms of marketing, it is seen that consumers do not make a real unbiased and free choice, as is the case with inferences about power. Ethical concerns aside, an increased consumption seems necessary to ensure the continuity of today's economic approach. For this reason, in the omniptic society, as in the panoptic society, the masses are kept under control and to ensure this continuity, the societies are directed to consumption. In other words, while surveillance was made for workers to work more efficiently in the modern period, today there is surveillance for consumers to consume more. Everyone's surveilling on everyone is possible today, especially thanks to social media tools. In other words, while surveillance and power are in question in both cases, but it changes depend to surveiller subject. When a consumer exhibits his moment of consumption on social media, he can also aim to announce himself to the society through this sharing, since he knows that ordinary people like himself are also surveilling. Considering that consumption has become an image creation tool today, it should be considered normal that this understanding further fuels consumption. As a matter of fact, the increase in exhibitionism and consumption today also explains this situation. However, it should not be ignored that consumers do not create their own consumption philosophy in this process. Considering factors such as the increase in resource use and the damage to the environment, consumers should consume according to the essence of the issue, not according to what is seen in the surveillance society. This shows that although the postmodern consumer should not appear to be "rebellious" in the surveillance society, he should consume by separating from the omniptic structure and developing a real consumption philosophy. In other words, there has been no change in the structure of power or economic systems in the process from the panopticon to the omnipticon. This means that in a capitalist system, it is not possible to create a consumption philosophy through the tools that the system develops. On the other hand, it means that consumption should be evaluated through philosophical and economic alternative approaches for a sustainable solution.

Undoubtedly, it is not an easy process for the individual to separate from the society he lives in and the worldview of that society. However, in order to develop alternative philosophical perspectives on consumption, it is understood with this study that the systems that are ignored today should also be taken into account. However, developing an understanding of consumption philosophy through each alternative system is wide enough to constitute the subjects of different studies. For this reason, studies that will develop the understanding of consumption through alternative economic and philosophical systems constitute the suggestions of this study.

References

Addis, M. & Holbrook, M.B. 2001. "On the conceptual link between mass customisation and experiential consumption: an explosion of subjectivity." *Journal of Consumer Behaviour*, 1(1), 50–66.

Addis, M. & Podesta, S. 2005. "Long life to marketing research: a postmodern view." *European Journal of Marketing*, 39(3/4), 386–412.
Arnold, S.J. & Fischer, E. 1994. "Hermeneutics and consumer research." *Journal of Consumer Research*, 21(1), 55–70.
Bauman, Z. 1999. *Küreselleşme*. İstanbul: Ayrıntı.
Bentham, J., Pease-Watkin, C., Werret, S., Çoban, B. & Özarslan, Z. 2016. *Panoptikon: iktidarın gözü*. İstanbul: Su Yayınları.
Berger, P.L., Berger, B. & Kellner, H. 1973. *The Homeless Mind*. Middlesex: Penguin Books.
Bitirim Okmeydan, S. 2017. "Postmodern Kültürde Gözetim Toplumunun Dönüşümü: 'Panoptikon'dan 'Sinoptikon' ve 'Omniptikon'a." *AJIT-e: Online Academic Journal of Information Technology*, 8(30), 45–69.
Campbell, C. 2005. "The craft consumer." *Journal of Consumer Culture*, 5(1), 23–42.
Campbell, J.E. & Carlson, M. 2002. "Panopticon.com: online surveillance and the commodification of privacy." *Journal of Broadcasting & Electronic Media*, 46(4), 586–606.
Demir, A. 2017. "Panopticon ve synopticon geriliminde özgürlük paradoksu." *Kaygı Uludağ Üniversitesi Fen-Edebiyat Fakültesi Felsefe Dergisi*, 28(28), 55–65.
Doyle, A. 2011. "Revisiting the synopticon: reconsidering Mathiesen's 'the viewer society' in the age of web 2.0." In *Theoretical Criminology*. London: Sage Publications.
D'Urso, S.C. 2006. "Who's watching us at work? toward a structural–perceptual model of electronic monitoring and surveillance in organizations." *Communication Theory*, 16(3), 281–303.
Foucault, M. 1995. *Discipline & Punish: The Birth of the Prison*. New York: Vintage Books.
Galic, M., Timan, T. & Koops, B.-J. 2016. "Bentham, Deleuze and Beyond: an overview of surveillance theories from the panopticon and participation." *Philosophy & Technology*, 30(1), 9–37.
Goulding, C. 2003. "Issues in representing the postmodern consumer." *Quantitative Market Research: An International Journal*, 6(3), 152–159.
Han, B.C. 2017. *Şeffaflık Toplumu*. İstanbul: Metis.
Harrison, R. 1989. "Jeremy Bentham." In *The Invisible Hand*, eds. Eatwell, J., Milgate M., & Newman, P. London: Palgrave Macmillan.
Hume, L.J. 2008. "Bentham's panopticon: an administrative history 1." *Historical Studies*, 15(61), 703–721.
Kavut, S. 2021. "Dijital kimliklerin ve the circle filminin Goffman'ın benlik sunumu kuramı bağlamında analizi." *Erciyes İletişim Dergisi*, 2(Special Issue for 4th Cultural Informatics, Communication & Media Studies Conference), 63–80.
Lida, Y. 2008. *Technological Panopticon and Totalitarian Imaginaries: The 'War on Terrorism' as a National Myth in the Age of Real-Time Culture*. www.nodo50.org/cubasigloXXI/congreso04/lida_180404.pdf. Date of Acces: 24.06.2022.
Lyon, D. 2001. "Surveillance after September 11." *Sociological Research Online*, 6(3), 1–6.

Mathiesen, T. 1997. "The viewer society, M. Foucault's panapticon revisited." In *Theoretical Criminology*. London: Sage Publications.

Mills, C.W. 1956. *The Power Elite*. New York, USA: Oxford University Press.

Nebeker, D.M. & Tatum, B.C. 1993. "The effects of computer monitoring standards, and rewards on work performance, job satisfaction, and stress." *Journal of Applied Social Psychology*, 23(7), 508–536.

Pease-Watkin, C. 2003. "Bentham's panopticon and dumont's panoptique." *Journal of Bentham Studies*, 6(1), 1–8.

Raaij, W.F.V. 1993. "Postmodern consumption." *Journal of Economic Psychology*, 14(3), 541–563.

Shearing, C. & Stenning, P. 1985. "From the panopticon to Disney world: the development of discipline." In *Perspectives in Criminal Law: Essays in Honor of John Ll. J. Edwards*, eds. Doob, A.N. & Greenspan, E.L. Toronto: Canada Law Book, 335–349.

Sprague, R. D. 2007. "From Taylorism to the omnipticon: expanding employee surveillance beyond the workplace." *John Marshall Journal of Computer & Information Law*, 25(1), 1–36.

Steadman, P. 2009. "The French Revolution and the creation of Benthamism." *The Journal of Architecture*, 14(2), 287.

Steadman, P. 2012. "Samuel Bentham's panopticon." *Journal of Bentham Studies*, 14(1), 1–30.

The New York Times. Accessed 10 February 2022. Available at: https://www.nytimes.com/2013/07/21/books/review/the-panopticon-by-jenni-fagan.html.

Thomas, M.J. 1997. "Consumer market research: does it have validity? Some modern thoughts." *Marketing Intelligence & Planning*, 15(2), 54–59.

Tynout, A.M. & Artz, N. 1994. "Consumer psychology." *Annual Review of Psychology*, 45(1), 131–169.

Wallas, G. 1923. "Jeremy Bentham." *Political Science Quarterly*, 38(1), 45–56.

Yılmaz, S. & Yengin, Y. 2021. "Analysis of emotional approach of digital surveillance in film studies." *Communication and Technology Congress – CTC 2021 (April 12th-14th, 2021 – Turkey, Istanbul*, 233–244.

Ziady, J. 1993. *Resistance and the Possibility of Freedom: Foucault, Merleau-Ponty and Subjectivity in Tension*. Honors Thesis Department of Politics Oberlin College.

Zizek, S. 2006. *Biri totalitarizm mi dedi?* Ankara: Epos.

Index

About the Contributors

Nihat AKBULUT completed his undergraduate from Ankara University Faculty of Political Sciences Department of Finance in 1995, completed his master's from Ankara University Finance (Public Economics) Department in 2014, and received his doctorate from the same department in 2021. He worked as an auditor in the Ministry of National Education between 1999 and 2007, as internal auditor for the Head of Internal Audit Unit in 2007–2009, as the education consultant of the Turkish Embassy in London between 2009 and 2012, and as the head of the Internal Audit Unit between 2013 and 2016. He still continues his duty as a senior internal auditor (A4, CGAP).

Mahmut Nevfel ELGÜN is an assistant professor at Business Administration Department in Necmettin Erbakan University. He received his bachelor's degree in Economics, Anadolu University. He received his PhD from Institute of Social Sciences, Afyon Kocatepe University. He lectures on Marketing, Logistics, and Production Management. His research areas are Logistics Villages, Neuro Marketing, Social Media Marketing, and Production Management. He has several published articles, book chapters, and papers in his field.

Pınar Fulya GEBEŞOĞLU works as a senior treasury expert at the Ministry of Treasury and Finance and delivers lectures in her areas of expertise as a part-time lecturer in several universities. Her academic publications focus on business cycles, economic crises, financial markets, insurance and private pensions sectors, and other topics in financial economics. She serves as an insurance arbitrator at the Insurance Arbitration Commission of Turkey and teaches insurance, private pensions, and economic crises in both undergraduate and graduate-level courses.

Çağrı HAMURCU is an associate professor in the Department of Finance, Banking and Insurance at Aksaray University. He received his BA from Hacettepe University, Faculty of Engineering, in 1998. He completed his master's in business administration from Gazi University in 2005. He completed his PhD at Kırıkkale University in 2015. Çağrı Hamurcu conducts academic studies, especially in the fields of behavioral finance, financial markets and institutions, and investments and portfolio management.

Mohammed HASSOUNA is a PhD candidate in the program in migration studies in the University of Granada, Institute of Migrations Research. His research areas include the economics of refugees and the impact of social integration in the host country on the economic situation of refugees. His studies revolve around business administration and economics. He did his bachelor's in business administration and a master's in economics, and the master's thesis was about discrimination in the labor market.

Esengül İPLİK is an associate professor in the Department of Business at the Adana Alparslan Türkeş Science and Technology University. She completed her PhD at Çukurova University, Adana/Turkey, in 2017. Her research interests lie in the area of management and organization and organizational behavior.

H. Çağatay KARABIYIK was born in 1988 in Turkey. After bachelor's degrees in economics and public administration, Karabıyık completed his master's degree with the thesis in the field of neuro-marketing in 2016. In 2020, he earned his doctorate with his thesis in psycho-marketing, in which he adapted the Nobel Prize-winning Anchoring Theory to the field of merchandising. Apart from these, Karabıyık has educations from different institutes and universities in the fields of neuroscience, psychology, economics, and intelligence. Believing that humanity can only develop with science, art, and philosophy, Karabıyık has 36 publications consisting of novels, philosophy, and economics books, theses, articles, book chapters, and conference papers. Currently living in Turkey, Karabıyık works as a certified public accountant and provides training and consultancy services in the fields of merchandising and marketing strategies at international level.

Iyad S. M. *KHAMAYSA* is PhD in Social Sciences (Migration Studies), with a dissertation titled "The Traumatic Experiences of the Catastrophe Nakba After 72 Years as Perceived by The First Generation" (Evaluation: Excellent Cum Laude 2022) from the Institute of Migrations Research at the University of Granada, Spain. He is a reviewer in PLOS *Global Public Health Journal.* He has considerable research published in Arabic, English, and Spanish. Dr. Khamaysa is an expert in statistical analysis software and research methods. He is a member of the International Sociological Association (ISA), the Palestinian Union of Social Workers and Psychologists (PUSWP), and International Humanities Studies (HIS).

Muhammet KUTLU graduated from Atatürk University, Department of Economics, and completed his master's degree from Erzurum Technical University, Department of Economics, with the thesis titled "Analysis of income distribution and determinants: TRA1 sub-region sample." The author continues his doctoral studies at Atatürk University, Department of Econometrics. The author conducts research on applied micro-econometrics and applied macro-econometrics and has been working as a research assistant at Atatürk University since 2016.

Şeyma ŞAHİN KUTLU graduated from Atatürk University, Department of Economics. She completed her master's degree at Atatürk University, Department of Economic Policy, and her doctorate at Bandirma Onyedi Eylul University, Department of Economics. The theses of her doctorate is on the relationship between monetary policy and asset prices; her research areas include monetary policy, environmental economics, and unemployment. She works as an assistant professor at Bandirma Onyedi Eylul University, Department of Economics.

M. Zaenul MUTTAQIN, S.Sos., M.Si, is a lecturer in Public Administration Study Program, Cenderawasih University, Papua-Indonesia. His interests and areas of expertise are in public policy and policy communication. His latest article is "West Nusa Tenggara Tourism Policy Learning in Responding to the Covid-19 Pandemic."

İlhan Can ÖZEN graduated from the Economics Department of Bilkent University in 2004 and received his MA in Economics in 2006 and PhD in Economics in 2010 from Johns Hopkins University. He conducted his thesis on the specific area of labor migration and its society-level health effects. The special areas that he focused with his thesis and his post-thesis work have been development economics and health economics. He has been working as an assistant professor in the Economics Department of the Middle East Technical University and carrying out research on the health and health capacity effects of migration patterns, in the special case of Turkey. He is a member of the Advisory Committee of Health Economics and Health Policy Research and Application Center at Hacettepe University. He is still carrying out independent research on the topics of health economics, development economics, and political economy.

Dr. Cem ŞAHİN is an expert at Central Bank of Republic of Turkey. He received his undergraduate degree (BA) in Economics from Middle East Technical University, Faculty of Economic and Administrative Sciences in 1998. He completed his master's degree in Economics and Econometrics from the University of Exeter in 2008. He received his PhD in Economics from Middle East Technical University University in 2015. Dr. Baki Cem ŞAHİN conducts academic studies, especially in Asset Pricing, Corporate Finance, Applied Financial Econometrics, Microeconometrics, Monetary Economics, and Banking.

Mehmet ŞENGÜR completed undergraduate study in economics at Abant İzzet Baysal University (2008). He worked as a research assistant in Economics at Eskisehir Osmangazi University Faculty of Economics and Administrative Sciences from 2009 to 2016. He earned his master's in economics at the Eskisehir Osmangazi University (2011). He received his PhD in Economics at the Dumlupınar University (2015). Currently, he is working as an associate professor of economics at Eskisehir Osmangazi University. His main research interests are poverty, income distribution and inequality, savings, economic growth, consumer demand, and inflation.

Osman Bahadır SİNAN received his BA from Ankara Faculty of Political Sciences, Department of Economics, in 1993. After graduating, he worked as assistant specialist in the Capital Markets Board of Turkey in 1994. He received his Specialization in 1997, and in 2002–2003, he completed the Capital Markets training program at Pennsylvania University Whartoon Business School in the United States. He still works as the chief specialist at the Capital Markets Board of Turkey in Enforcement Department. He completed his master's in Beykent University Business Administration in 2010, and in 2011 he started at Istanbul University, Institute of Social Sciences, Department of Economics. He completed the PhD program in 2015.

Javier Tamayo TORRES has been working as an associate professor in the Department of Management-The University of Granada since 2009. He is also a member of research group IADE. His area of interests are Ambidexterity and Organizational Behaviours, Manufacturing Flexibility, and Quality.

Cenk TUFAN, PhD, is a member of Faculty of Applied Sciences at Akdeniz University. Tufan has been conducting research on organizational behavior, strategic management, and knowledge management fields. He has focused his recent researches more on leadership and behavior. He has also conducted studies with researchers of different specialties in such areas as marketing, finance, and economics. Apart from his academic career, he also has expertise in the foreign trade sector. In this context, he has a 20-year managerial history at Turkish customs.

Berna TUNCAY obtained her BA in Finance from Istanbul Bilgi University in 2003, and her MA in Economics and Finance from Bogazici University in 2004. She also received her MA in Economics in 2011, MS in Finance in 2012, and Graduate Certificate Degree in Statistics and Mathematics in 2014 from the University of South Florida. While teaching a wide range of economics and finance courses at the University of South Florida, she earned her PhD in economics in 2014. She held a research scientist position at Moffitt Cancer Center and Research Institute in Florida for one year between April 2012 and March 2013 to apply econometric models to the field of health economics. She won the Provost's Award for Outstanding Teaching at the University of South Florida in April 2014. After completing her PhD, Berna Tuncay joined IMT Institute for Advanced Studies Lucca, Department of Economics, as an assistant professor in May 2014. She moved to Istanbul in 2016 and worked as a faculty member in the Department of Economics at Koc University between June 2016 and May 2020. She is currently an assistant professor in the Department of Economics at Ozyegin University. Her major areas of research are Applied Microeconomics, Industrial Organization, Health Economics, Public Health, and Applied Econometrics.

İlksun Didem ÜLBEĞİ is an associate professor in the Department of Business at Çukurova University. She completed her PhD at Çukurova University in 2016. Her research interests lie in the area of management and organization, organizational behavior, and research methods.

www.ingramcontent.com/pod-product-compliance
Ingram Content Group UK Ltd.
Pitfield, Milton Keynes, MK11 3LW, UK
UKHW041834031026
15587UKWH00002B/772

9 781793 646248